AF676220

DON'T LET THEM DOWN

ONE DAD'S BATTLE TO PROTECT HIS CHILDREN IN A FAILING SYSTEM

A documentary novel about love in a toxic relationship and the functioning or malfunctioning of justice at the Family Courts and Social Services

Written by:

ROBYN WELSH

Don’t Let Them Down
One Dad’s Battle to Protect His Children
Documentary Novel
Publisher: Lanternwalk Books
Author: Robyn Welsh

© Robyn Welsh, 2026
All rights reserved.

This work is protected by copyright. Reproduction, distribution, public communication, or any use of the book in whole or in part may only be done with the prior written permission of the author and publisher, except as otherwise permitted by applicable law.

This book is a documentary novel. It was inspired by real events and experiences; however, the characters, names, locations, dates, and any identifiable details have been changed or created by merging multiple sources.

The narrative reflects the narrator’s subjective perspective and should not be considered as a legal opinion, expert advice, or a psychological or psychiatric diagnosis.

CONTENTS

FOREWORD

Every book has a life of its own, they say.

And every book has a reason, a strong motive to be born.

This documentary novel was written for several reasons. One simple reason more than a few missives is written is that some things can no longer be kept in. Enough is enough – in this case, of the stereotypes and a mindset that is fixated on one or two aspects. Of the double standards. Of the summarily and uncritically judgmental behaviour. Of the frequently biased social welfare system and the extreme, fatal automation of the justice system. Of the narrow-minded attitudes. Of the total lack of any presumption of innocence, both as a legal term and in practice. The other reason is less important: my own therapy. To document everything in the hope that one day I could understand what had happened to us.

I had a son. Conceived with passion, raised with love, he grew up to be a wonderful, honest, and pure-hearted man. That man is no more. A shadow of his former self now. In every sense.

This novel is about a relationship between a young couple, which rapidly turned toxic. It shows the positive and negative reactions of society, but also seeks to identify the reasons for the rapid change and to find solutions. It raises questions and describes fears. It uncovers wounds and expresses hope for their healing. This is the story of Jack and Cara, a story that is perhaps not so unique, perhaps not so rare. A story that is one of the boy moms' worst nightmares.

Acknowledgements and Dedication

I owe a debt of gratitude to my family and friends for every word of kindness and comfort, and the quiet patience with which they stood by us. We thank the following organisations, who, directly and indirectly, advised, educated, and informed us, and guided us to recognition: Justice for Fathers, Accused.Me.com, Family Needs Fathers, Mankind Initiative, and PAIN. We thank everyone, celebrities and ordinary people alike, who did not withhold the truth, who were not afraid to bring the abuse they had suffered into the light, and who bore witness to it through various channels. And we thank the Almighty, who was with us through it all, even if it didn't always feel that way during the darkest hours of our nights – we thank Him for keeping us.

"Blessed are the poor in spirit, and those who know not the meaning of the words 'red flags', 'mirroring', 'love bombing', 'flying monkeys', 'gaslighting', and 'hoovering'.

Blessed are those who do not end up in court, because they have a good marriage.

Blessed are those who live not in a relationship where love is merely a disguise, and its very name when spoken conceals something entirely different.

Blessed are those who know nothing of the various categories of domestic abuse and violence.

Blessed are those who know not the meaning of 'coercive control'.

Blessed are those whose relationships do not compel them to use internet search engines to research psychological disorders.

Blessed are those who survive all that is done to them by those who are less than healthy.

Blessed are those who still have faith.

INTRO: THE GIFT – DECEMBER 2022

I took her for a scan. It was my Christmas present to her because I knew she'd like to go, and I hoped it would make her happy and maybe ease her inner anger and pain. I didn't let go of this hope for a long time. Maybe I still haven't.

A 4D scan. We upgraded at reception, so we could keep all the pictures and video footage from the examination. Although she protested at the time.

"You really shouldn't do this for me, it's already so expensive!"

But I could see she was happy about it.

The first attempt didn't work out. These 4D scans don't seem to go smoothly for anyone. Maybe it's true that foetuses don't like ultrasound exams. The baby turned away almost immediately, covering her eyes and face as soon as the probe touched her mother's belly. For a good ten minutes, the sonographer tried to get a view of that little baby face so she could capture a photo, but eventually she gave up and sent us for a walk around the car park. For a while, we trudged silently alongside each other. I found a minced pie in the car and offered it to Cara, and she accepted. I was thinking that sugar makes babies more active in the womb, and she was terribly thin anyway, nothing but skin and bone. Her belly wasn't that big either. She could easily button up her normal winter coat at 29 weeks. She was 40 kilos. At least, that was her weight at the start of that pregnancy, just like the previous one, and she couldn't have been much more by this point, although she claimed to be over 50. She said she'd gained a lot of weight, but there's no way she'd have been offered a seat on the tube.

We avoided sensitive topics of conversation. All topics, in fact. It was cold and very windy. Nobody in their right mind would feel like taking a stroll, so we silently did our laps of the car park with coats pulled up to our chins. Then, to break the increasingly awkward silence, I gave her the latest gossip on the neighbours. Partly to take her mind off things, and partly to avoid a conversation about the past and about me, or my son. The neighbours had been her neighbours too, for almost a year, and she hated them as she generally hated everyone. She enjoyed my tales of their misery.

- "Guess what, Carol's divorcing. And their 18-year-old daughter is pregnant. There's no way to know who the father is," I told her.

Her eyes lit up, and without a second thought, she directed her suspicion onto the only adult male in the family, the girl's stepfather.

- "He must have knocked her up. Al!"
- "I don't think so," I said a little awkwardly, thinking not everybody's that depraved… In most of the population, it's not typical for stepfathers to impregnate their stepdaughters. Why jump straight to the most terrible conclusion? Once again, I was shocked by this feature of her thought process and chose to remain silent, but she kept on, clearly excited by the topic.
- "Oh, come on, that girl's so ugly, and she's the size of a cow! There's no way she had anyone. Who'd shag that? She never set foot outside the house. She never came out! Who else would have gotten her pregnant?"

I didn't want to argue. I wouldn't have known what to say anyway. I hadn't a clue when the girl from next door went out, or where, or who with. I didn't watch them in that way. And anyway, the girl wasn't even ugly. A bit chubby for sure, but I wouldn't call her ugly at all. In fact, I think she has a positively sweet face. Once again, I was shocked by Cara's endless capacity for *schadenfreude.*

- "Well, I don't know, I don't think so. Or rather, I still can't picture Al doing something like that," I said quietly. "But let's go back in, maybe the baby's turned around".

She nodded enthusiastically and turned in at the corner of the building, cutting across the pavement. This put her in front of me again. She liked walking ahead of me, even if only by a few steps. At the clinic, several people were now waiting, so they sat us down on comfy leather sofas. As usual, Cara looked at the people around us at length, scrutinising them one by one. Then she made comments about them, as she always did. She spoke loudly in Hungarian, visibly enjoying the fact that nobody apart from me could understand her. And I would still always get embarrassed if someone spoke to me in Hungarian in front of the Brits, the people who were born here. This was deeply ingrained in me at my first job in England, when I was severely scolded by my boss for speaking my native language with a Hungarian cleaner in the corridor. She said, it was one of the rudest things I could do. "Talking in a language that most people in the room don't understand, it just isn't the one thing! And somebody who lives and works in England should at least speak English in front of others; that's the minimum." It was clear and logical. I accepted it and took note. So now, I started shifting uncomfortably on the sofa. Cara grew louder and more uninhibited as the families in the waiting room and the girl at the reception desk began to notice us, giving us sidelong glances at the sound of this unfamiliar language. I thought it likely that they all shared my ex-boss's views and considered us both terribly rude. Tactless and backwards. I don't like it if people think I'm rude. Or if I can't fit in. I replied to Cara in a somewhat reluctant whisper, then took out my phone as if I'd just received a message I needed to read urgently. This worked. She soon took out her iPhone and started browsing, as was her habit. Luckily, we were called in soon after that. The baby still refused to show her face. Cara was moved back and forth on the examination table; they made her raise her hips, turned her onto her right and left side, but the baby continued to cover her little visage with her arms. Then, to let us know how little she enjoyed what was happening, she turned abruptly towards her mother's spine. The sonographer laughed.

- "Looks like it's time for another walk!" she said. "But don't worry, there's plenty of time. We're open till six."

She held out a paper towel for Cara to wipe the lubricating gel off her tummy, then courteously helped her down from the table. The scan came with satisfaction guaranteed; that is, a guarantee of success. This meant the sonographer would keep trying to capture the 4D images until they were perfect. If it doesn't work out on the day, you get another appointment. Well, that's something at least, if this baby-watching session's costing almost 100 pounds. I thought about that, and about both of us going back out into the cold.

But instead of walking – because Cara was hungry – we got in the car and drove over to the McDonald's next to one of the filling stations. Cara bought a meal deal for herself, paying for it out of her own pocket. We queued for so long that, in the end, the clinic called, and we had to hurry back. Cara got into the car, eating with such gusto that she didn't even notice the barbecue sauce dribbling onto her chin. I told her to wipe it off before we went in for the scan. She used her phone's camera as a mirror to see how messy she was, and where, then gave a self-conscious little laugh. "Still a little girl, such a little girl" was the thought that came to my mind. Unrefined. Brutally open and honest. Wounded too, like a wild animal, but she doesn't talk about who wounded her, and how; she just watches and listens. And if she doesn't understand something, or if she misunderstands, she attacks immediately. That's what I was thinking. Yes, I still see her like that, even two years later. A wounded little wildling, a charming, but impetuous little girl.

We returned just in time, and now we don't have to wait. The scan succeeded this time. The hamburger and chips had their effect, along with the fizzy drink. Complex carbs seem to count for more than simple sugar. They're quicker and more effective at waking up cells and organs. Now the baby turned outward, finally showing her impish little face with a pointy little nose, a beautifully curved, tiny mouth, and eyes shut tight. She even seemed to smile.

- "The heartbeat's strong, regular, and loud, as you can hear", smiled the sonographer. "The baby's a normal size, and everything seems to be working perfectly. A well-developed, healthy foetus."

Cara lay happily and peacefully on the table. Her eyes were on the screen, but she kept turning to me with new evidence that this little girl would also be just like her father, just look at her nose, her mouth, how similar they are, and how beautiful!

This is my weak spot, yes. Foetuses and newborns, babies and infants. When I was young, I wanted to be a midwife, and all my life I've loved really small children. I like nothing more than cuddling them and teaching them all sorts of things. Helping develop their motor skills, showing them new toys, singing to them, and watching their minds open! Babies. Tender little lives, plunged into this wily, noisy, and alien world. Little ones, who can still be taught about love simply and honestly, by touch. For whom nothing too complicated, and who are so easily made happy. A full tummy and a smile, a cuddle, rocking, kindness, and comforting – that's all they need. And since this isn't impossible to achieve, and I know I can give them all this, anytime, my relationship with them makes me happy, too. More than anything else on this earth.

- "What a cute little baby!"

So, I went out to the car, moved, and was in very high spirits after we'd chosen the five images to be printed. Cara also seemed to be in a good mood. It wasn't awkward talking to her anymore, so we gossiped, and Cara even asked me what was happening at my workplace. My guard was down, and I didn't hold back, talking, for example, about what a hard winter it was, much harder than the last, and how so many of the old patients were dying that year.

- "Too many are dying", I sighed. Pausing for a moment after that sentence because I saw Cara give a nod.
- "Everybody dies," she said, smiling.

It was dark in the car; dusk had fallen. We'd spent a good three hours at the clinic, and it was the end of December, a gloomy winter evening, so I didn't see her smile fully, only in profile. Cara didn't look at me but just stared ahead and out of the window.

- "Well, I hope not everyone! Sure, they won't all be due…" I answered, laughing a little awkwardly. Because what can you say to something like that? "If everyone dies, who will I nurse?" I added.

Cara was still smiling, and she didn't turn properly towards me. I just saw her glance briefly to one side as I started the car.

- "Who do you want to nurse from six feet under?" she asked in a cheery voice and laughed.

I didn't understand the question at first. I was turning onto the main road, and I paid attention to the traffic. So, at the time, I didn't reply. I don't think I reacted at all. And Cara quickly changed the subject. The baby and what it would be called, what it would be like, and how much like its older sister it might be. I forgot the brief exchange between the two of us and that strange sentence. It only crossed my mind again when I'd dropped her off at her house and finally returned home myself. Sitting at the kitchen table. I looked at the ultrasound pictures she had given me from among the five photographs she'd received. I looked at both images again and again, then downloaded the app needed to access the rest of the photos with my email and sent them to Cara as soon as possible. It was only then that the sentence came back to me. This time, however, it flashed through my mind like an illuminated billboard. Constantly, repeating in an endless loop:

"Who do you want to nurse from six feet under?" The question echoed within me.

My son, who may or may not be the father of that little baby, was just coming down from his room with my grandchild in his arms.

- "Everything okay?" he asked.

- "Of course," I answered. "The dates match up less and less. The due date has moved back another few days, and you'll really need a DNA test to know for certain whether the baby's yours. But otherwise, everything's fine. A healthy, sweet little baby."

Jack acknowledged what I'd said, scowling but not making any comment.

I played with my grandchild a little longer before my son took her back to Cara. And I only started talking about what had happened later that evening, when it was just my son and me sitting in the kitchen.

- "You know, something strange happened this afternoon, too. Something very strange was said." I told Jack, and then I repeated the exchange with Cara. And the question. My son went pale.
- "I can't believe it!" he said. "I didn't want to tell you about this, but we had a terrible row a few days ago. Cara said she didn't want to scare me, but she had to tell me because she couldn't keep it to herself, that I should watch out. After all, I'm going to have a very difficult year. Because she dreamed that something was going to happen to you, some tragedy… I didn't listen to the end. I told her to shut up. I said she'd regret it. And I told her that if anything happens to you, or you die, she'll see a side of me she never knew existed! I said I'd had enough of that talk. Told her to stop it. I never thought she'd start all that with you, too."

My son seemed really agitated, so I had to take the edge off the situation somehow. So, I tried to make a joke out of the whole thing.

- "Okay. OKAY. No worries. We don't have to take this so seriously. Anyway, it's kind of her, no? At least she's warning us," I laughed. "I'll make a will. It's about time I did that anyway… Of course, I'm planning to live awhile longer and enjoy my retirement, but who knows? That sort of thing could come in handy."
- "Stop it! You're not going to die. Try to ignore this crap! Cara's crazy, saying stuff like that to you. This just proves it. Forget about it!" Jack closed the conversation as he opened the fridge to make himself supper.

And I did my best. For days, weeks, I tried to forget about that sentence. Especially the emphasis, and the smile:

"Who do you want to nurse from six feet under?"

But while it was still fresh in my mind, that question just kept gnawing at me. A couple of days later, I had the rare opportunity of picking up my grandchild to take to my son for the court-designated paternal visit, because Jack wasn't yet back from work. She opened the door straight away. She must have been waiting to see when I parked in front of the house. Cara's dress was messy; she had some crumbs or morsels of food in the corner of her mouth again, but I said nothing. I switched on the voice recorder because I wanted a record of the explanation I was after.

- "Cara, I'd like to ask you something", I said softly, and waited for her to nod.
- "Go ahead!"
- "After the scan, did you really tell me I'm going to die?"

There was silence. The question itself was spoken quietly, and I looked directly into the eyes of the young woman, whom I usually saw as a defenceless little girl, and who I'd always tried to think of as a diamond in the rough until then. I didn't release her from my gaze, and it was impossible not to notice the strange light that flashed in her eyes for one tenth of a second. Then her pupils dilated, turning her eyes entirely black. It was obvious to me that she knew exactly what I was talking about. And I suspected what her answer would be.

- "I don't remember", she said simply and smiled.
- "Ok", I replied. And I smiled back. Then I repeated the words, the same way she had spoken to them two days before: "You asked who I'm going to nurse from six feet under, Cara. I'd like to know what you meant. Do you think I'm going to die soon?

She looked wonderingly straight ahead, no longer looking me in the eye.

- "I don't think I'd have said anything like that. But I don't remember exactly", she replied again, still smiling. Then she quickly changed the subject. But later, once I'd taken charge of Elsie and walked down the stairs with her, she returned to the subject, eager to explain what she'd said and what she'd meant. She wrote it down in a WhatsApp message half an hour later, too. I'd already arrived home by the time I got it:

> *"I didn't mean that you'd die straight away tomorrow or soon. I just said it because I don't really know why I said it, but what I said to Jack, that something will happen to you, it's true that I said it to him because I'd dreamt about it for a week ...and whenever I dreamt stuff all the time and told Jack it always came true soon after. It was the same with the pregnancy. Back in May, I dreamt I was running on the sea with Jack and you and the little one, and I was pregnant with a baby girl. And then it really happened. It was the same with your father, I knew something would happen, but I didn't say anything, and then you wrote that he wasn't well. I didn't want to tell Jack about this thing with you either, but I did so you'd both know before it was too late, and you could go to the doctor for a checkup. Don't take what I said to heart, it's just that this world isn't safe for anyone anymore (sad emoticon)."*

That's all Cara wrote.

"Ok. Thanks!" I replied.

Obviously, I wouldn't take it to my heart, especially after that. Of course not.

That was how December ended. After that, the two of us didn't talk much. I didn't have anything to say after that little episode. Cara did, but I couldn't have cared less what she thought. It was too much. I'd simply had enough. I no longer saw her as just a very damaged little girl. After the past year and a half, I couldn't see her as just that. And I no longer wanted to get to know her better, or to save her.

To retain any love or humanity at all – I knew – I had to distance myself from her. And I also felt that I couldn't afford to take any more blows from her, assuming I could still get up off the floor… Because every single confused statement of hers felt like a physical blow, even if the confusion wasn't about or directed towards me.

PART I – THE ILLUSIONS

Rose-Tinted Glasses - Love bombing

"Everything was fine until the wedding day." That's what I always said, to everyone, and I've stated this in writing more than once. But it wasn't even true. It wasn't *strictly* true. The problem was always lurking in the corner like a well-fed cat in a half-lit room where we never turned on the lights, so we didn't notice it. We didn't want to turn on the lights. Sometimes the half-light feels good; it soothes you without hurting your eyes. A dimly lit room takes you back to the womb, where light only filters through occasionally, where all the sounds of the outside world are muffled, where there is nothing but softness and warmth, and a heartbeat is all that can be heard.

> **"Never become so thirsty that you drink from every cup that's handed to you. That's how you get poisoned". It's a shame I'd never heard that saying before, and it didn't occur to me in time. Not early enough for me to pass it on to my son.**

Jack yearned for love more than anything. Once, he said nothing else mattered to him anymore.

> *"I just want someone to come along, at long last, someone to love me and stay by my side. To love me, and never want to leave."*

Jack's plan was that if he didn't find a loving partner by the age of 30, then he'd adopt two or three children, so he'd have a family, someone to love, and so he wouldn't grow old alone. It's a fundamental human desire to love, and nobody blamed him for that. Nobody warned him. It would have been premature and rude to tell Jack that there are worse things than being left on the shelf. That miserable knowledge – for those who have it – is something that people acquire for themselves through experience. And nobody wants that for the one they love. Mothers who love their children don't want their children to learn this lesson. Instead, they try to believe in true love again. Because there are positive examples. People who love each other, sincerely, and who truly live together (and not just side-by-side) their whole lives. Why couldn't it work out? It could work out for him, too. For my son. If only it would! So, I said nothing to Jack. When he and Cara were getting to know each other, I just paced up and down in that dimly lit room. And when the problems arose, triggering the sensors in my mind and my soul, as if the feline presence had activated them, I quickly fed the cat and turned off the lights again.

So, it's not true that there weren't any problems. But certainly, the beginning of the relationship was indeed beautiful, wonderfully beautiful. Cara herself was beautiful. Enchanting, charming, fragile. Gentle and kind, quiet and cheerful. That was what she was like, how she showed herself to be.

The quiet. The quietness. We didn't know exactly what it meant. We believed it was part of her personality, her being. That Cara was essentially like this. Quiet and refined. We believed this, we wanted to believe this, for many long weeks and months.

I saw a young girl online recently who lived with a python. This girl often posted photos and videos of the enormous reptile to dispel what she considered a misconception: that snakes are emotionless beings who don't yearn for tenderness or cannot appreciate it. The giant snake slept next to the girl for weeks on end, curling up against her. In the photos, the girl smiled happily and triumphantly. Until someone with a better grasp of ethology wrote to her that the snake wasn't snuggling up to her because it felt any kind of love, or the need to feel loved and accepted, no! Snakes can fast for weeks if needed, and if they spot a larger prey item, they shimmy up to it to gauge its size, determine whether they can eat and digest it, and estimate its weight. How long would the snake need to fast before it could digest her?

Little did we know that this may have been precisely what lay behind Cara's quietness. And this could be the purpose of her shimmying. That sort of thing didn't cross our minds then. But now I think – because I can't imagine it being anything else – that her quietness was simply an act of observation: we were being thoroughly and painstakingly frisked.

The charm, kindness, gentleness, and cheer were all part of the enchantment. The fragility was just a disguise.

Cara weighed 40 kilos, together with the kitchen sink, as the saying goes. That might have given us reason to suspect anorexia nervosa, but we didn't because Cara ate with gusto and visibly enjoyed life. She didn't vomit, so I didn't suspect bulimia. And as I said, we were living in the half-light. The benevolent hope that everything would be lovely. Peace, a safe harbour at last. The fast-flowing mountain stream broadens into a placid lake on which rowboats gently rock. Happiness.

Cara bore the marks of cuts on her skinny arms. Eight or ten faint, whiteish lines. Scars. I remember exactly what I thought when I first noticed them: "Ok, there's no need to bring this up right." The thought of an anxiety disorder, or some other kind of disorder, could have crossed my mind at this point, but it didn't. Nothing like that occurred to me. I didn't know anything about Cara's past; I didn't know the girl at all, but I did have plenty of good friends who hadn't had an easy childhood and adolescence, and who bore the same scars. I'd seen scars, many kinds, and scars never shocked me. I thought I'd investigate, but later. Someday we'd find out what happened. I thought Cara would eventually open up, let us in, start talking, tell us when she was wounded, and how. I thought that whatever it was – if necessary, and if possible – I'd make it better. I'm a nurse, no stranger to injury of any kind. Quite the opposite. Maybe I'm just the person to help.

Jack and Cara met online through a dating site. For two months, they talked and chatted for hours at a time. It was a month before I learned of

Cara's existence. I may already have suspected that something was going on, but that was when Jack told me. That was when it became public knowledge. Jack ordered 30 red roses and sent them by international courier to the centre of Europe, to the country and the address that Cara gave him. Afterward, their relationship grew serious, and Jack planned to invite the girl over so he could get better acquainted with her in person. As we were living under the same roof, he told me about this, but he didn't have to ask my permission; he just felt I should know. I was happy with the news. There was no precise date; the time of the visit was still to be decided, but one afternoon in late November, Jack sat down with me for coffee at the kitchen table and announced that Cara was arriving in two days.

- "What? How? So soon?"
- "Well, that's how it's worked out. Cara's been laid off, and her circumstances aren't too good right now either. She wants to move out of the place she's been living, but doesn't want to move back in with her parents, so this seems like the perfect opportunity for us to get to know each other. I wouldn't like to wait any longer", said Jack.
- "Ok, well, that seems to make sense. How long will she be staying?" I asked.
- "I don't know, we haven't discussed it yet. Until Christmas, I suppose. But we'll see. She might even stay for good", my son said with an awkward smile, and he seemed very happy.
- "That's not how it usually happens," I replied softly. But I didn't want to discourage him, so I quickly kept my mouth shut. And I gave my blessing to the plan: A girl's coming to stay with my son for a few weeks, and she'll be living with us.

All I knew about Cara was what Jack had told me, and what he himself knew about her: that she was 19 years old, trained as a hairdresser, with three brothers, a mother, and a stepfather, and she'd left home when she was 16. I'd seen a photograph of her and been given links to her social media accounts, so I could see her videos and albums. In fact, that evening, after Jack spoke to me, Cara also wrote me a kind, short letter in endearingly broken Hungarian, expressing her joy at finally being able to get to know me in person.

- "And apparently, she's still a virgin", Jack said to me, blushing and lowering his voice a little across the kitchen table. "She's a really sweet girl, you'll see!"
- "I hope so, son," I replied, and hugged him.

I so wanted everything to work out the way he wanted. It was so good to see him happy at last! He'd been so calm in the previous few weeks, whistling in the kitchen, pottering about with a broad smile on his face. How great it would be if this mood became permanent. That was all I could think about.

- "I'm picking her up at the airport, she's coming with the morning flight, it lands at 8:00. So please wake me at half-five because it's an hour and a half's drive, Jack asked, and I said okay. I'd be on night duty the next day anyway, so I'd phone to make sure he got up in time.

It was only when I asked why Cara was flying into the airport farthest from us that I learned Jack had paid for her ticket, too. Because Cara didn't have any savings at that time, but she'd pay him back as soon as she started work. That's what they'd agreed. And because that was the only destination with tickets available that day. Flights were operating infrequently due to COVID-19. I raised an eyebrow when I found out that Jack had paid the girl's airfare, but I wasn't really that surprised. Jack was very chivalrous and generous in all his relationships.

So, Cara was coming. Two days later, she was here. She arrived with a pink hard-shell suitcase as hand luggage. In it were some knickers, a pair of jeans, a few tops, and a party dress. That was all her possessions. Plus an iPhone, the only thing of value besides the 100 euros in her pocket. I wasn't surprised that Cara was travelling so light, as far as I knew, she was only here for a visit. Jack, on the other hand, was surprised because, as he later told me, he'd also paid for a checked-in suitcase because of the cold weather, so Cara would have space for some warm clothes. However, there was nothing warm to wear in the small cabin bag. On the other hand, alongside Cara's passport were her birth certificate and a settlement permit from the country she had come from. Because she was an immigrant in that country, too. But we didn't know that yet. I was a little surprised to see these documents, but I didn't say anything. I thought that must be just another habit. There must be people who always carry these kinds of documents wherever they go. Who knows? And anyway, there were other surprises in store for us. I was more concerned with those.

Cara put her personal documents on the table as if she wanted to show them to us. Jack looked at the photo in the passport, smiled, and turned the official document towards me. Cara's surname on her passport was completely different from the one on her social media profile and the one she'd introduced herself with. When Jack asked in surprise if the name she'd given us wasn't her real one, Cara shyly asked us not to be angry; she didn't want to confuse us, but she really loves her stepfather and usually uses his surname. This made sense; we accepted it. Cara didn't mention, however, that her stepfather never officially adopted her. She also didn't mention that the legal name in her documents was her mother's. She didn't consider it important to tell us these things, so we only found out much later.

The girl had literally nothing to wear, so over the next few days, Jack bought Cara some winter clothes. Winter came early that year, and it was already cold in the first week of December. Jack gave Cara his credit card so she could shop online and buy everything she needed. So, Cara bought sweaters, trousers, and shoes, a coat, and make-up for herself. In the first week, Jack took her to the hairdresser, cosmetician, and nail salon. "So she'll feel good in herself and be happy," said Jack. They moved into the little room, the two of them, and happily slept side-by-side on the single bed. Cara wasn't a virgin; that became obvious on the first night. But Jack wasn't disappointed. He said he'd found it hard to imagine that such a beautiful girl was still a virgin at 19 anyway, and that Cara had laughed and said she was sorry that Jack misunderstood, she'd been talking about her star sign… That didn't ring true for me, because we already knew that Cara was born in mid-August, which made her a different sign altogether, but I didn't say a word. I don't think Jack even noticed this fib.

There were already a good few bright spots in that confounded room of ours; the lights came on from time to time, but I pretended not to notice them and just hoped there wouldn't be any problems. In truth, I tried every day to figure out how I could signal to Jack that he should think about the fibs – that nothing Cara had said about herself so far was really true – but I was afraid that Jack would see this as me interfering in his relationship at the very beginning, and react like an adolescent, an adolescent who's being prevented from exerting their independence. I didn't want my doubts to cause him pain. So, events moved on…

After two weeks, it became clear that Cara would stay for longer than a few weeks or a month. One day at breakfast, they told me that they'd both like it if Cara stayed with us longer. There wasn't much point in her going home when we were all getting along so well. And why should she go back to a country where no one and nothing awaited her? She'd left home three years before. She'd terminated the lease on the apartment she'd been living in, and her employment contract had terminated. Jack was clearly happy, walking so high above the ground you could use him to catch birds. And Cara was glowing with joy. "*I've found the best family ever!*" she would say to her mother and relatives on the phone. "*If you only knew what kind, decent people they are! Jack, and his mother, too! I'm loved here, I've got everything, I'm with the best family ever!*"

Cara was placid, kind, very grateful, and seemed very happy about everything. She spoke politely, never swore, cuddled the dog, taught Jack to dance, joked, smiled constantly, and laughed a great deal. Cara's presence was like a breath of spring in the house. A fresh breeze, bursting with life. But like on most spring mornings, when nature is still stirring into life, and we don't know what seeds the birds dropped from their beaks in the autumn, and what wildflowers will sprout in the middle of the lawn, Cara's life also held many secrets.

When she arrived, we didn't know, for example, that one of her older brothers lives not far from us in London. Cara talked about him, telling us she hadn't seen her brother Mike for years and that she'd love to visit him. The boy didn't have a good marriage because of his wife; he couldn't get a job or even find casual work. He was caring for his son, who was then three years old, Cara told us. The poor lad didn't even have a telephone; he just used borrowed phones whenever he could, so Cara gave him her own iPhone.

- "I don't need a phone anyway, I hardly use it", Cara said to me. "And if I do need one, I'll borrow your son's…" she laughed.

I tried to talk her out of this act of generosity. A phone's a personal thing, and as far as I could see, she was very attached to it. I told her that her mother would probably want to be able to call her. But Cara was determined.

- "There's the laptop, and Jack's desktop PC too. I can use those for browsing the web, and I always speak to Mum over the internet anyway", she answered.

I didn't have any more arguments. A few days later, we went to visit her brother Mike, and Cara left her brand new telephone, her only valuable possession, as a gift.

The next day, she asked for the password and logged in to her social media accounts on Jack's computers and phone. Cara then read all of Jack's messages from the previous three to four years. She looked through all the photos and albums and went through the private groups in Jack's accounts with a fine-tooth comb, but we didn't know this at the time; we didn't suspect; it wouldn't have crossed our minds. My son worked, and Cara stayed at home, lying in bed with the laptop on her knee. Usually, she said she had a stomach-ache, so she stayed in bed for hours each day. When she got up, she bathed, ate something, and went shopping. She couldn't work or look for a job because she didn't yet have pre-settled status, an immigration permit, or NI number, and anyway, the second wave of Covid was underway. A partial lockdown was in force across the country, with mandatory home working. Seventy percent of the population was working from home or on furlough. Job opportunities were virtually non-existent. The shops were barely open, and fast-food restaurants and service-industry outlets like hair salons and beauty parlours were operating with limited hours because of Christmas.

Jack and Cara planned what Cara would do once she got pre-settled status, and lockdown was over. It should have been a no-brainer that she'd look for work as a hairdresser, because although there are lots of hairdressers, almost every salon is always advertising for staff. Jack reasoned that she'd be able to make a good living, because a man's haircut is 15 pounds for twenty minutes of work, and a woman's costs 40-50 quid for barely an hour of effort. Surely Cara would be earning good money once she started working. But as they talked about this and delved deeper into the subject, and Jack started talking about which nearby salons might have openings they could ask about, Cara became hesitant. A few minutes later, she admitted that she hadn't gained her certificate or even completed the course. Her stepfather had paid for the expensive hairdressing equipment, and she'd started the practical training, but she'd been treated badly at the salon where she was serving her apprenticeship. They didn't let her outside, even for breaks, so after a few weeks, she sold her tools and spent the money on a puppy. Giggling, Cara said her stepfather still didn't know she'd sold the equipment and that the puppy had been bought with the proceeds. Returning to the subject of her training, she thought she should finish it sometime because she really liked the profession; it was just the way that her boss and coworkers treated her that she couldn't stand. Maybe here she'd find somewhere better? If so, she'd be happy to start again.

- "She'll hardly earn anything as an apprentice", I said to Jack that day when I was alone with him. "But that's the least of it, the smallest problem. What worries me far more, and what you should be thinking about too, is that so far that girl hasn't told you the truth about anything; and today we found out she conned her stepfather too..."

Jack didn't reply straight away, but just bowed his head and only spoke up a few moments later.

- "Yes, that's pretty bad. But she's still very young. People do stupid things when they're young... She might have come to her senses since then."

I could have argued with him; this story wasn't – couldn't be – an old one, because Cara had told us several times about how sad she was that she couldn't bring the puppy to live with Jack. She even planned to have her ex-boyfriend send it after her. But I didn't want to argue with Jack about this. Better to plan for the future, I thought, agreeing that this must be far more important.

We found a language school because Cara didn't speak a word of English, and if she planned to find any kind of work in the future, she'd obviously have to learn the language first. Cara concurred and happily agreed to enrol. She and Jack went to the interview together. I was ready shoulder the financial burden of the English lessons, I'd have paid for the course. After taking a test, Cara was told she could join the beginner's class that was starting in January. But a couple of days later, in the morning, Cara decided it would be a shame for me to spend so much money, and anyway, the school's so far away, she'd have to go by bus, and it's cold. She'd rather learn English by herself! Don't worry, she said, everything's out there on the internet, and she'd watch TV, and we'd buy books. She learns languages easily, she added, smiling. And I believed her in the end. She already spoke 3 languages at 19: German, Romanian, and Hungarian. Why shouldn't I believe her? Like everything else, it was so easy to take her word for this, too.

Cara also claimed that she could cook very well, in fact, or at least everyone had praised her cooking so far. So – she said, laughing – from now on, she'd take care of Jack. Now there was no need for me to take care of my son, not even when it came to what he eats. I smiled, but I was happy she was so enthusiastic. However, it soon became clear that things weren't exactly as she described them in this regard, either. Cara asked her mother for recipes over video calls, and as she cooked, they discussed what she should or shouldn't mix while she stood at the stove. As far as I could tell, Cara couldn't cook any food except schnitzel. But she was infinitely enthusiastic and cheerful, kind, and charming. And she seemed happy. So innocently happy. She was 19 years old. We turned a blind eye to the fact that she hadn't told the truth again, and that she couldn't really cook. So what? What of it? She'll learn. Anyway, it's the thought that counts, isn't it? And her intentions seemed to be real. She's still a little girl, I thought. Always. And I tried to remember what I was like at 19, what thoughts went through my head, how I lived, how I behaved.

It was the third week of December, and Cara had been living with us for three weeks.

- "We've decided to get married," she said to me one morning, with a broad smile on her face. Beside her stood Jack, holding her close. "We'd like to do it as soon as possible. We don't want to wait at all, it's best if we hold the wedding straight after Christmas!"

It was the year of the global pandemic, the second wave, everything was closed, including the registry office, and every marriage had to be registered at least a month in advance. And it was already upon us, only one week to go until Christmas. With the best will in the world, getting together an ad-hoc wedding was a hopeless undertaking. I had to tell them this. Cara looked bitterly disappointed.

- "But anyway, you've only known each other for three weeks, there's no need to hurry, you've got plenty of time," I added. And I tried to grab onto something, because suddenly I was overcome by the feeling that someone had pushed me onto a moving express train. "Winter weddings aren't as pretty, anyway. At least wait for spring!"
- "But there's nothing to wait for. What should we wait for?" she said. "We love each other, we're good together! We want to live together properly, officially! And we want to grow old together. Don't we?" She cuddled up to my son, who nodded and held her even closer. He kissed her and squeezed her tightly, his face betraying an unearthly state of bliss. Literally, it was like he was somewhere else in the universe; he wasn't with us. And Cara continued:
- "And we haven't only known each other for three weeks, it's been almost three months! We spoke for hours every day online before I came. Sometimes we spent the whole night together! There was even a time when Jack fell asleep, and I stayed up all night

just watching how your son sleeps. Because he's so beautiful. The most beautiful man. The most beautiful person I've ever seen."

I didn't have any more arguments or counterarguments, and it might sound silly, but I liked Cara's enthusiasm, too. It wasn't her flattery – I found that repulsive – but her youthfulness, her energy, her sincerity. Or what I thought to be sincerity. That's what I liked. Although this, too, was nothing more than a vain hope. For her side of the story, like everything else, was a subtle half-truth. Because by "talking," she meant she had gotten my son to talk while she listened. By the time she arrived here, she knew everything about us, while we knew almost nothing about her life…

My daughter warned us. Both of us. Both my elder sons had more than a few reservations of their own, too.

– "Mum, be careful. Mum, this is very quick. It might be too good to be true. Mum, that girl's got a strange glint in her eye; she's not a calm personality. She looks disturbed; in fact, pretty much everything about her seems to be disturbing… And Mum, you hardly know anything about her. You don't even know her family. They're both still very young. They don't need to get married yet. Let them get to know each other, live a little, travel around!"

Unfortunately, my children also messaged their brother with their opinions. And Cara knew the passwords and read every single message that was sent to Jack. She had a free pass to all his social media accounts and emails. And she used it. But she hadn't yet revealed this. We didn't know, we didn't notice, that Cara was watching us, all of us. She read everything, screened every message. And she paid attention to everything, down to the last hyphen. But she kept it buried deep down, in her silence. Back then.

Silence. Not a little buddy. Not a good friend. Unless you create it for yourself, just for yourself, when you're alone. In communities and relationships, silence isn't a good sign, not a sign of peace. Wise people say: a person in silence is thinking about something. And it's better to know what's going on in people's heads, better if they speak out, if they express what they're thinking and what they'd like. For everyone to be happy and live in peace, it's not silence we need, it's monologues, confessions, and lots and lots of dialogue.

- "We'd like to have children, you know, which is also why we want to get married as soon as possible. Jack really wants a child, children, and I'll give him that", Cara said to me one morning as she came out of the bathroom.

Her face was glowing. Jack wasn't home; he'd gone to work. I'd just gotten up and was about to drink my coffee. I was lost for words, although there was so much I had to say about that! But how?

- "You've got loads of time for that. Live a little first, have fun, learn! Travel, see the world!" was all I could stammer. "There's still loads of time to start a family. You're both very young!"

But Cara just laughed. All she wanted to do was to make Jack happy, she said. And when she found out that you could buy pregnancy tests off the shelf, we had to buy one every day. I asked about her menstrual cycle and tried to tell her that it's only worth doing a test if she's already missed a period, but she'd recently asked me for tampons and sanitary towels, so that certainly wasn't the case. But Cara couldn't be talked out of this either. Every day, she wanted to know precisely whether or not she'd conceived.

Before Christmas, Jack bought a symbolic ring so he could at least go through the motions, and he got ready to propose to Cara. Jack even called the girl's family to ask for Cara's hand in marriage "officially" via video chat, as there was no other way. That was when we saw Cara's other two elder brothers, her mother, her stepfather, and the uncles and aunts living in her home country "in person" for the first time.

There were lots of them. And although they unanimously offered their congratulations, they also said it would be better to wait; there's plenty of time. I was happy about their good sense, seeing that at least they thought as my family did. They should live a little; they're still very young. But Cara used the same arguments against them as I did, and Jack confirmed his intentions. That evening, Cara announced to her family again that she had found the best husband ever, and the best mother-in-law, and there was nothing to wait for. She wasn't going to miss this opportunity, and she was certain that it was the right decision...

"We'll live our lives together, have lots of children, and be happy!" Cara cuddled up to Jack like a little cat during the video call, too.

Cara knew exactly what Jack longed for, what he wanted to hear, what he wanted to see, and how he pictured the future. And Jack seriously believed he'd found the one, his soulmate for life. Jack believed it. I didn't. But I didn't know how to get it through to him. In fact, I wasn't even sure if it was my job to get it through to him at all. After all, it was his life; he had the right to make decisions, the right to make mistakes. He was an adult, and at that time, Jack hadn't asked for my advice and opinion. That's why I kept quiet. If I'd known what was coming, I wouldn't have kept quiet even if Jack had seen it as intervention, even if it harmed our relationship. But it's too late to think about that now. Much too late. We've been through hell and high water, crossed every line. At the time, I felt I was doing the right thing by not interfering with my own opinion. And now, it doesn't help to know what a huge mistake that was.

Cara had beautiful hair. Huge, long, luxuriant locks, a wavy storm of golden-brown hair. But in the middle of December, she got it into her head that she wanted to go to the hairdresser and get it bleached. I kept asking her why.

- "Have you ever been blonde?"
- "No, never. I don't even know how it would suit me," she replied, laughing.
- "Why then? Why do you want to bleach your hair?"
- "Because Jack likes blonde hair better!" she whispered to me, flashing a conspiratorial smile.
- "No, he doesn't! He's never had a blonde girlfriend."

- "Well, that's just it!" she giggled, "but I know. He goes for blondes!"
- "I don't think so", I said pleasantly. "I've no idea why you think that, but you should still ask Jack if that's really true. I think he loves you just the way you are!"

But Cara wouldn't listen.

- "Believe me, this is what he needs," she said, "it'll be great! I'm sure that Jack will love me even more like this! He prefers blondes!"

I felt embarrassed and unsure how to reply. I hadn't read Jack's private messages to his friends, so I had no way of knowing that he'd once said something to the effect that he liked blonde girls. All I knew was that my son was so in love he couldn't see past his own nose and was walking with his feet six feet above the ground. Everyone could see that. Two weeks after Cara arrived, Jack quit the job he'd been doing for three years. He reasoned that he'd had enough of it anyway and wanted to do something different. He didn't yet know what, but he'd decide after Christmas, he said. However, the real reason was that he wanted to be with Cara 24 hours a day. Cara couldn't stand being alone. Every afternoon, she complained to him that she was lonely, had nothing to do, and was bored. Then, when Jack worked afternoons, and they spent the mornings together, she'd beg him not to go, but to stay with her instead.

- "Let's enjoy ourselves a little. Jack can look for a job after Christmas; he's got plenty of time to work. Let's let him relax a little; he's so tired anyway, you can see", Cara said to me.

I didn't really agree, but they were both adults, so I didn't have any say in their decisions, and neither did they ask for my opinion. But I was worried. Not least because Jack really loved his job, and although he was tired, I knew he loved what he did, that he enjoyed looking after the old people in the community. He liked being a home carer and spoke a lot every day about his experiences with the different patients. And everybody, the families he visited, and the agency that employed him, liked him a lot. The job wasn't just a daily chore for Jack, but a part of his self-esteem and his personality. An important part. But now, nothing else mattered except Cara. Jack couldn't see ahead, nor to the left or right. His vision had narrowed as if looking through a kaleidoscope. Still, I tried to speak to him about his decision before he made it final and handed in his resignation.

- "What's going to happen, son? How will you support yourself? What will you do? You've got plans, you wanted to buy a house, a car. Your last paycheque's going to run out soon, and you'll use up everything you've saved so far."

But Jack laughed at me, theatrically opened his wallet in front of me, displaying his credit cards, and showed me his savings on his phone, including the money he'd invested in stocks and shares during the past few months.

- "Mum, I know what I'm doing. I'm a grown-up, I've got money. Even if I don't work for a year, we'll still live comfortably. But you don't need to worry, I'll look for a job. Everything will be fine. I'm just going to rest for a bit. A few weeks. Then I'll look for something. You know I wanted to leave that company anyway…"

What could I have done? Pretty much nothing. A grown-up man, free to make his own decisions.

The days went by quietly, happily, and very quickly. My eldest son and I were working full-time, so Jack and Cara had plenty of time alone together. When we were at home, they went out sightseeing, shopping, and driving. Cara said that back home, she'd almost gotten her driving licence. She'd passed the theory exam and taken a good few lessons, but the course was cut short when she came to be with Jack. But she really loved driving. She asked Jack to take her out a few times to a quiet road by the national park, to practice so she wouldn't forget everything she'd learned. After that, Jack took her out for a drive almost every day. He was surprised that Cara didn't know how to use the gearstick and clutch, but Cara told him she'd learned on an automatic. So, Jack taught her to change gears and said she was pretty good at it. Cara was a quick learner, and it wouldn't take much for her to pass her test. I just hoped they didn't get caught by the police first, driving all over the place. Although Jack had started to apply for Cara's provisional license, it hadn't arrived yet, and there was still no news of when it would turn up.

Cara insisted on her plan but eventually took my advice, and one afternoon, she asked Jack for his opinion about bleaching her hair. What would he say if she were blonde? Jack told her she was beautiful as she was, no need to add or change anything. But Cara was determined to see a hairdresser at any cost. I didn't understand, but once again I told myself she was still very young, still just getting to know herself, so let her do what she wants.

Late one afternoon before Christmas, Jack took her to the best hairdresser in town, who refused to bleach Cara's hair, saying it would just ruin it. She didn't want to be responsible for that. Cara's hair, she explained, wasn't the kind that could be bleached to an attractive blonde. Finally, at the girl's pleading, the hairdresser carried out some kind of test, but the result just confirmed that even the weakest solution of bleach would severely damage the structure of her hair, and the hairdresser reaffirmed that she wouldn't take on the job. She applied highlights to Cara's hair using a technique called balayage and told her that this was the most she could do with the colouring if she wanted it to stay pretty. Cara was bitterly disappointed, but there was nothing she could do. She asked to have her hair straightened, then they came home. They spent 4 hours and 100 pounds at the hair salon. In the end, Cara didn't like her own hair at all.

- "Well, it wasn't worth paying so much for that," grumbled Cara. "That hairdresser's totally stupid, and she didn't do anything for all that money. Look at it now. Can you see any difference? It's just the same as before."

In truth, I could see a difference, and no, it wasn't just the same as before. But I couldn't tell her that. Because Cara's hair had lost its character. The beautiful, thick locks had been ironed into straight, thin strands of hair. A style that otherwise fitted in perfectly with the trend, with highlights. Out and about, eight out of ten girls were walking around with the same head of hair at that time. Nothing special, a totally generic look. "You're still very pretty", I said to Cara warmly, and Jack tried to convince her that she was beautiful just the way she was, but to no avail; Cara didn't believe him or me. And she never got over the visit to the hairdresser, which she saw as a failure. The first morning after the festive season, she went to the shop, bought a home dye kit, and bleached her hair in the bathroom. Her whole head turned orange.

RED FLAGS

For the weekend before New Year's Eve, I invited Jack and Cara to the small town where I'd recently bought a little two-bedroomed house. Before Cara arrived, I'd planned to finally move away from my grown-up sons and provide for my retirement, while they lived their own lives and eventually started families of their own. Everybody would live happily ever after. It was a cosy little house, which I'd managed to buy with a 10-percent down-payment on a mortgage, in a small town near the sea. I still had almost twenty years until retirement, which is exactly when the mortgage would be paid off. I repainted it and slowly, but surely, furnished it. A little cottage, a cosy home of my own. I was very happy, after so many trials and tribulations, to have somehow got myself and my life on track. The dog scampered happily around the beach and the parks; we explored the area together. I liked being there in that town. At first, it felt strange, the peace and being alone, but I'd raised four children, and it felt good finally to be doing what I wanted. I worked, read, slept, went for long walks, and got to know new people. I wanted to finish that year by sharing a little joy with everyone, so I invited the young ones to take some time out with me on the weekend. Cara and Jack enjoyed themselves. They, too, went for long walks in the late December sunshine. We chatted, and everything was peaceful. We went down in two cars. I wanted to see in the new year there, and they wanted to return to the capital to party. When it was time to say goodbye, they waved happily as they descended the stairs.

- "Your house is lovely", said Cara, smiling, and she hugged me. "And don't be sad that we're going now. We'll come and see you a lot. We'll visit. You won't be able to get rid of us!" she added, laughing.

I wasn't sad. Cara couldn't have known it, but I like being alone. I often need silence. I think that's how it is for everyone who deals with people in their job. And that was how the first week of the new year went by, nice and quietly. I did up the house and enjoyed my annual holiday and the peacefulness that came with it. Then, on one of the last few days, the phone rang unexpectedly. My son was calling.

- "Hello, is everything ok?' I stammered, sensing from his voice that he was in a very good mood, almost beside himself with happiness. He didn't even want to wait for me to reply.
- "We've got something to tell you!" he added straight away, and the next moment, Cara was on the other end of the line, screaming into the telephone.
- "Happy New Year GRANNY!!! Granny! Do you hear me? Imagine, you're going to be a granny! You're going to be a granny. Are you happy?"

I was happy. All the strange little episodes aside, I was happy at the news. How could I not have been happy? My son was untroubled. In the past few weeks, his face had been glowing, calm, and smooth-skinned. I knew he'd been longing for this for years. To have a family of his own, children. Jack had spoken about this since he was a teenager; soon after starting work, he'd be sure to get to know someone, start a family, and have lots of children. Jack wasn't like other men, and he certainly wasn't like his peers. He wasn't interested in football or other sports; he didn't go out on the pull or drink with his mates, only a maximum of three or four times a year, on birthdays. Jack didn't go to parties, to the pub or disco, he wasn't a party animal. He didn't want to travel and see the world that much, and he didn't have any grand plans or ambitions. He just wanted a little house, a good car, a job he enjoyed that paid enough to live on, and a family, lots of children that he could love and raise.

So, I was happy to hear the news. I was happy that Jack's dream was coming true, that all this seemed to be within reach. And of course, I was happy because I, too, was already ready and yearning for grandchildren. All my other children were older, but my eldest son hadn't settled down yet. My daughter was married, but she and my son-in-law wanted to build a life together and enjoy it before starting a family.

Jack and Cara switched to video and showed me their pride and joy: the positive pregnancy test. The two pink stripes shone out, clear and irrefutable. They could see I was happy, my eyes teary. We were all very happy. When I returned to the capital, we celebrated the big event. Cara didn't drink a toast with us, of course, because "even that one sip could be damaging". Her face glowed; she was beautiful. We called Cara's family and my daughter's to share the news so they could share in our celebration. Not long after that conversation, my daughter called me on my own phone.

- "Mum, Mum, this is very early. Very fast!" she said, with genuine concern in her voice.

I knew that myself, I didn't need to be told. Cara had arrived barely six weeks ago. Three weeks ago, they'd started talking about the wedding, and three weeks after that, they were already expecting a child. Early, very quick. But it was their life.

- "This is how they wanted it. This is the life they've made for themselves. How could I interfere in that? This is happy news, Sophia", I told my daughter, calmly and kindly. A child is a blessing. All we can do is congratulate them and be happy for them. And hope that everything works out, that it'll all be fine..."
- "I don't agree", my daughter said, simply and coherently, the way she always argued. "Mum, this is my little brother. Who, by the way, is the nicest person I know. He doesn't deserve to be conned and hurt. I'm worried, and I'll only stop worrying when everything really is ok. When I see and feel that everything's fine."

I understood my daughter, I understood her train of thought, and I knew her way of thinking. I hadn't expected any other reaction from her. And to be honest with myself, I should have recognised that somewhere, deep down, I shared her concern. But there was nothing we could do. The two lines were already there on the test strip. "Behold, children are a heritage from the Lord, the fruit of the womb a reward" – a true saying that came to my mind. And under the circumstances, there really wasn't anything to do but grasp at hope.

- "Let's hope everything will be fine", I said softly into the phone.
- "Well, I hope so too", sighed Sophia. Then we didn't talk about it anymore. We exchanged a few words about other things, then put the phone down.

We had to decide how to make things work for everyone. I, we, spent days thinking about this. Of course, the wedding had become urgent as well. We might as well do it as soon as possible, given how things have turned out. Cara came from a traditional family, or so she said, and she was Catholic. That's what she claimed to be, anyway. In keeping with our values, we also believe a child should be born in wedlock, if possible. There were plenty of questions, and they all needed an answer. We couldn't put off the decisions for long.

- "You can't stay here with a child. You know that, don't you?" said my eldest son.

He and I were the official tenants of the flat. We'd taken out a lease on the little maisonette a few years ago, and it was the first home we'd had to ourselves since moving here from Hungary.

- "The landlord wouldn't agree to it, and 45 square metres isn't big enough for four adults and a baby!" added George.
- "Of course, not", I replied. "I'm already thinking about what to do. We'll figure it out, don't worry, son."

But the young couple had no chance of moving out and renting a flat on their own. Cara didn't yet have pre-settled status or even an NI number, so she had no employment contract and, of course, no income either. My son had just quit his job, so he couldn't show any proof of income either. Even if we scraped together the deposit and didn't tell the landlord the young couple was expecting a child, they still wouldn't have been able to rent a flat independently. No letting agency, or even a private landlord, would have given them the time of day.

So, there was only one option left for us. To move out to the country together, to my house, and they'd live with me until they found their feet and were able to make a home for themselves. I'd already found a job down there before Cara arrived, and my plan had been to move in the early spring. The notice period at my previous job was two month and I handed my resignation to my boss in December. I'd planned to move at the end of February, but since August, I'd been going down to the little house for a few days every week so I wouldn't have to take all my stuff there and furnish the house in one go. I was getting it ready at my own pace.

We decided this was how it would be. They'd move in with me. They both thanked me profusely. Cara smothered me in hugs and seemed very grateful.

- "This is really kind of you, thank you so much! You know it's only a few months until the baby's born and we get some money. And when I start working, we'll move away. But you're a granny, it's great that you'll be there at the beginning, to look after the baby while everything's shaping up", said Cara and laughed.

And at every video call, she continued to tell her family that she'd found the best husband and mother-in-law ever, and how lucky she felt, how she could hardly believe that all these good things were happening to her.

Everything really did seem ideal. Doable and pleasant. We started planning what else we'd need, but in fact, the house had everything we needed, since I'd already furnished it. I'd intended one of the bedrooms as a spare room and bought a double bed for it, thinking that if my daughter Sophia and her husband came to stay, it would suit them, too. So, there wasn't really anything else to buy, perhaps just some cupboards. We decided that Jack and Cara would have the larger upstairs room, the spare room, which overlooked the garden, because it had the double bed. I'd stay in the smaller, street-facing bedroom, which was more than big enough for me. We also decided to move at the end of January, and I'd commute, travelling up to work for three days a week when my shifts were scheduled. Jack sprang into action almost immediately, looking for work on the internet. He found a home care agency, just like his old workplace, in the small town. We went back for two days for the interview. The interview went well, Jack got the job, and we celebrated. Jack finally felt secure financially, too. He was happy to have a job again and earn money.

Cara was happy, too, and clearly understood that Jack had to work now that the baby was on its way if they wanted a home of their own. I relaxed too. Everything seemed to be turning out well; there was no need for me to worry so much. This girl probably really does adore her husband, and I'm overthinking. I think too much anyway. There were a few days left until the move, and we spent them joyfully packing and getting ready.

On one of those days, we woke to find that Cara had cut her own hair. It wasn't really short, but it came down just above her shoulders.

- "It was ruined by the bleach", she said. "I had to do something with it, I couldn't leave it like that, it wasn't even nice to touch".

Her mother was dismayed when she noticed it during that day's video call.

- "Oh, my little girl, what's happened to your beautiful hair? Why did you have to cut it off like that? Just look at it now! When will it grow back? It'll take ages!"

But Cara laughed and said the same to her as she had said to me.

- "It's only my hair. What are you all so worked up about? It'll grow back. Don't worry about that!"

That incident aside, everything seemed fairly settled. But then something else happened to jolt us out of this happy, expectant state of mind for a while.

With only a few days left to go, in the last weeks of January, I was on night duty. It was past midnight, and finally, I could take a break and check my phone. This is when I'd usually spend a few minutes losing myself in social media newsfeeds, looking at photographs. A time when I don't have to answer questions, reply to letters, place orders, or solve problems, just surf the web as I please. This is usually how I spend my mid-work breaks because there simply isn't time for anything more meaningful. But now, a message was waiting:

- "Mum, I'm really sick, we're going to A&E".

This kind of message is every mother's nightmare. Well, certainly it was mine. I tried calling my son's phone, but he didn't pick up. Cara had received an almost brand-new telephone for Christmas from Jack. I called her number too, but she didn't answer either. A few minutes later, I got a text from her.

- "We're here at the hospital, down in A&E". That was all.

I spoke to my shift manager, who let me go. I got changed and rushed down to A&E. Jack was sitting in the waiting room looking pale; next to him, Cara was shaking. Neither of them looked great.

- "What happened?" I asked, but Jack just shook his pale head, and Cara looked down at the ground. I lost my temper.
- "What happened, son? Cara? What happened? What's wrong? What's happened to Jack?"
- "It's not my fault!" snapped Cara. "Don't blame me", she said with a sudden defiant flash of the eyes.

It was a strange reaction, out of place, the way Cara immediately lashed out at me. It sounded off to me at the time, but I didn't have time to deal with that right away. I took a deep breath and tried to keep my voice calm.

- "I'm not blaming anyone. I'd just like to know what happened."
- "Oh, for pity's sake, at least don't start arguing here. Mum, it's better if you go back to work," Jack said, and when he looked at me, his expression was alarmed, unsettled. I thought something must be wrong. Something had to be very wrong if Jack had come to the hospital of his own accord, if he'd decided he needed to see a doctor, and if he felt the question I asked really wasn't helping. Maybe what happened wasn't the most important thing. I had to pull myself together.
- "I didn't come down here just to go back to work a few minutes later. I'm here to be with you. You texted me that you're unwell. What's that matter?"

They sat silently in front of me for a few minutes. But when they finally started talking, all I found out was that Jack had experienced chest pain and breathlessness, so they'd decided to come to the hospital. They'd been sitting there, waiting, for two hours. COVID was a factor, but the waiting time at A&E was usually at least four hours anyway. I phoned my manager and explained the situation. If that's how it was, she said, I shouldn't go back to work. They'd get the work done, better for me to stay with my child… I was truly grateful for that.

We waited another hour. Thankfully, Jack's condition seemed stable, and he was breathing easily, which is why he wasn't prioritised at triage. But he did seem tired, exhausted even, and terribly pale. We bought drinks from a vending machine, but none of us spoke much. When we were finally called into the examination room, a series of tests was run. Blood pressure, heart rate, and oxygen saturation. The tests showed nothing out of the ordinary. His pulse, measured at 160 on arrival, also seemed to be returning to normal. Now it was only 120. His blood pressure was normal; they took blood and urine samples, and the ECG and chest and abdominal CT scans showed no abnormalities. The duty doctor asked Jack about the episode. How it started, how long it lasted, whether he was still experiencing symptoms, and how much better he felt compared to when he arrived at the hospital. Jack had to answer these questions, and only then did I learn the details. Not everything, of course, just that they were arguing. Later, I also found out why. Days later. Jack told me how it happened.

Jack had arrived home late because he'd been to settle things with his old employer, picking up the documents he needed to start at his new workplace. When he got home, he found Cara chatting with her ex-partner in the kitchen. Later, it turned out that this wasn't a one-off; they'd been chatting daily, exchanging a raft of messages since the New Year, the two of them, Fred and Cara. Jack asked for Cara's phone and scrolled through the chats. Of course, he didn't understand what they were talking about because Cara wrote to her ex in German, but as was her habit, the girl sprinkled her messages with smileys and other clearly affectionate emoticons, and even long strings of hearts and heart smileys. Harsh words were spoken, then Cara burst into tears, saying she wanted to go home for a few days or a week to decide how things should be… That was when Jack began to feel unwell.

- "But there's Covid! You might not be able to come back, or even go, as the borders are closed. Even if they let you out of the country, it might be months before you can get back in, and… And we want to get married! We're about to move. You want to go now? Now you want to decide what you want?"

Jack tried to explain to Cara, and mainly to understand her, and what had happened, but then – Jack told me – he suddenly felt really sick and couldn't talk anymore.

Hearing the story, I felt sick too, and for days afterwards. They were planning to move two days later. Cara was carrying my son's child. They were both preparing to marry. They'd told everyone they were completely happy, and Cara seemed to be happy too. And then, suddenly, she doesn't know what she wants? Does she chat with her ex-boyfriend every day? She doesn't know how things should be, asks for more time, and wants to go home to decide. Luckily, I hadn't known about this narrative back there in the emergency ward, because I don't really know how I'd have reacted.

The duty doctor issued his discharge summary in the small hours and made Jack promise to get some rest. "Take it easy, mate," he said. Jack was to keep things light and avoid stress. He was discharged. Cara crossed herself and burst into tears when we stepped out through the hospital doors and finally were able to set off home.

- "Don't be angry, please! I love you. I don't know what happened to me. I don't want anything to happen to you. I'll die if anything happens to you. I want to live my whole life with you," she gasped between sobs, clinging to my son's shoulder.

Jack didn't say a word, just hugged the two of us. He'd always had long arms. And a big heart.

The next day, all was peace and quiet. Cara promised Jack she wouldn't talk to her ex-partner, either on the phone or via Messenger, and showed him her phone to prove that she'd deleted him from everything. Fred was no longer a friend on her social media. She'd even blocked him.

- "It's over. That's the past. I don't even know what was up with me. I don't know why I started talking to him again. You're the only one for me. I want to live my whole life with you. We'll have a child, a baby, babies, and we'll grow old together. I'm sure it's just the hormones…", Cara would say. "And I'm not going away, why would I? I don't know what was with me that day, but don't be angry, please! It's all just those stupid hormones.

Two days of peace. We took a deep breath and relaxed. The day of the move arrived. I set off in the early afternoon. We loaded everything we could into the bigger car, but it was obvious we'd have to go back for a few bits and bobs some weekend. We agreed that Jack and Cara would set off early the next morning in the smaller car, when it was light, so they'd arrive safely without having to drive in the dark, and I'd be able to get their room ready for them in the meantime. I'd cook them something nice for lunch. I arrived in the small town, a three-hour journey from London, in the early evening. I let the dog into the garden, and she ran around happily. I freed the cats from their box, too, and fed them. I pottered about serenely, tidying up, and by around ten at night, I'd finished the unpacking. I was just getting ready to take a bath when I got their message:

- "We've left, we'll arrive after midnight", Cara wrote, with a smattering of smileys.

I called Jack. His phone was on speaker because he was driving.

- "Hi, what's happened? Weren't you supposed to come in the morning? Your car isn't in good shape; it's pitch-black outside and cold!

Jack didn't reply.

- "But we didn't want to wait until morning, we want to be there with you now", said Cara, and laughed.

I didn't laugh. I sighed instead, but said okay. I asked them to be careful, to drive carefully, and arrive safely. Then I had a bath, quietly relieved that I'd already got everything ready. I'd even pulled on the bedclothes and made their bed. I was still in the bath when their next message arrived. They'd broken down on the motorway. There was a long tailback at one of the roadworks, and they'd had to shut down the engine, but Jack left the lights on while they were sitting in the traffic jam, so the battery went flat, and now the car wouldn't start. If that was even the problem. Because they didn't know precisely what the problem was. And nor could they say where they were. Somewhere on some motorway, next to some exit… Then I lost my temper. Not enough to raise my voice, but I certainly spoke forcefully.

- "What was the point of that? Why couldn't you just stick to what we agreed? If you'd come by daylight, the battery wouldn't have gone flat even in the traffic jam, and you wouldn't be in this mess!" Jack didn't answer, staying silent again. "Why did you have to force it?" I asked Cara. She bridled.
- "I haven't done anything! Now it's my fault again, is it? I didn't say we should go. I didn't care when we went. Jack didn't want to stay. He said we should go to your place today!"

We all knew this wasn't true. It wasn't Jack who'd been calling the shots in the past few weeks, whatever they did together, whatever it was about. Jack had been tired that afternoon – I'd seen it, I knew – he'd been happy that they'd only be leaving the next morning, and he wanted to say goodbye to the neighbours. But I didn't want to argue anymore; I was already regretting bringing it up in the first place. I needed to focus on resolving the situation. Jack said his phone's battery was on 15% and would run out soon, because he had nowhere to charge it. He asked me to call for roadside assistance because he didn't know the number by heart, but if he tried looking it up on the internet, his phone's battery would drain even quicker, and they wouldn't be able to do anything at all. Cara's telephone had already died because they were using it to play music in the traffic jam. Great. It was already past midnight. I called the two breakdown services that I knew. The second promised to get there faster, perhaps because I told them the young lady in the car was six weeks pregnant. Because the young couple couldn't say where they had broken down in the deep, dark night, the dispatchers called Jack's phone to locate them using GPS. Finally, they identified the location. Jack didn't have coverage for this kind of incident, so I had to pay in advance, by credit card over the phone… But that didn't matter at the time. Not long after that, the mechanic found them and charged the battery. That was all that mattered. They reached the house, me, their home, at three in the morning. I waited up for them. But they didn't ask for anything to eat, just went straight up to their room to sleep. Cara marched upstairs indignantly, without greeting me or even glancing at me. The next day, before she would smile again, the three of us had to discuss why I blame her for everything when nothing's her fault, and why should I blame anyone for anything anyway? I had to apologise, which I somehow managed to do, although it didn't really seem appropriate to me.

After a few days, everything was back on track. Jack picked up his new contract at his new workplace and started his training. A daily routine started to emerge. Jack and I tried to work in a way that wouldn't leave Cara feeling too alone and abandoned. They went into town a lot to walk, shop, and eat. I gave them plenty of time to themselves, as I usually worked four nights a week, sleeping after and between shifts in the afternoon. They lived upstairs, with me on the ground floor. They had their own space. Jack, Cara, and I only met when they came down to use the kitchen or the bathroom, and that was about it.

More Red Flags

Everything seemed calm; it looked like things were settling down.

Cara started worrying about her pregnancy, but I tried to reassure her.

- "It's so strange that I don't feel anything", she would say to me. "I should feel something, shouldn't I? But there's nothing. No morning sickness, no nothing. It's like I'm not even pregnant...
- "It's still very early days", I smiled. "You'll feel all sorts of things before long; you might even miss how things are right now!" I said, trying to comfort her.

Then one afternoon, Cara called her mother, who asked about her symptoms, and when Cara said she had no complaints, in fact, she was feeling great, with a good appetite and no aches or pains, her mother just said

- "Well, then, I doubt very much that you're pregnant, my girl! Whenever you were pregnant before, you slept all the time… You slept whole days when you're pregnant, without getting out of bed."

We were all sitting at the kitchen table. Jack looked in bewilderment at me and at her, too, his wife-to-be. But Cara looked away. From both of us. After the video chat, we sat in silence for a few minutes. Then Cara broke the silence. She sighed and admitted that this wasn't her first pregnancy. She'd already had two spontaneous miscarriages. She fell pregnant with the first baby, she told us, when she was 16. The second was six months before, not long after her relationship broke down with her ex, Fred (the one she'd flirted with on Messenger a few weeks ago). But, she told us, she hadn't wanted that baby anyway…

Cara showed no embarrassment as she told Jack and me all this. I had to turn away for a moment so she wouldn't see my face. I didn't know how much of what I was thinking was written across it. Jack said nothing for a few moments, then gently placed his hand on Cara's.

- "It's okay, sweetheart, it's good that you told us. Now at least we know everything about you", my son said gently.

I wasn't so sure about the second part, but I didn't say a word. I was thinking that, practically, not a single word of what Cara said was true. And how much had come to light unexpectedly and taken us by surprise.

What else didn't we know? And how much was there that we'd never know? Perhaps that was the first time I let the light come on in that dimly lit room and didn't allow the sensors to shut down again. From then on, I started paying attention, although I'd never even heard the expression 'red flags' at the time.

Because Cara was really worried about whether she was pregnant or not, whether the baby was okay, or what was happening to her at the time, we tried to get to see a doctor or gynaecologist. But in that small town, we still didn't know anyone or anything. To be precise, we didn't even know where the local hospital was. We searched the internet and finally came across a private ultrasound clinic. The global pandemic was in full swing, so we had to book in advance and take every precaution, complying with all the rules when we accompanied Cara to the scan. I wasn't allowed inside, so I waited for them outside in the car. Jack was only allowed to go inside with Cara because she didn't speak English, and someone had to translate. But they were given a photo of the scan. A tiny ball inside a larger, pear-shaped black cavity. Alongside the tiny, pea-sized ball, computer text: Yolk sac. So, Cara was five weeks, three days pregnant. There was nothing to see of the baby yet, not even a heartbeat, but the sonographers said that, based on a visual examination, everything was fine and normal for this stage of pregnancy.

Cara happily pottered about the flat. All was calm. They went shopping together every day, and they cooked. In the evening, they watched films. Things were going nicely. "Everything will be fine," I thought again. Or at least, that's what I kept telling myself. And I knew that was what my son was hoping for, too. But the following weeks revealed that something still wasn't quite right.

The second weekend after our move, I arrived home to find that Cara had cut her hair. Not just a bit this time. All of it. She was completely bald. Not even a few millimetres remained of her hair, nothing at all. Just her bare scalp. I was on my way home when she sent a selfie she'd taken after the haircut. In the selfie, her almost bald head was still blonde – or she'd just coloured it with Photoshop, I don't know – but by the time I got home, she had no hair left. Just bare skin. She was like someone who'd escaped from a concentration camp. Alarming. But even like this, she was still pretty. Think Sinead O'Connor at twenty years old. Very, very young – I thought again. This girl is terribly young. She has no idea what to do with herself. I tried to explain to myself. At the same time, I felt sure that something was very wrong with this latest act. If a woman shaves her hair off, there's always a reason for it. A serious reason. I knew that too. But still I tried to reassure myself.

- "Oooh, my little one, oh my God! What have you done?" asked her mother, too.
- "Oh, come on! Come off it! I just wanted something new", laughed Cara. Then she added, "My hair was burnt out from the bleach, it was ruined, I had to cut it off… But don't worry, it'll grow back soon! A year from now, it'll be just like before, you'll see! My hair grows really fast. Until then, I'll get some wigs!" she laughed, loudly this time.

The next day, she was having second thoughts, of course. She didn't say anything, but I could see it. I saw how she stood staring at herself wide-eyed in the mirror. She must have talked to Jack later about how scared she was about what she'd done to herself, and how sorry, because that day Jack told her every half-hour that she was still beautiful, that he still loved her, and wouldn't ever leave her. Especially not because of that. She needn't worry, he'd stay with her for eternity.

For my part, I had a lot on my mind, for example, the terribly cold weather. It was early February, still the depths of winter. How cold her head would get! And that it was almost time for the wedding. And that something didn't add up. Something was off. But what? What should I do? Should I do anything anyway? And if so, what? Just wait and see? Pay closer attention to her? Or what should I pay closer attention to? I hadn't a clue what to do, or if I did or said anything, how I should do or say it. Should I keep quiet, or start shouting?

The next day, Cara ordered her first two wigs on the internet. Two shoulder-length hairpieces. One was blonde; the other, chestnut-brown.

In the next few days, I tried talking to her a lot to find out if there was any other reason for mutilating herself in that way. I didn't ask direct questions; I'm not that tactless. I just tried to get a little closer, to better understand her. But she didn't say too much, as usual. She never strayed from the superficial to the meaningful, even in these conversations.

Dark Winter Nights

Until the end of February, I still had to work two weekends at my old job, so the young couple had plenty of time to themselves. Cara swapped friendly messages with me while I was away and always waited up for me when I came home. Jack started to work and enjoyed exploring the area and getting to know the new families. Cara was at home in the meantime, but was only left alone for a few hours, and didn't mind. This was when the pregnancy symptoms promised by her mother kicked in: Cara slept a lot and threw up every morning, but otherwise, she was generally in good spirits. She no longer liked cooking; she couldn't stand the smells of everyday food preparation, the odour of cooking fat and oil, even the aroma of chicken soup. She craved certain foods, so it was Jack's task to procure them from little corner shops: aubergine hummus, Romanian beans, processed ham. But these usually remained untouched in the fridge. By the time Jack returned with the goods, Cara craved something else. So, most of the time, they ended up at McDonald's or one of the takeaways in town. Or they ordered food for home delivery. There was a Chinese restaurant on the corner, and they ate there a few times, too. This didn't bother me, quite the opposite. I could put myself in Cara's shoes; I still remember my own pregnancies. Even after 30 years, I still had vivid memories of my own cravings. I was glad Jack could afford it all and pamper his wife as much as he wanted, without worrying about money, now that he had a job again. Whenever I called them, their voices were cheerful and carefree. So, everything was fine, but during the last shift of the second weekend, in the middle of the night, I got a message from Cara informing me of a new problem:

- "Jack's really unwell, he's on the loo for the third time, and his stomach's really hurting. He said there's blood in what came out, too… Can you come home? When are you coming home?"

I rushed to the telephone and called them. Jack didn't want to talk, but Cara desperately asked what she should do.

- "I don't know what to do, he's so sick. He got sick suddenly, from one moment to the next. It must be because of the oil you used to fry the meat two days ago," stammered Cara into the phone. "Because that oil's been on the stove for ages and it's full of bacteria…" she said.

For a moment, I was lost for words. I didn't reply, and Cara must have thought I hadn't heard or properly understood what she'd said, so she repeated it:

- "That oil was rotten. Do you hear me? The oil you cooked with. You should always change the oil; you mustn't fry things in it more than once! Then leave it to stand. It's full of bacteria!"

I still didn't really know what to say to this. It took me a while to gather my thoughts:

- "There's nothing wrong with that oil. I fried some potatoes in it once. I've been cooking for my son for 28 years, and he never gotten ill from my cooking. There's no way that oil made him ill."
- "Yes, there is! And don't tell me there's nothing wrong with it, it stinks! That oil's dirty; you should have poured it down the toilet ages ago. Anyway. I don't know what to do here. Your son's so sick! He just came out of the toilet. I looked, and everything's covered in blood. Even after he flushed, the toilet stayed red!"

I swallowed hard.

- "I'm going home in the morning. Until then, give him fluids, make some tea, or boil some water and make him drink it in small sips. There's paracetamol in the kitchen cupboard. Give that to him. He knows how to take it, so his stomach won't hurt…"

I left for home in the morning as soon as the shift had finished. I made it down quickly on the motorway; on weekdays, there's hardly any traffic heading to the country, everyone's hurrying to the capital. Jack was lying on the bed, curled into a ball, his knees pulled up to his chest. He had terrible stomach cramps. His face was pale, his lips drained of blood, almost white. He wasn't vomiting or even nauseous. I was sure that this wasn't a simple stomach upset. And I was also certain that this wasn't caused by the oil I'd left on the stove. I called the ambulance. It came within five minutes, and I was very grateful for that. They examined Jack and decided to take him to the hospital. We were still in the third wave of Covid, so nobody was allowed to go with him. But Cara and I went afterwards and managed to get into the hospital through a side door. The ambulances were lined up outside A&E. We couldn't go in there, but we found the winding corridors leading to the storeroom, which came out behind the A&E reception and waiting room. The waiting room was packed, and everyone was very busy. This meant that, luckily, nobody was looking back to see if anyone was coming from the direction of the wards. We made it to the examination rooms unchallenged. There, we stumbled onto Jack when we heard his voice as he talked to one of the nurses. We waited for the nurse to come out, and sneaked in. Jack said he was feeling better and had been given medicine. Cara threw herself over his chest. "Oh God, just don't let there be anything wrong with you," she kept saying. We were able to talk to Jack for a few minutes, but the nurse came back and very quickly ordered us out of the building. Jack was sent home after a few tests. He phoned to say he was being discharged, so we waited for him in the car outside the hospital. He was prescribed three kinds of antibiotics and painkillers. By the evening, he was feeling better. A few days later, we received the stool test results by post. The result was also reported to the council, and Jack had to send back a list of the restaurants they'd ordered from, where they'd eaten, and what. The infection was caused by a bacterium that thrives in meat prepared in commercial kitchens where hygiene regulations aren't being followed. It's impossible to catch it at home, in a household setting. We forgot the incident in a few weeks. And I put that terrible conversation about the bad oil to one side, like all her other unpleasant remarks. "It must be the hormones talking!" This excuse may even have slipped into my subconscious. I accepted and used Cara's own explanation for her behaviour. She never apologised for suspecting me and blaming me for the oil.

Cara could be very charming, almost enchanting. She sang in the bath, danced in the middle of the living room, used awkward, old-fashioned words, and always clowned around. Often just to make us laugh. Jack was in love like he'd never been in his life. He filled the room with tea lights and lined them up on the side of the bath. On Valentine's Day, he scattered rose petals on the bed and on the bathwater. At night, if Cara was hungry and woke him up, Jack would happily go downtown to the all-night Burger King or McDonald's for a hamburger or whatever Cara fancied at the time.

I made arrangements for the future and helped as much as I could with whatever they asked me to do. We sent the online application for Cara's pre-settled status again, because three months had passed since the first application, but we hadn't heard back from them. Because of Covid, the language schools had closed, so I found an English teacher who spoke Hungarian and who could give her lessons online. I registered her with our GP, arranging for her to be accepted without pre-settled status or an NI number. I phoned the midwife, so she'd receive prenatal care. I translated during phone conversations like an interpreter. I wrote to request an appointment at the registry office to apply for a marriage license. They set the date as 21 April. Cara wanted the wedding to be earlier, but she had to wait because of the pandemic. "At least you'll have time to find a really beautiful wedding dress!" I comforted her. Because the wedding dress shops would only open from the 1st of April, like every other shop selling non-essential goods, we wouldn't be able to arrange anything until then anyway.

Cara sometimes cooked, maybe once a week, but she didn't do much else; she complained of stomach pain, back pain, and was always tired. So, I washed, cleaned, and cooked for them. Both of them. Cara usually slept until noon, because even if she got up in the morning, she'd fall back to sleep after Jack had gone to work. Jack went to work early, making coffee for himself at six in the morning. Cara was usually up until two or three in the morning, browsing the internet and watching videos. After midnight, Jack usually fell asleep beside her. Cara laughed at how short a time Jack was able stay awake at night, despite being a man. "Jack is like a baby, he falls asleep the minute his head hits the pillow", Cara would say... But back then, there was still love in the way she talked about Jack.

One morning, Cara was scared because she'd found a brown stain in her knickers. She sat crying on the edge of the bed, and, unusually for her, called me up to their room.

- "My lower tummy hurts. I think I'm going to lose this baby. It was like this with the other two! First just a brown stain, then my tummy hurt, and I started bleeding. I don't know what I'll do if I lose this baby..." she said, frantically.

Cara was very scared, so we booked a private scan for that afternoon. The baby was eight weeks old, now completely baby-shaped, nice and plump, with a strong heartbeat. We couldn't hear the heartbeat, the sonographer said it wasn't recommended before week twenty, because the frequency used would be too high, and it could harm the foetus. But they showed us the baby's heart, where it was located, and how steadily it was beating. Cara finally relaxed. But she stayed in before for a few days, even while she was awake, to be sure that the baby was safe.

- "Listen", she said one morning the next week, "I might have some kind of infection. Maybe that's what caused the brown stain, not the baby. I don't feel too good down there either, but it can't be good for the baby if I've got a urinary tract infection. And that can only be because you wash my knickers together with yours. I think I caught something from you. It's almost certain. So, could you not wash them together, please?!"

This was another remark that left me speechless for a moment. I'd never washed her clothes together with mine, and I've washed knickers at a high temperature all my life... What's more, there was nothing wrong with me. I swallowed hard, and it took a little time for me to find my voice and inform Cara of these facts. She just ignored what I said and continued, saying that she'd never had any problems until she moved in with us, or before she got pregnant, and she must be more sensitive down there now.

- "It doesn't matter if you haven't got any symptoms", she said. "I can still catch a disease from you, so please promise that from now on you'll wash the knickers separately..."

I repeated that this was what I'd always done, but I promised all the same. Just to reassure her. But a few days later, the conversation had moved on, and Cara never mentioned any infection again, nor did she ask us to take her to the doctor about it.

The days went by peacefully. Sometimes we went out for a walk together, but Cara didn't much like leaving the house since cutting off her hair. Now she had three wigs, but it didn't help because they weren't very comfortable to wear, she said. Her scalp itched under them, and the wigs were heavy; she might even be allergic to them, because they weren't made of real human hair. Nevertheless, Cara was always happy to go shopping. To make sure she got some fresh air, Jack would sometimes sit with her in the garden. Quite a lot. Every afternoon when he got home, or in the mornings when he was on an afternoon shift. The weather was good. The winter was mild in that little seaside town, and spring came early that year, with warm sunshine and a soft breeze.

At the very end of February, our dog had puppies, seven tiny little mutts. Cara joyfully assisted with the birth of the puppies and sat down with them every day in the little fenced-off corner of the room, stroking them and watching them grow, open their eyes. She even had a favourite among the seven puppies, and said she'd love to keep it if she wasn't expecting a baby. Cara was also at peace with the cats, though she was wary of them in general. She said that when she was little, a cat had scratched and even bitten her, and she hasn't trusted them since. But our old cat, the seven-year-old tortoiseshell, who was mainly my son's, slept upstairs with them in the big room, and Cara was on increasingly good terms with it.

Cara finally started English lessons with the teacher I'd found online, who taught students and adults online. In principle, the course should have consisted of two 90-minute sessions a week for Cara, with the lessons paid for by me. But after two weeks, the teacher recommended switching to three 45-minute lessons because the girl couldn't manage any more. She couldn't concentrate for more than 30 minutes at a time, so we agreed on that. Cara clearly enjoyed the English lessons at first, but after a few weeks she started to complain that there was no point studying with this teacher because he hardly taught her anything, just asked questions, and he didn't speak English to her, only Hungarian…

"And anyway, it costs too much", said Cara. There would have been free English classes – available to all immigrants – had it not been for the global pandemic. We tried to explain to Cara that this was the only opportunity to learn at the time, but she just scowled.

- "I can learn English by myself. I'll watch videos", she still maintained.

And from then on, from the end of March, Cara just sought excuses for why the agreed-upon time was no good for her, why she didn't want to attend the lessons. The impending wedding and her pregnancy were a good excuse for this. The best excuse.

During one of the video calls at the end of March, Cara talked to her mother about the birth. I was stopped in my tracks again by a sentence that I overheard by accident.

- "But you can't have a natural birth, my little one. You know you had that spine injury. At the hospital, they told us if you ever get pregnant, you'll need to have a caesarean, or you'll end up in a wheelchair", said Cara's mother.

We hadn't known about this either. When we asked, after the call, Cara told us that when she was a little girl, she'd fallen out of a tree and broken her spine. She hadn't needed an operation, said Cara. She'd just been given a belt that she had to wear for a few weeks, and then it healed. But she couldn't remember anyone saying she wouldn't be able to give birth naturally because of it. And she was very upset. With her permission, I wrote to her stepfather and mother, asking them to send the hospital discharge summary on the spinal injury, because it looked like this would be needed as the due date approached. They sent the report, and it arrived by post the following week. It was in German, so we had to get it translated into English. I didn't mind paying the hundred pounds because an official translation was needed and it was a specialised medical text. It turned out that the fall happened when Cara had turned 16 and had already had her first abortion. So not in her childhood, as she had told it. The report also mentioned that Cara had received psychotherapy for a brief period after the fall. However, nowhere in the report did it say that she needed to take any special precautions after healing, or that she couldn't give birth naturally. According to the medical opinion, her spine wasn't broken; there was just a crack on one of the vertebrae, and she had to wear the belt for six weeks.

You always have to wait for the right moment to ask delicate questions. Cara was usually in her best mood when we went shopping and when the weather was fine. We were preparing for the wedding, and needed to get loads of stuff, so we went for a look around the shops one afternoon. At last, the third wave of Covid was officially over, and the larger shops had opened again too, so we could look at clothes. We planned a girls' day out at the shopping centre, as Jack was working that day too. Still, I only dared to ask my questions to Cara cautiously, after a successful day out, in the car on the way back, and outside the house, when I'd turned off the engine.

That was when Cara told me about how she got her injury. She hadn't fallen out of a tree, as she said before, and yes, she admitted, it happened when she was a little older. What really happened was she didn't climb a tree, but a fence, and jumped down from there. When I asked why, she laughed and just said it was because she hadn't wanted to go to school. She'd hoped that if she jumped off the fence, she'd break her leg, but unfortunately, she landed on her back.

- "Well… That didn't work out too well", she said with a grin. "But at least I got what I wanted. I was out of school for a few weeks because of it…"

I wouldn't have known what to say to this if I'd wanted to. But Cara was visibly in a good mood that day, speaking freely, so I struck while the iron was hot and asked about the scars on her arm, too.

- "That really was a long time ago, when I was a child", she said. "You know, I'd never felt pain. I wanted to see if it would hurt, if at least that would hurt, if I cut my arm. But even then, I didn't feel that much. So, I tried cutting my arm with a knife until it really did hurt at last…"

– "Dear God…" I replied, but Cara probably didn't know what I was thinking, because she just continued to smile serenely at me, and after that, she just looked straight ahead. Even then, the corner of her mouth was turned up in a smile.

She gave Jack a completely different explanation for the scars on her arm, but I only found out months later. To Jack, Cara said that she got the scars when her stepfather locked her in her room for doing something she shouldn't have. And they only let her out when she started slashing herself.

Whatever really happened, I felt sorry for her. I felt pity, sympathy, and love for Cara all at once. Whenever I looked at her, I saw a little girl who was very fragile, vulnerable, and probably hadn't had an easy life, or childhood either. Until she was seven years old, she'd been raised by her grandparents in Transylvania. Her mother worked abroad and couldn't have her taken out to join her and her brothers until after she was seven. Her grandmother loved her, but her grandfather disciplined her a lot and even beat her once – this is what Cara told us. I wanted to make her present and future better. I was determined. And I believed that love and care would be enough for this. More than enough. Cara made my son happy, and that's all I saw; that's what I kept sight of. My son's wife is the mother of my grandchild-to-be. I wanted them to be happy. For a long time, together. Perhaps forever. I pushed the past to one side as if it had never happened. Cara's past. I believed in a clean sheet, a fresh start. I didn't want to remember, or I had forgotten, the certainty that there's no such thing as a clean sheet, even at birth. Sadly, nobody starts their life on this Earth with a spotless scorecard. It's already marked with generational traumas (blessings and curses), only pencilled in so they can be erased, but clearly visible, nonetheless. Eliminating this legacy, healing, takes a lot of work. And I'd also forgotten that while a fresh start is often a gift and an opportunity, like everything else, it takes willpower, and that needs to come from the person who wants a fresh start at anything. A persistent, incredibly strong, determined will, a conscious effort, and a long series of consistent actions.

The Wedding - A few Weeks of Happiness

Maybe there was no will, maybe no determination, or perhaps there just wasn't the motivation for any kind of new start. I didn't know what was missing, and I still don't.

The registrar had scheduled an appointment for mid-March, so Jack and Cara could register their intent to marry. A cold wind was blowing that day, with storm clouds gathering in the sky. The town was decked with already-blooming daffodils, but there were no other signs of the approaching spring. Cara set off for the appointment in a miniskirt and tiny leather jacket. Jack wore his best shirt. The local city hall is a barren, grey, concrete monstrosity, the product of who knows what architectural style, but by all accounts, a grim, unfriendly building. It was still only partially open to the public, so we had to hunt down the entrance to the registrar's office. This was at the back of the building. By the time we found it; after going around the whole fortress, we were chilled to the bone. And despite having an appointment, we still had to wait. For a long time. I was there not because they couldn't have arranged things by themselves, as adults, but because someone had to translate. Jack couldn't do it because he was one of the prospective newlyweds, and they had to enter the office separately and declare their intention to marry independently. For this, Cara needed an interpreter. The registrar looked over the documents, checked them, and asked loads of questions.

"Has Cara decided, of her own free will, that she wishes to be married? Is she sure?"

Cara looked at me, rolling her eyes, as the registrar turned away to photocopy the personal documents.

- "What's the point of all this?", she whispered

But she sat patiently at the plexiglass screen. The register asked for her mother's name, and then her father's. Cara gave me an awkward laugh.

- "I don't know. I haven't got a clue", she said.
- "What do you mean?"

- "What do you mean, what do I mean? I don't know, period! I haven't a clue. I don't know my father's name!"
- "But isn't your surname from your father? I thought it was", I asked, a little confused myself now.
- "No, that's my mother's name. I don't know my father's", said Cara, still smiling. The registrar listened attentively, but a little suspiciously, to this dialogue that she didn't understand.
- "We have to say something…" I said quietly to Cara.
- "Well, let's just say I don't know," she riposted with a giggle.

On the spur of the moment, I asked the registrar for Cara's birth certificate, which I'd only seen once before on the evening when she first arrived, and placed it on the table in front of me. It really didn't show her father's name. The place for that was crossed out with a single line. I looked at Cara again, then glanced at the registrar and saw that she was waiting patiently. Although suspicious and unable to understand what we were talking about, she watched us placidly with doe-like eyes. I put the documents back on the counter in front of her.

- "Cara doesn't know her father's name", I said softly. "It isn't known." The registrar nodded.
- "Okay", she said, and made a note of this. Cara sighed.
- "So, is everything okay? Or what's going on?"
- "Don't worry, everything's okay", I answered. And I put my arm around her.

Again, I wondered what else we didn't know yet. But I tried to reassure her and myself.

Cara and Jack decided the wedding day would be the 21st of the following month, in the hope that by then, everyone would be able to make it, the restrictions would be lifted, and family members would be able to travel again. Cara couldn't wait to see her family, and we were looking forward to seeing my own daughter and son-in-law, who'd be coming home from abroad for the big day.

The young couple left the building happy. Now that we had a date, we could start planning around it. The letters started flowing about who was coming, where they'd be staying, how long they'd be here for, and where we should hold the dinner. The ceremony itself would be in the registry office, which they showed us. According to the pandemic rules at that time, a maximum of 30 people were allowed in the room, which was very tastefully decorated with flowers and curtains. This room wasn't cheap, but any other venue would have been even more expensive, even if we'd been able to find a mansion or church suitable for holding a wedding. And it was uncertain whether such a place could open by then anyway. We looked at a few candidates online, but their websites said all public venues would open only for May events. And everybody's event had already been delayed for two years. Most of the nicer public places that hosted such events had already been booked well in advance. So, the young couple quickly accepted the room offered by the registrar, and I paid the fee. Thirty people aren't a very large gathering, but we weren't expecting more family members than that. And we didn't have any friends from the local area yet. There'd be room for all of us. This would do us fine, I thought.

So, in the first week of April, we started the preparations in earnest. Cara's mother had sent money for the wedding dress in early March, but Cara had already spent it on other things. Cosmetics, sweets, and summer clothes were ordered online. So, when we finally found the right wedding dress, I paid for it with my credit card. Cara was very grateful for that. She thanked me and urged me not to worry, her mother would send more money, and she'd pay me back out of that. We stepped happily out of the clothes shop and into the street and took photos of each other outside with the pretty grey canvas suitcase containing the beautiful, snow-white satin bellflower-shaped dress. I bought her a matching crystal-studded belt and tiara, and a petticoat. Jack bought his own wedding suit: beautiful, deep-blue trousers, a jacket, waistcoat, and matching tie, and shoes to go with it. He paid for these himself. We got lucky because one of the biggest high street chains was going out of business, so we got Cara's reception dress and my own dress for the occasion in the closing-down sale.

Cara was happier than ever during this period, walking on air. Every day, she bought something, created the invitations on the computer, composed the dinner menu, searched for music to play as she walked up the aisle, and hunted for other tunes for the party that would follow. Cara happily made her plans. I managed to sell the puppies, and with the proceeds, I helped Cara do her shopping. I also used some of this money to buy garden decorations. I'd decided to make it a garden party because all the good venues and restaurants that we could afford were booked solid. I bought a marquee, which Jack erected on the patio one afternoon. We took pictures of this, too, amid much laughter; everyone was in such a good mood that day. Later, I bought the barbecue, garden tables, and chairs. We bought pans, new cutlery, and glasses. We looked for a hairdresser who would fit Cara's new wig and style it beautifully on the morning of her big day. We looked for a makeup artist, too, but Cara said she was too expensive, so we didn't need her in the end. Cara said she'd put her own face on, and she's pretty good at it, so we bought new makeup. Finally, we ordered the wedding cake. What else? Cara's mother made me promise to buy a guest book so all the guests could leave their best wishes after the wedding. My prospective co-mother-in-law said she'd pay for this, because it was her wish and her gift to our children. I ordered the guest book online. A dainty white A5 volume, leather-bound with a golden silk ribbon. We were nearly ready, with everything planned and organised. Now, with seven days to go until the wedding, we just have to wait for the big day to arrive.

In the last week, however, it turned out that, unfortunately, things wouldn't go exactly as planned. Cara's parents wrote to her, saying that they couldn't make it after all. The wedding was too soon, they said. They didn't have time to prepare. Cara's mother couldn't get time off work, Cara's brothers were still at school, and the principal wouldn't authorise their absence during term time, not even for a few days to celebrate with their family.

Meanwhile, my daughter Sophia, after ten years of childless marriage, called me up one morning in tears, sent a video, and announced that she was pregnant. I was over the moon, of course, and I totally understood that they couldn't travel in that state. But still I was dismayed, and a little scared. Who'll come? How many of us will be at the wedding? How can I make sure everything's wonderful, and everyone feels happy and blessed, if there's hardly anyone there, hardly any loved ones and relatives, to give their blessing?

I tried to comfort Cara, but she didn't really need it. She'd clearly accepted that her family wasn't coming, and she seemed to be taking it well. She was sad for maybe a few hours, then said not to worry, the family would attend via video chat. It is what it is. This was her wedding, and it didn't matter how few people were there; everything would still be wonderful! My two elder sons were coming, and Cara's brother Mike, to whom she gave her telephone, would travel down from London. The witnesses would be there, a young colleague of mine and his wife. And maybe the neighbours would come over too. That's at least ten people for sure.

- "At least we don't have to find accommodation for anyone. There's enough room for everyone in this house", said Cara.

Two days before the wedding, we bought the barbecue food: meat, salad ingredients, and potatoes. I prepared everything and marinated the meat. I ordered the taxi to bring Cara's brother and my sons down from London. The night before the wedding, I decorated the marquee and the front garden with flowers, ribbons, and tea lights. It was all so beautiful! I laid the tables too, finishing up at three in the morning. On the morning of the wedding, when Cara woke, I told her to close her eyes and led her downstairs. Then, when I said she could open her eyes and showed her around the house and garden, she almost burst into tears.

- "My God, how beautiful it all is! I'd cry, but I've already done my makeup, and I don't want to ruin it," she said. "But how beautiful you've made it. All by yourself, wow! Thank you so much, really!" She hugged me and rested her head on my shoulder.

And I was overjoyed to see her so happy. I thought it was worth all the money, all the effort, to see her eyes light up like that. Then, Cara quickly ate breakfast, and I took her to the hair salon. In just two hours, the hairdresser, Nancy, conjured a beautiful mane of hair onto Cara's still almost completely bald head. The long, thick locks of the wig reached down to her waist, and you couldn't tell that it wasn't her own. It was worth every penny. This hairpiece was made of real human hair, with no plastic at all. The best quality. Nancy said so too.

Early that morning, Jack rushed out to wash and decorate the car. My son was so excited. He stayed constantly in touch with the taxi carrying his big brother and future brother-in-law. He came and went in the kitchen, laughed, went out into the garden, checked the oven, inspected the salad in the fridge twice, to make sure there would be enough. Then he showered, got dressed, and went out into the street ready to greet his siblings, his future brother-in-law, and the witnesses as they arrived.

My colleague and I dressed Cara together. She looked stunning, like something out of a fairy tale. At 17 weeks pregnant, her bump was barely visible, if at all. She was just beginning to fill out. Her waist and bottom were a little more pronounced, and some soft flesh had appeared on her arms. She was perfect, like a princess! Then everything happened very quickly. The cake was delivered at the last minute, and the boys arrived at the same time. We had half an hour to greet everyone, and then we had to leave for the registry office. When Jack saw Cara in her wedding dress, he flushed red and almost cried. At that moment, he was the happiest person on earth!

We hurried across town so as not to be late. We even went past a no-entry sign. The witnesses honked behind us, but we just laughed. Jack went ahead in his own car with his brothers and brother-in-law, while I took the bride-to-be. Jack had to go into the room first with the registrar, while Cara and I were stopped and had to wait in the lobby. We handed the camera to the brother-in-law, and I held the phone so the whole family could see the event on a video call. Cara clutched her bouquet, a small one with brightly coloured, scented roses. In the end, she didn't wear the veil, saying it looked silly on her, so there was only the tiara on her head and the white pearls in her hair. She was enchanting, with peach-like skin, not yet twenty years old. The music started, the familiar melody struck up, and the door opened. Jack stood at the table, facing the registrar, and he and everyone else turned towards Cara. She walked into the room, a little self-consciously, but with a broad smile. Confidently, happily, almost dancing. There was nobody to lead her up the aisle. I followed behind, accompanying her.

It was a short ceremony. Although she didn't speak English, Cara repeated all her vows nicely and clearly. And she laughed throughout, even when signing the register, as the photographs show. On the way home, we changed vehicles. The newlyweds went in Jack's car, while I took the boys and the rest of the small family contingent. The witnesses followed on behind. The beer cans tied to the exhaust pipe rattled joyfully on the tarmac, and we honked the horns of our three little cars continuously to banish the evil spirits.

Afterparty, gathering storm clouds

We were lucky with the weather. The sun didn't shine, but at least it didn't rain. The boys got to work grilling the meat on the barbecue, while I served little bite-sized sandwiches skewered on cocktail sticks, as an appetiser. We raised our glasses, the music played, Cara and Jack danced cheek to cheek, I spoke with the witnesses, and their three-year-old son played with the remaining two puppies. It was a peaceful, pleasant afternoon, and everyone seemed happy. Jack and Cara cut the cake, and everything was as it should be at a normal wedding. They held the knife together, kissed each other, and theirs was the first and biggest slice. As dusk fell, we lit the tea lights and turned on the illuminated garlands decorating the sides of the marquee. Cara and Jack canoodled, the boys talked among themselves, and laughed a lot. Everything, and I mean everything, was like a fairy tale. I made the beds for our guests, and we fell asleep contentedly. The next day, after the guests had left, I took my eldest son Joe home and spent the day with him. Then Jack, Cara, and I were alone in the house again, and life returned to normal after a few days. The newlyweds postponed their honeymoon because of Cara's condition and lingering travel restrictions, but they still managed to spend a few happy days together. Jack took time off, and they went on day trips and picnics. I continued to work. I wasn't at home much.

The week after the wedding passed in total peace, and we had no idea it was the last week of the happiness and calm we had so wholeheartedly yearned for. On 28th April, one week after the wedding, everything suddenly became a problem. Cara changed, a complete reversal, as if she was no longer the same young woman we'd known a few weeks before, and certainly not the one we'd met a few months previously! Almost overnight, Cara became irritable and reticent. She avoided spending time together, wouldn't talk to me, and avoided eye contact if I spoke to her. She spent all the time upstairs in her room, chatting in German on the phone, with – it seemed to me – various people. If she dropped something or if something went wrong, for example, when cooking, she would swear with words I'd never heard her use before. And somehow, everything became intolerable for Cara. Including the dog's barking. At work, Jack got messages like this from her:

> *28th April*
>
> *Hey, that fucking dog barked at me again. It comes up here, and barks, then goes away and barks there too. I can't stand it. I can't take this. Please let's move out!*

Jack replied that he was very sorry, and she should tell me to tell the dog to be quiet, and of course, they'd move out just as soon as they could.

Cara wrote to me the same day and then told me again, while she was cooking in the kitchen (and I was still drinking my first coffee after waking up), that she was sure I understood her need to move out as soon as possible, because they were now married and needed a home of their own. Because they were a separate family now. I didn't have any objections to that, did I? Of course not. I understood perfectly. But I'd spent more than 3000 pounds on the wedding, and Jack had spent loads of money too. The two of us had paid for everything. Even the taxi that brought Cara's brother down and took him back, the hairdresser, the cake, the dress, the food, and everything else. I couldn't understand why this move had suddenly become so urgent. And I didn't know how I could help them move out at the drop of a hat. We had no money left, literally. After the wedding, all my credit cards were maxed out. I tried to explain this to Cara. There was no money to rent a separate flat, and anyway, that's not what we'd discussed. The plan had been that when she started working, and they had two incomes, they'd rent a house. I reminded her that she herself had said she wanted to stay with me until the baby was born, because it was safer that way.

– "Yeah, but you don't get it. I can't stand it when the dog barks, and I don't want to bother you either."

- "Hey, you don't bother me. I'm hardly ever at home; I work so much."
- "That's just it. You don't get to sleep or rest."
- "Of course I do. You two don't bother me, I told you. But if I'm bothering you, and you want to be alone together more, I'll just work even more. It's no problem! I can work five or six days a week if necessary."
- "No, that's not what I'm talking about! It's just that we're a separate family now, and we'd like to live separately."
- "I understand that, but you need to understand, too, please, that there isn't enough money for that. Jack doesn't earn enough, and all his savings are gone. Please don't ruin him. If you move out now, you'll both be ruined financially."

That last sentence was a serious mistake. From that point on, Cara turned it against me. She claimed that I'd accused her of ruining Jack. Bitterly offended and hurt, she asked how I could say such a thing. She would never ruin the man she loves, the father of her child. And if that's what I believe, if that's really the case, she'd rather leave because that's not her at all. She'd rather leave and move back in with her mother. So, nine days after the wedding, she wrote to Jack that she wanted to divorce him…

I knew nothing about these messages. I only saw this one six months later, after the solicitor advised us to search Jack's phone for evidence of Cara's motives. Cara introduced the topic gently at first, but between five and nine in the afternoon, she bombarded Jack with messages as he worked the afternoon shift.

"*16. May*

- *I can hardly wait until we move out.*
- *What's happened? Is something wrong, my sweetheart?*
- *Nothing, I can hardly wait is all. I don't know what your mother's fucking problem is. She's sad, doesn't say a word. Yesterday she was still laughing, but she's been like this since I told her we're moving out. I'll tell her we're sorry, really, but you wouldn't want to live with your mother-in-law, your partner, and your child either.*
- *We'll go as soon as we can afford it. You know that's what I want, too, and I'll work more if I have to, so we can make it happen. If my*

mother's in a bad mood, there'll be another reason, not just that we want to move out. She might have other problems, too.

- *I don't know. You might see it like that, but I don't. Especially after what she said yesterday: that if we move out, we'll go bankrupt. I don't know why she says things like that, and how long she thinks we're going to live here. All I want is for us to move out. When the baby comes, I'll be really tired, and I won't be in the mood to see her tired and sad every day because she has to work. And you know that fucking dog barks at any old shit, I won't be able to stand it.*
- *Ok, I'll talk to Mum, forget it for now.*
- *Forget it, me? What? Okay, you stay with your mother. I'll sort out the paperwork. I've had enough of you lot treating me like shit. I'll divorce you. Fuck you! Treating me like that.*
- *I'll find a house, and we'll move out before the baby arrives.*
- *Your mother ruined everything.*
- *There's no need, you can stay with her. I'm divorcing you.*
- *Please, don't divorce me over this. I'll sort everything out.*
- *But I couldn't get divorced, I still love you. You're everything to me. I'll ask my mother to send 1000 euros so we can rent a flat.*

That was how Cara closed the conversation. Her mother never sent 1000 euros, of course. Perhaps she didn't have that much money to send. She was raising three other children, Cara's brothers, two of whom were still minors at ages 16 and 11. Besides them, Cara's mother also regularly supported Mike, her grown-up eldest son, who still didn't have a job. Since March, Cara had been getting about 50-100 euros a month, or more like every two months, and the money for the wedding dress was about half the actual cost. Her mother could give her that much, but she didn't have the means to send 1000 euros, even if Cara asked. I don't know if she ever did, or if she just told Jack she would.

One thing is certain: from that day on, from 1 May, the dramas became a daily occurrence. It was like being on a rollercoaster. In the first half of the week, Cara wanted to move, or if she didn't want to move, then to divorce and go back home; but then in the second half of the week, she felt fine and didn't mention anything like that, in fact, she laughed and clowned around like in the old days, before the wedding. There were also days when her mood changed during the day. She'd wake up in the morning in a good mood, but in the afternoon – usually when Jack went to work – the dog and the cat were the problem, or it was me being at home, or not being at home, and where had I gone without her? Cara bombarded Jack with messages every day during this period. She didn't just complain; she asked what he was doing, when he was coming home, and whether he could bring this and that when he did. And there were days when Cara woke up in a bad mood and stayed grumpy for the whole morning, but then she'd eat something and ask me to take her shopping in the afternoon. Then she'd cook happily for the rest of the day and be almost kind as evening came.

Cara either spoke to me or she didn't, but this was impossible to predict. To be honest, I hadn't a clue how to cope with these situations. I always had to play it by ear. Usually, I tried to be kind and keep on Cara's good side. For example, once, when she was in a good mood, she said she'd like to learn how to knit or crochet properly, because her grandmother had started teaching her when she was still alive, but she'd forgotten since then. There were a few balls of wool in the house, so we knitted, overjoyed to have found something to do at last. I showed her how to knit and started teaching her. I bought some crochet hooks, too, because she said she could remember that better. But in the end, she left the box unopened. Two days later, she seemed to have forgotten the whole thing. She wasn't interested in knitting or crocheting. When I asked again if she wanted me to show her once more, she said no, she wasn't very good at it. And anyway, the whole knitting and crocheting thing wasn't much fun, so let's leave it.

Cara often said she liked reading, so I bought her a few German books. But they sat untouched on the shelf. When she was in a good mood, we chatted in the kitchen and watched videos together. And I recommended films for her to watch that I was sure she'd enjoy. But Cara rarely watched films and never watched television. She mostly slept, browsed social media, messaged Jack, and spoke to him on the phone. She rarely came downstairs. Less and less frequently, in fact. Only occasionally, when she felt like cooking. The weather was glorious in May. I always invited her out into the garden when I went, and I told her about the flowers. And

Cara, when she came out with me, just sat quietly at the garden table watching me plant, mow, and rake. But she never asked any questions or commented on anything I said to her. On the rare occasions when the sun was shining brightly, and she was prepared to come out at all, that is. But usually, she felt cold and preferred to stay indoors. In May, we still had the heating on so she wouldn't feel cold, but the window in their room was open night and day so they'd get fresh air.

Cara really longed for the baby to arrive, and she painstakingly monitored her own pregnancy and that of others, too. Back then, she was still on good terms with my daughter Sophia, and they exchanged messages several times a day in the family group, discussing morning sickness and everything else. What cravings they'd each had, where they'd get their maternity trousers and nursing clothes, that sort of thing. A bunch of amiable conversations was born. This made me so happy. But this idyllic state didn't last long. Her friendship with Sophia ended when Cara began making increasingly frequent and critical comments about Sophia's handling of her pregnancy. Cara brought up the fact that Sophia drank cola to calm her nausea, and let the sonographer amplify the baby's heartbeat, when Cara had been told this could endanger the fetus. Whatever my daughter said to Cara, she tried to find fault with it and succeeded. And then she'd air it in front of everyone. Sophia had waited a long time to get pregnant, and she was 16 years older than Cara, so she decided she could do without the stress. She wrote that she wouldn't be talking to Cara much and asked me not to hold that against her.

It hurt that my daughter and daughter-in-law didn't get on. I kept thinking how things could have been, what a beautiful friendship they could have, two young women expecting together. That in itself is an opportunity for a meaningful friendship. I was sorry it turned out that way, but I understood Sophia, who chose peace. And I didn't urge her to work on their relationship, especially after Cara made some very strange comments about Sophia's unborn child. Once, for example, she said and later wrote to me in a message:

> *"That baby definitely won't be healthy. I'm sorry to have to tell you this, but you know your daughter Sophia isn't*

> *young anymore, and I don't think she looks after herself properly. Whatever, let's hope the baby is born alive and won't be too sick."*

I was speechless. I couldn't believe Cara was saying these things about my own daughter and future second grandchild. Not knowing what to say, I just swallowed. And of course, I said nothing about it. I never told Sophia about these comments. A few months later, during the search for evidence, when Jack asked me to go through his messages, I discovered the motive behind Cara's malignance. I understood, although I still find it impossible to truly understand and accept it, even now. That May, Cara wrote to Jack about Sophia, my daughter's, and Jack's sister's pregnancy:

> *"I can't believe it! Why did she have to get pregnant at this moment? If they've waited ten years for a kid, they could wait a little longer, no? Why does she have to be pregnant at exactly the same time as me?"*

Back then, I didn't know about this message, but I did sense what was (or could have been) behind it all, Cara's attitude towards my daughter and their relationship. Jealousy, fear perhaps, and the craving for more attention. So, I tried to give her more attention to keep the peace and maintain the calm. We took Cara for a private ultrasound scan every month, and she also had genetic screening on the NHS, early in May. We found out that Cara and Jack would have a daughter, and that the baby was likely healthy. The scans were necessary to make Cara happy and reassure her that the baby was developing well, and she wasn't going to miscarry. And Cara *was* happy, always attending the scans with joy. Jack wanted a daughter, and Cara danced with joy in the car park when it was revealed that she was, in fact, having a girl. She even laughed as she told her mother, who had consistently guessed it would be a boy, that she'd been wrong.

So that was how that sunny May ended. Jack and I had suddenly found ourselves riding this rollercoaster, and we never knew what would await us every morning after we woke up. Would she be up or down, or both? Cara wanted to leave, wanted a divorce, started making threats, started blackmailing Jack, and using filthy language that she'd never used before. She swore and cursed. She changed so much that once the question just slipped out of my mouth: "Cara, what's happened to you since the wedding?" She never answered. Of course, how could she? All I could do was look for the answers myself.

Once, a few days before the wedding, on 17 April to be precise, when something – I can't even remember what it was – had annoyed her and sparked a minor argument, Cara sent me a message:

> *"I'm sorry about what I said. Help me, please. I don't want to be like this with you. I love you like my mother. I know you mean well, and it doesn't bother me. I'm happy you worry about me, but I can't stand it; it hurts me, too, that I'm like this with you when you haven't done anything. It's just I don't know how to manage these hormones; I'm not like this. This isn't me, you're right, I'm really depressed..."*

This message was in my head, in my heart, in my mind constantly. It was all I could think about. But it was the last message to contain any apology or plea for help, and nine days after the wedding, Cara changed completely. And with that, our lives also changed. We had no idea what we were faced with, no idea what would happen from day to day after that. All hell broke loose, and I had neither the power, nor the tools, nor the strength to prevent it. I could only delay the storm, very rarely, but even that wasn't entirely up to me. I'm sure of that.

The June Incident

The morning started out peacefully, with no sign of any drama in the making. I had the day off. It was my father's birthday, and I was going to call him after lunch via video chat to wish him many happy returns, as I do every year when I can't make it to Hungary for the occasion. It was a fine, warm summer evening, with plenty of sunshine. I was in good spirits as I got ready for the call, which, as usual, was going to be joined by Jack, my daughters, and my eldest son. We also told Cara there would be a family event after lunch.

It was approaching noon. Cara was upstairs, and Jack was cleaning. He reloaded the washing machine and hung out the previous load to dry. I was cooking, tidying up, as we pottered about together.

At noon, I heard a heated exchange. It wasn't too loud, but I went out into the garden to avoid overhearing any of it. But it soon turned to shouting. Then I heard Jack's footsteps coming down the stairs. I also heard him looking for me in the kitchen, so I went into the house. Jack looked at me with a furious expression.

"This is too much", he said. "You know what's happened now? Cara read my Facebook messages and saw that last year I was talking with my mates about how much more reliable and stable mature women are than young ones. And she got so upset, she told me she wants to get divorced and go home. She doesn't want to live with me like this anymore! Can you believe it? She wants a divorce because of an old message that she read! She wants a divorce again. I think I'll go out for cigarettes and some fresh air, because I haven't a clue what I'm supposed to do!", said Jack. But he didn't move, just continued, still upset. "Mum, I tried to reassure her, I told her everything and said that it was months ago that I wrote to Matt, months before I got to know her, before she came, before we got married. But she won't stop! She started shouting, and now she's crying. And she's started packing. She says she's read other messages and she's had enough. Mum, we just got married! What should I do now?"

Jack looked at me, and I could see the tears welling up in his eyes. His face twisted as he tried to hold them back, not to cry in front of me.

"What?" I asked, shocked.

"I don't know, Mum, I don't understand. Total hysteria. She wants a divorce. She wants to leave, and she's started packing. She says she's called her mother, who's sending her the plane ticket. I said what about the baby, and she said she doesn't want to raise a child with a man like me. I should forget I'm the father; she'll bring her up alone. Mum, do you understand? I don't know what to do. I've no idea what'll happen…" Jack gulped, shook his head, and sighed. "Oh well, I'm going out for cigarettes… Back in a minute. Or not. I don't know…"

Jack left the house, and I could hear Cara packing upstairs. She slammed the cupboard doors and shouted about Jack, and to Jack, calling for him to come back because she hadn't finished yet, and what a rotter he was, how could he treat her like that? Cara screamed hysterically and cried, then finally she slammed the bedroom door.

That was the last straw for me, and, in hindsight, I regret not thinking my actions through more carefully. But I was thinking of the foetus in Cara's belly, and what would happen to the baby. I thought about my unborn grandchild, what she could be going through in the womb of a mother who was fuming, shouting, and lashing out. Strangely, this crossed my mind as the most important reason to end this storm. I felt no anger, just incomprehension and bitter disappointment. Why was Cara doing this? When the door slammed, I ran upstairs. I hadn't really thought about what I was going to say, but the words just came out as I went.

- "Cara! Are you out of your mind? What are you doing? Why are you shouting? Didn't your mother teach you how to behave? Do I have to teach you? What's the matter with you?"

I said this as I entered the room. My voice was raised, perhaps I was shouting.

- "Cara, why are you doing this?"

She was sitting on the bed, her back to the door, facing the window. There were no tears in her eyes, but she was very upset.

- "I'm leaving," she shouted back. "If you knew what he wrote about me… I'm not staying here. I'm leaving!"

I stepped over to the bed, and she pulled away from me as if frightened of what I'd do to her in the next moment.

- "Cara, don't be silly! What makes you think he wrote anything about you? And why are you reading his messages anyway? Why are you ruining everything? Please, don't hurt my son. Don't ruin everything!
- "I've read everything! Not just what he wrote to his friends, but what your family wrote about me," she was on the attack. "You can't accept me. I'm not welcome here. Jack doesn't love me. You don't love me. I know everything!"
- "Cara, have you lost your mind? You just had the wedding; you got married six weeks ago!"
- "Yeah, well, if I'd known all this, I wouldn't have married your son! I didn't even want to marry him… And now I want a divorce. I'm going home. I've written to my Mum. She said she'll send the plane ticket."
- "Cara, are you thinking straight? You came here to get away from there. You fled, and now you want to go back to where you came from? You left your mother at 16. Now you want to move back home?"
- "Yes, I'm not staying here a minute longer," she shouted into my face. "And don't you threaten me! Would you hit me? A pregnant woman? Shame on you! What kind of a person are you?"

Cara jumped up from the bed and ran out of the room. I was left standing in the middle of the room, totally paralysed. Frozen. I hadn't even been close to lashing out at her, either physically or mentally. I was standing about two metres away from her, I hadn't raised my hands, and I've never hit a young adult woman, especially not a pregnant woman…

I heard the door slam. I followed her downstairs but didn't catch up. Through the window, I saw Cara running barefoot down the road in jeans and a T-shirt. Jack wasn't home yet. When he came, I was still half-paralysed, and all I could tell him was that Cara had just run off.

- "What? Where?"
- "I haven't a clue", I replied. "But go after her! She hasn't got any shoes on, and I don't know where she could have gone. She ran across the road, but she couldn't have gone far."

Jack snatched the car key from the kitchen table and stormed out. I couldn't tell him how it happened, why Cara suddenly ran out of the house. I couldn't tell him, because there wasn't time, and even I didn't understand what had happened and what was happening at that moment.

I sat down at the computer and wrote a message to Cara's mother that her daughter had run out of the house barefoot, and we didn't know where she was. Later, I got a tongue-lashing from Cara about this. How dare I write such things! Wasn't I ashamed of myself for worrying her mother like that? And on top of it all, she told everyone I'd tried to hit her. That's what she told Jack, too. Anyone who knows me would know I'd never do such a thing. It would take a lot for me to even raise my hand at someone. I don't even know what it would take. But not many people know me, especially not here. So, Cara could say, and later did say, whatever she liked about me. And sure enough, some people believed her, and I had no way of defending myself. Words can hurt, too. I'm aware of that. And maybe my words did hurt Cara. But at the time, I couldn't just do nothing, just stay quiet and back away from the conflict. My home, until then a haven of peace and calm, had turned into a war zone. I couldn't stand by and let that happen. At the time, I couldn't let it go. Maybe today, things would go differently...

About half an hour later, the two of them returned to the house, Cara and Jack. They went straight upstairs and shut themselves in their room. I wanted to follow them, ask Cara if she was okay, if everything was okay, and reassure her. Reassure them both. But they shut the door in my face. So, I was left standing outside the door, and although I didn't want to eavesdrop, I wanted to know what was going on. And to prevent another tantrum if necessary. But there was no more noisy arguing. I could only hear Cara's voice. Jack said nothing. And Cara didn't shout, just spoke softly, in a measured and infinitely cold voice. She gave Jack an ultimatum: either they would move out immediately, or she would go home. She couldn't live in my house a minute longer, she announced. She said, Jack needed to choose between her and me.

- "I love you", said Cara. "You're my husband and the father of my child, and I don't want to leave you. But I can't live with your mother a minute longer. She wanted to hit me. Your mother

> never accepted me, and nor did anyone else in your family, so either you find a flat where we can move in together, or I'll go back to my mother and only come back to you when you've found somewhere for us to live. You, me, and the baby. I'll come back to you when you write to me that you've found a flat where it'll be just us. I'm not living here anymore, and if everything stays the same, I want a divorce. Your choice. Delete the people you know who wrote bad things about me from your phone and cut all ties with them. I don't care if they're family or not. And you need to delete your ex-girlfriends, too. From Facebook, Instagram, and everywhere. But the most important thing is for us to move out. Because that's the only way I'm staying in this country. I'll talk to your mother, but only when it's necessary. After what happened today, don't expect me to be nice to her and chit-chat with her. Just the bare minimum. You can tell her if you like. Until we move out, that's how it'll be".

What made this so spine-chilling was the way Cara said it all so utterly soberly and calmly, telling Jack repetitively, clearly, and without raising her voice. Later, Jack started to reply quietly, but I couldn't hear what he said. Cara repeated every single sentence at least three times. She spoke to Jack like a teacher, using a tone almost exactly like teachers or parents use when talking to their children. Perhaps to make sure Jack clearly understood. And there was no longer any emotion in Cara's words. No tears, no offense, no confusion. She was totally in control. It was terrifying to hear. Inexpressibly so. Measured and cold. So cold, my blood turned to ice, my heart stopped. I stood at the door and thought this can't be happening! This doesn't happen! Surely this isn't happening to us! I stood, frozen, with no idea what would happen next.

For a few days, Cara refused to talk to me. She avoided me when she could. She simply stayed upstairs and didn't come out of her room until I'd left for work, and as soon as I returned home, she immediately went upstairs from the kitchen or bathroom, or wherever she happened to be downstairs. The next day, Jack asked what had happened, and I told him everything. They had no chance of moving out, so we had no idea what to do. What *could* we do? I'd have been happy, very happy, if they could move out. The sooner the better. But they couldn't.

I think Jack tried to explain this to Cara. For the umpteenth time. And after a few days, things seemed to be calming down. But from that point on, I was the enemy. The main, and effectively the only, enemy. The root of all evil, the cause and originator of everything bad. The biggest or perhaps only obstacle to their happiness. Everything about me, everything in the whole wide world related to me, became unbearable for Cara. My dog, my cat, my garden, my neighbours. And anything I said or did was always a problem for her.

And the rollercoaster shifted up a gear. Ups and downs. Sometimes a week would pass peacefully; sometimes it would be only a few days before the next argument. Of course, Cara believed that the reason for every conflict was that they didn't have their own home. If they didn't live with me, everything would be different. The main grounds for any apology, if there was any, were the pregnancy and its symptoms. The "*don't be angry, I don't know why I'm like this, I don't understand it myself, I don't want to hurt anyone, it must be the hormones*" monologue became a part of every cycle from then on. By the end of that summer, I knew it by heart.

At the Gates of Hell

"Get stuffed!"

Who would have thought that this little phrase would be the one to make me blow a fuse? This simple curse, 100 or 1000 times milder – and less malicious – than the many I've heard in my life and tolerated without batting an eyelid? There wasn't anything special about it. Cara was just expressing her momentary anger in her own way, and she had every right to. Perhaps I had even enabled her. But still. These couple of words were somehow so vulgar, so common, it floored me. Or maybe it was just the last straw that broke the camel's back.

It wasn't spoken; there was no vocal emphasis. It was written in a message on some social media channel. It landed in my inbox. I asked her a question and offered help. These two words were the reply. Concise. I was just going out to walk the dog when I received and read it. My throat constricted. By the time I got to the beach, I was finding it painful to breathe; it felt like some terribly heavy, stone monster was sitting on my chest. I clambered out of the car, let the dog off its lead, looked up a support group online, and called the number on their website. Live Fear Free was the organisation's name, and it specialised in domestic abuse. I felt shame as I keyed in the number on the screen, but I couldn't take any more. I couldn't take any more of the whispered hatred, the brusque or non-existent answers, the downcast eyes avoiding me, the locked bedroom door, and the whole atmosphere this created. I couldn't bear to see the fear in my son's eyes, the pain, and the disappointment. I couldn't take any more of the questions echoing inside my head: Why is she doing this to me and to us? What did I do wrong? What should I have done differently? Why didn't it work out? What's wrong, and what can I do to make things better, to change the situation?

The helpline answered immediately. They took my details, asking who I was, where I lived, what I worked for, and how old I was. And I held up well for that. I answered the questions in turn. But when the young lady at the other end of the line asked what was wrong in a gentle and deeply understanding voice, the dam burst. I started to cry. I told her everything. The past month and a half. The day-to-day silent terror, the blackmail, the accusations, the threats. I described what I had done, what Cara had done, and the responses. To the help, the care, the love. My doubts, the feeling that it might be my fault. My questions about where I'd gone wrong. I spoke, sobbing, into the telephone, stopping occasionally when my voice cracked. The sea roared beside me. The dog happily ran after its ball. Luckily, there weren't many people on the beach. The long, beautiful stretch of beach has enough space for so many people. The young lady couldn't help but she advised me to keep a distance, and if the emotional abuse turned to physical abuse, I should call the Police. I thanked her and expressed my hope that this would never happen.

From 3rd June, the situation got progressively worse. Cara didn't manage to dial down the anger that she was feeling towards me now. Whatever I did, she found fault with it.

> *"Tell her not to bring me flowers or buy cakes! I don't need them, tell her, I don't need anything from her. Tell her to leave me alone!"* Cara said and wrote to Jack.

She still wasn't eligible for any support, and she didn't have a penny to her name, just the 50-100 euros her mother sent every month. She remained totally dependent on us, financially too. We took care of her every need. Maybe she found this hard to bear, too. I would have. So, we tried to give to her and do things for her without notice. She never had to ask for anything. But if she did ask for anything, we gave it to her. And she never had to show gratitude. For anything.

I did the shopping mostly. Jack was barely earning. He had a new job and wasn't working many hours. In addition to the daily necessities, whenever I saw something in the shops that I knew Cara liked, I bought it for her. Spring onions, Eastern European deli meats, fruit. She was pregnant with my grandchild. And I loved her. I still thought she could be my daughter. And I was still always trying to adapt to the situation, still trying to understand her.

On 5th June, Cara received her pre-settled status. It was early in the morning, and I was watching the news on TV. She came downstairs holding the phone and showed me the email. She was happy. And I was happy. Finally, we've managed to sort it out! After six months, she was finally legally resident in the country! Finally, we wouldn't get threatened over the phone that every medical examination, all treatment, including the birth, would have to be paid for out of our own pockets! It had been worth all the emails to our MP, to the Citizens' Advice Bureau. Somebody had done something, and bingo, all of a sudden, the government decided to grant her pre-settled status. The way was clear from here. The same day, I applied online for her National Insurance number so she could claim Social Security and maternity benefits when the little one was born. I don't remember if she thanked me, but I wasn't expecting her to.

I suspected that she didn't know or understand what I was doing. Even I was learning how to navigate the bureaucracy. I spent hours online trying to find out what arrangements were needed to make sure everything would be okay. She still didn't speak English, and she was only 19.

She didn't want to study English. The online English classes and private language lessons stopped before the wedding because Cara wanted to get ready for the big day, and she said that, alongside everything else, the lessons were too stressful for her. After the wedding, she didn't want to go back to the English teacher. She said she felt bad about the money I was spending on the lessons, and "that woman only speaks to me in Hungarian anyway, she doesn't teach me anything. It's not worth paying for". I called the English teacher, apologised, and cancelled the pre-booked lessons. The teacher warned me too.

- "Something's not right, watch out for that young lady, something's off. That girl's pretty unstable. I had real trouble getting on with her, and I've got plenty of experience as a teacher. She can't concentrate. She's very distracted, very disturbed."

I didn't really know how to react. I could sense what the language teacher was talking about, but I tried to find a reason for every negative thing. To explain it away. "Oh, she's still very young. Her pregnancy isn't easy either." I made excuses. To myself, to the teacher, to the rest of the family. And, generally, to everyone. I didn't know what to do about her English. We'd discussed that, when lockdown was over, she could sign up for the free group lessons provided for immigrants. We applied online, and she was called for an interview, but for some reason, she didn't manage to log in to the required online application at the right time. She said she hadn't received the email with the download link. Having missed the assessment, Cara lost out on the free language lessons. It was hard to believe that someone who spends all her time browsing the web and is so tech-savvy would have trouble finding an email and a link, but what could I have said or done? I bought her some books and a German-English dictionary. I dug out my boys' old English language textbooks and notes, and I playfully spoke English to her in certain situations; basic stuff like: "Are you hungry? Would you like some water? Let's go out into the garden. How are you feeling?" Jack taught her words and phrases when he got home from work. But we didn't get much further than that. It was up to her to actually read the books and notes that I gave her. At my son's suggestion, they both watched Netflix in English for a while, but Cara said she found it tiring, and she was pregnant too, so it took all the fun out of watching films. She didn't watch television or read the newspapers. Cara spent most of her days in bed, up in their room, browsing social media or shopping online. She didn't do anything else.

The whole month was a series of ups and downs. A few days of peace followed by yet more problems. Not big problems, but thousands upon thousands of little niggles that Cara probably experienced as major annoyances. "The dog's barking. The dog is barking too much. Jack should come home from work because she's feeling very lonely. Jack shouldn't work so much. She'll ask her family for money so Jack can stay home with her. The dog's hairy, dirty, and smelly, so she can't eat or cook because there's dog hair everywhere, and it puts her off. I should take the dog to a pet groomer for a bath, and I shouldn't take it to the beach because it always comes back muddy." She sent pictures from the internet of how a dog should look and said that if I groomed our dog like that, she wouldn't have a problem. I didn't react but just sent a 'like' and bathed the dog. I bought an anti-barking collar, but this didn't solve the problem. We had to understand that she couldn't live like that; she wanted to move out. She pestered Jack to rent a flat for them. Jack explained that, here, to rent a flat, you need to undergo a credit check, and he wasn't earning enough. They wouldn't be approved, and they didn't have enough for the deposit anyway. Cara seemed to understand, and for a few days, she didn't mention moving out, but then everything started again from the beginning.

- "I'll ask my family for money for a deposit", she said.
- "But we still won't pass the credit check, I'm afraid", replied Jack. "But okay, let's try it and see. You never know", he finally relented. And the two of them started flat hunting.

Then other problems arose. Pregnancy-related ones. Cara's tummy hurt, and her back. The baby was constantly kicking, and that's not pleasant at all, Cara would say. She couldn't sleep properly because the baby was always moving around. And her back hurts. I bought her a pregnancy pillow, a U-shaped one, the biggest, the most comfortable.

- "I don't need something this expensive", she said. "A cheaper one will be fine".

But the cheaper one was only a few pounds less, so we chose the best one together. She used the pregnancy pillow for two days, then put it in the wardrobe because it wasn't comfortable and she didn't need it after all.

The cat shouldn't be allowed upstairs, or the dog. So, we bought a baby gate and installed it, but the cat jumped over it.

- "Why does the cat come up here? Why does it want to sleep with us?"
- "Because that's where it's always slept. It's been in the family for seven years. My son's cat. It wasn't a problem until now..."
- "But it shouldn't come upstairs! We need to do something about it! Anyway, look at the state of this house. Everything's dirty and worn. The carpet needs changing, and there aren't any proper cupboards for me to keep my things in..."

And this is how it went, in an infinite loop. A few days' respite, and then it all started again, from the beginning.

I tried to understand what was happening. I'm a nurse with 30+ years of experience. I worked on a gynaecology and obstetrics ward for four years. I was familiar with many illnesses and conditions that trigger mood changes, but I'd never worked with psychologists, and I knew little about the traumas and symptoms of personality disorders. But I knew what was happening wasn't necessarily okay. I tried to understand precisely what was going on in Cara's psyche, what was happening to us and around us, what situation we were in. I wanted to know what I could do to make things better, for Cara to feel better and be happier, or at least for our relationship to be like it was before the wedding. I knew what I already knew, the things she'd told me, about her arm and her spine injury, her family, her childhood, her more recent past and previous relationships. But it was only after the incident on 3rd June that I sat down at my laptop and wrote the following words into the search bar of my browser: self-harming, mood swings, depression, manipulation, controlling behaviour. There were plenty of hits for things I had heard of or knew a little about: borderline personality disorder, bipolar disorder. But this was the first time in my life that I had read about narcissistic personality disorder as well. Then I read everything I could find online about it. It all seemed to fit Cara, but overall, none of the syndromes rang completely true; each one slipped up somewhere. Or maybe this is just what I wanted to believe, or I hadn't been paying enough attention. I'm not paid or qualified to diagnose anyone. I'm not a doctor, a psychologist, a clinician, a trainee, or a therapist. I'm just a simple nurse, standing by to assist the doctors, trained to provide practical help in treating patients. Yes, I do have a sixth sense. With my skills, experience, and a certain intuition, I can often sense what a diagnosis will be. But this is not totally reliable, and certainly not official. The doctors I've worked with over the years have often asked for my opinion and questioned me in detail about a patient's symptoms. I've always appreciated this, but I've known my limitations and been conscious that it's not my job to diagnose, because I don't fully possess that ability or knowledge. That's why I was always cautious around Cara. I just read, researched, and searched, and I still wasn't sure about anything. But at least now I have a better idea of the problem and what the solution might be. I was less reassured, but I still felt a little better because I could see more clearly, which made our situation easier to understand. If this were just a spell of excessive emotional volatility or pregnancy-related psychosis, with no deep-seated problems, it would pass with time. If there were other problems, there would still be a way out. Because where there's a diagnosis, there is a treatment, a way out, too. Of every problem and every illness. I spoke to psychiatrists I knew, and to my friends. They tried to reassure me, too. "Take care", they said. And that's what I did. I grew cautious around Cara, my senses growing more alert.

In the last days of June, my son had to return to Hungary for a few days to address an inheritance matter and obtain a new passport, as his old one was expiring soon. I was worried about how things would go with just the two of us in the house, but, to my surprise, Cara and I got along fine. I cooked, and so did she. When I dropped Jack off at the airport, he asked me to take Cara a present when I went home, and he tearfully asked me to look after her, however she might behave. I promised. Jack didn't feel like going away at all. Cara treated him very kindly in the few days before his trip, and the mood between them was almost as it had been when they first met. She was quiet, smiling, gentle, and attentive to Jack. On the way home, I stopped in town and bought a heart-shaped cushion, flowers, and a little angel for Cara. I sent Jack a picture of them before I handed over the gifts. Cara was touched and burst into tears.

Messages of undying love went to and from between them that day. They both showed me their messages. The problems began on the third day, when I sensed that Cara was increasingly stressed about something. I asked my son what was up. Was there some kind of problem? Jack wrote back that everything was okay, but Cara was calling him every half hour to ask where he was, what he was doing, and who he was with. He couldn't pick up the phone every time and couldn't always answer because he was at the bank, dealing with the solicitor, or at the passport office. As a result, Cara was probably cross with him for not picking up the phone in time, and when he did, he told her he couldn't answer every time she called… I took Cara for a walk and to the park to see horses and feed the animals, to distract her and calm her down a bit. We had a nice time together, and that day everything was peaceful.

Two days later, there was another incident. Jack set off home on the fifth day, but that morning, he called me in a panic, asking if Cara had received flowers from someone? And if so, from who? He asked me to find out. I didn't know what he was talking about. Later, he sent me the messages that Cara had sent him. In one, there was a picture of a beautiful bunch of flowers and a few words: *Oh, my darling, you really shouldn't have! (Smileys, hearts) Thank you so much!* My son pleaded with me desperately.

- "Mum, I didn't send her flowers. I can't afford it, and I'm going home anyway. Please, find out who sent them."
- "But there aren't any flowers here. Nobody sent Cara flowers, and I haven't bought her anything except when I came back from dropping you at the airport", I answered.

My son found it hard to believe me, and I could hear in his voice that he was really upset, as if I were trying to protect him from something, hiding the truth. Finally, he wrote to Cara that he hadn't been able to send anything, but he was on his way home, and who had she gotten the flowers from? Cara replied with a dozen 'tears of laughter' emoticons. It had all been a joke. "*Don't be angry, I'm laughing my ass off now!*" she added. "*That was cool! You believed it, that's so funny!*" It wasn't funny for us. We both found it hard to believe that Cara was capable of such a stunt, and that she found it funny… To make Jack jealous, worried, and stress him out…

June became July, and our day-to-day life continued much the same. Ups and downs. A few days of peace, then silent terror. "*Let's move out, I can't take it here anymore. I don't want to live like this, the dog's barking, there's dog hair everywhere, etc., etc.*" They looked at houses but didn't pass the credit check. I applied online for a council house for them. There was a long waiting list, but at least it felt like I was doing something. They were visibly overjoyed at this possibility. "That would be best!" they both said. "It doesn't matter if we must wait. We'll get a place sooner or later!"

But a few days later, early one afternoon, I found my son alone in the kitchen. Cara was sleeping upstairs. Jack was sitting at the kitchen table, with his face buried in his hands. He looked totally desperate.

- "Mum, I haven't got any money left. All my credit cards are maxed out. I don't know what to do. Cara wants to go. She says if we don't move out before the baby's born, she wants to divorce and go home to Austria". His voice cracked, and he turned his head away. My adult son sat before me, clearly devastated.
- "Mum, I've tried everything… I tried to make her happy. It didn't work. And I've got no money left. I don't know what to do. She wants to leave. She even said I'm not a real man. That the child deserves a better father. And that if she goes, the child will never get to know me. I don't know what to do."

I didn't know either. It just felt terrible to see my grown-up son like this. The only useful idea I had was something a psychiatrist friend of mine had also suggested: If things get worse, tell the midwife. She'll help, Ruth, the psychiatrist told me. "The system here takes this kind of thing very seriously, so believe me, it'll be fine." I tried to put my faith in what she'd said, and I couldn't see any other solution anyway. We couldn't stay silent any longer; we had to talk about the mood swings, the constant tension that Cara created, her bad temper, and the fact that she never left her room all day. It was time to talk about this, so we decided to notify the midwife. Perhaps she'd be able to help, or at least give us some advice. I wrote to her that day, and she replied to the next day. She'd be coming round in a few days anyway, she wrote, so she'd talk to Cara then and assess the situation, see whether there was anything she could or needed to do.

That year, because of the global pandemic, district midwives made home visits instead of doing all the necessary examinations in the surgery. She visited every pregnant woman in person and measured their blood pressure, took urine samples, and listened to the foetal heartbeat. Cara's midwife was a very kind young woman called Lynn. A really gentle, motherly, young blonde woman. She was quiet, but assertive, and clearly very experienced. Lynn was persuasive and committed. She always stayed a long time, talking a lot with the young parents-to-be both during and after the examinations. While she wrote up her notes on the kitchen table, and afterward too, Lynn would answer all the questions my son and Cara asked, and many they didn't. She gently and thoroughly prepared the young parents-to-be for one of the greatest events in their lives. I know all this because for the first few months, they asked me to translate for them, so I was present at the visits. Although Jack spoke good English, he wasn't familiar with the terminology of prenatal care, so I served as an interpreter, which made the visits easier for everyone. I was flattered to be asked and was happy to take part. But still, I felt it would be best if I weren't there for her coming visit in a few days. Lynn agreed. She was preparing for a deeply personal conversation with Cara, so I retreated into my room while the three of them stayed in the kitchen. Of course, I could hear everything from in there, but Cara didn't know this, so she could speak openly. I wasn't eavesdropping, but it was difficult not to hear Lynn's questions, despite her soft-spoken way of asking. My room was only two metres and a narrow hallway away from the kitchen. I heard Lynn ask Cara how she was, how she was feeling, whether she missed her home country, her own family, and her mother. Because a pregnant young woman always needs their mother the most… I heard Cara burst into tears at this. And I remember feeling so sorry for her at that moment. Then I heard Lynn stand up from the kitchen table, perhaps going over to hug Cara. I knew she was comforting her because she spoke to her even more softly, almost murmuring. And I was very grateful to her for that.

- "This happens to everyone. During pregnancy, most women become really sensitive. You wouldn't believe how many people feel exactly the same as you! But know that everything will get better. This sadness will go away eventually, and we can help make everything easier for you until the baby's born, and afterwards too!" Lynn said it louder this time, so I heard it, too.

They agreed that Lynn would refer Cara to a doctor on Friday, the following week, and they'd go together. She would be there with Cara. They'd also request an interpreter so that Cara would understand everything the doctor told her and could fully express what was troubling her. I was truly, sincerely overjoyed at this. It made me incredibly happy. I thought finally everything would be ok, everything would be sorted out. And my son believed this, too. For a few days, Cara became much, much calmer, and the week after Lynn's visit was a truly peaceful one.

At the doctor's visit, however, Cara told the consultant there was nothing wrong with her. She was just a little sad, as she sometimes was, because she really missed her family. But she thought it was just the pregnancy hormones, and generally she felt great and there wasn't really anything wrong. She spoke to the doctors very persuasively, and although Lynn didn't believe her, there was nothing else she could do for Cara. Cara refused the assessment and the treatment. Lynn tried speaking to her honestly and kindly again, warning her that these downs would get more frequent as her pregnancy progressed, and things could get worse after the birth. She asked Cara to call her if she felt low or out of sorts, or just to send her a message. She'd be there for her. Cara promised.

Later that afternoon, Lynn sent me a message, apologizing. She felt something wasn't quite right, but if a patient says there's nothing wrong, they don't feel ill or in need of help, there was nothing she or the doctors could do. They couldn't refer Cara to a psychologist or psychiatrist, because Cara had announced to everyone, with a cheerful smile, that she was fine and had no need for help. *Anyway,* wrote Lynn, *I'll keep an eye on her and do what I can.* And she asked me to get in touch straight away if I noticed anything amiss.

Later, it turned out that Cara's mother had advised her to deny that she needed help because her mother told her that if she were diagnosed with depression, they could take the baby away. But we didn't know that at the time. Cara only told us about this several days later.

And from then on, everything continued as before. Ups and downs. At the end of July, Cara announced that we were right – Jack and I – and there was no point in moving out before the birth. She was seven months pregnant at the time. "Time to settle down and get ready for the baby to arrive", she said with a smile. And she hugged me. Warmly, lovingly.

- "We'll get by. We'll be fine here if you let us stay. Then we'll move out a few months later, when the baby's bigger."
- "That's great", I replied. "I think it'll be safer and more comfortable for you, too."
- "Yes," Cara smiled at me, "and then we could do what you suggested. You've already moved downstairs, so we can move into the two upstairs rooms! We'll do them up, Jack and me. Your bedroom will be the nursery, and we'll stay in the big room. We'll just do it up a bit."
- "No problem", I replied and hugged Cara. "I'm going away for four days anyway, so you can get everything ready upstairs."

We agreed, and all was peaceful. I went to visit my father and celebrate my daughter's birthday, while they took all my furniture and my remaining belongings from upstairs, into the dining room, which we never used anyway. That became my new bedroom, opposite the front door, adjacent to the living room. Jack bought some click-together flooring and laid it in my old room. Then they went shopping with the small amount of money he'd inherited from his father and furnished the nursery. They bought a changing table from Ikea, and plants and lamps. They set up the cradle that Cara and I had bought together in the spring, along with the white cupboard. They turned all this into a splendid little nursery and even made a video of it. In their own bedroom, they took up the fitted carpet, and Jack laid beautiful, brand-new, grey click-together flooring there too. Before leaving, I'd bought them two big white wardrobes with mirrored doors on my credit card. While I was away, Jack assembled these, too. The stairs got a brand-new carpet. I'd bought this for them too, but we laid it together after I got home. The house was sparkling, everything was clean, new, and modern. Now we could just sit back and wait for the baby in peace. I truly believed everything would be fine from then on.

August came. Cara's birthday was in the middle of the month, and we were getting ready for it. Back when I'd been visiting my daughter, I'd bought her some new German books and a few gifts, so we only needed to get some balloons and a cake. In the morning, Jack went to work but promised to be home by early afternoon. "Cara sleeps until noon anyway, then she eats, and I'll be back by then". And that's how it was. I decorated the living room, and Cara was greeted by balloons, the cake, and the presents. Cara woke up very sad and stayed that way all morning. She only told Jack how much it hurt that her mother didn't call her that day, or even write her a single message. After that, of course, she cried when we asked her to close her eyes, led her into the living room, and began singing "Happy Birthday." She saw the balloons and started crying. Only a few tears, but they seemed genuine.

- "My God, how beautiful! I've never had such a beautiful birthday. We don't celebrate it in my family. But you really shouldn't have spent so much… you shouldn't have", she kept saying.

It was early afternoon, a fine, warm summer's day. Cara was snacking on the cake and leafing through the books. She'd taken the balloons up to their room. Her gift from Jack was an appointment to get hair extensions at last. Her hair had grown to five centimetres, so now it was possible to apply the long extensions she'd already picked out. She looked exotic and beautiful with her brown skin and long, black tresses. Cara took a load of selfies like this, and some pregnancy photos together with Jack. The hair extensions only lasted a day; the next day, Cara took them out, saying she couldn't sleep with them in because they were heavy and pulled at her scalp. But after she removed the artificial hair, she was left with curly ringlets that suited her, and she liked herself that way. She looked exactly like a cute little black-haired goblin. Charming and sweet. We had some happy afternoons that week.

We had one more week of peacefulness left, but we didn't yet know that, so we were happy. It was great to fall asleep at night knowing that everything was fine, there was nothing to worry about, no arguments, no friction.

But at the end of August, Cara suddenly said she wanted to move out after all. I thought I'd misheard her at first, but she tried to explain.

- "I know we said we'd stay here for a few months, but I can't help it, I've changed my mind. Look, the dog's barking again. I couldn't sleep again today because of that. And when the baby's born, it's going to wake her up too, and we'll just argue about that constantly. It's no good living together. Everyone who's married moves out and lives in their own house. That's how it should be. There are cats here, you know, and I don't like cats. I'm scared of them, and you won't take them to the animal shelter even though I've asked you to, and it would be easier that way. You need to get rid of the animals, you can't travel with them and don't even think about us looking after them, because we've got our own life, you know..."

Cara spoke incoherently, her train of thought wandering. I tried to make her understand that she'd be giving birth within a month, perhaps in a couple of weeks, so even if we could afford it, that wouldn't exactly be ideal. But Cara wouldn't budge. One day, I wrote her a message, in a polite, reasonable tone, asking her to be patient. The reply came:

"Get stuffed."

At the other end of the helpline, the social worker took down my details and recorded, somewhere, what had happened and why I had called them, but of course, there wasn't much she could do to help. All she could say was that it was certainly serial abuse, and I should do everything I could to protect myself. I should avoid the abuser as much as possible. That was when I realised, I really wouldn't mind if they moved out. If only they would go! It was a shame about the money we'd spend doing up the house, but that wasn't wasted either. The improvements would remain if they went, I thought to myself. It was only my son I was worried about. How would Jack manage if he had to pay for everything himself? What would happen if he couldn't even work because he constantly had to rush home so Cara wouldn't feel lonely? I worried that, sooner or later, he wouldn't even have a job because no employer would put up with that… I had trouble dealing with my own thoughts during that period. I didn't want to watch my son slide into poverty.

Waiting for the Birth

I worked as hard as I could. I took on 5-6 night shifts a week. I wanted to set aside a little money in case Jack lost his job or needed anything if I had to support them. We had nothing in reserve, only debts. Almost all my credit cards were maxed out, and all of Jack's, whose money had run out. We had barely a penny to our name. We lived on what I earned, from one paycheque to the next. Jack was dismissed from his job. He had a zero-hours contract, but at the interview he'd agreed to work at least 36 hours a week, and he couldn't keep his side of the bargain. The agency was also in trouble. It started laying people off, and later declared bankruptcy, but we didn't know that at the time. We only felt the first effects of the decline. Jack was among the first to be let go. He started driving for Uber and took on all manner of home-delivery work to make a little money. But the large, 12-year-old diesel Audi he used wasn't exactly economical for this work, and he constantly feared something would go wrong with it and the cost of repairs would be astronomical. Granted, nobody worried too much about these things, but preparing for every eventuality often gave me sleepless nights. I was troubled by the thought that I wouldn't be able to help. I was tired, exhausted. My nights weren't restful, and nor were my days. With five or six night shifts a week, I could sleep only four to five hours each afternoon.

– "We want to live alone. We want to move out!" Cara brayed.

- "You are alone, I'm never home", I replied. "And when I am at home, all I do is sleep!"

That wasn't entirely true. When I came home from my shift, before going to bed, I cleaned the kitchen, loaded the washing machine, hung out the washing, did the gardening, and took out the rubbish. Then, when I got up in the early afternoon, I cooked something and took the dog for a walk. Once, to avoid doing everything myself, I tried leaving the house and kitchen untouched. I didn't wash their dishes or clean the shared parts of the house for two or three days, hoping that Cara would notice and figure out what she needed to do. Well, she certainly noticed. She wrote to Jack immediately, saying the mess in the house was unbearable and that she'd like the three of us to sit down and write down who does what and how we could make sure everything's clean and tidy. *Because your mother doesn't clean, and we can't live like this*, Cara wrote to Jack. I didn't know about this message either. I only saw it months later when Jack gave me his telephone. The 'sitting down and talking it over' never happened. All I noticed was that while I'd stopped cleaning, no one else was doing it. Then, on the third or fourth day, when there was no clean cutlery left, I washed up. Later, I swept and mopped the floor, because it wasn't possible to live in the house the way it was.

I should have set boundaries and created a system, but I'd neglected to do so. At first, because she was suffering due to her early pregnancy, later, because she took every comment I made as a personal attack. Was I scared of her? No! I wanted to protect Jack from her outbursts and mood swings. I fought tooth and nail to keep the peace and maintain some semblance of normalcy in my family. I failed to set boundaries. That was a mistake. I didn't want to be a bad mother-in-law. I still had vivid memories of my own, who constantly criticised me for not keeping things tidier. I always had a list in my head of the kinds of mothers-in-law I didn't want to be, and I thought that if I stuck to it, everything would be fine. That was a serious misapprehension. I compared Cara to myself. I think that was the biggest mistake of all.

I paid the bills too, including the council tax for all three of us, and I paid the mortgage. Jack had chipped in when we lived together with his elder brother in the rented house, and back then we'd split the rent three ways.

When he and Cara moved in, we agreed on an even lower amount. This was good for everyone. Jack kept his dignity; he wasn't sponging off his mother, and they were contributing something to the bills. But during one night shift, I received the following message from Cara:

> *"It would be great if you didn't take offence at this. I'm writing because Jack would never say this to you, but we won't keep paying you to live here, because we can't. Certainly not as much as we've been paying until now. You have to understand that the baby's coming, and we need all our money, so we won't pay until I'm working too. If you want, and if you really need it, then I'll give you half the money I get after the baby's born, but I can't give any more, nor can Jack, because you wouldn't want him to work more so he could give it to you. Because if he works more, he won't have any time to be with us, his family. So please understand, we won't pay you anymore just to live here."*

This came as a bolt out of the blue, but after a few hours thinking it over, I'd understood and accepted it. And provisionally, I said ok. When they move out, they'll have to pay for everything themselves anyway, so it's best if they can set a little aside in the meantime. I won't say it didn't hurt, of course. But I understood, or at least tried to understand, Cara's way of thinking. Jack was furious when I mentioned the message to him. He said he wouldn't go along with it. He'd keep paying, and when Cara got her first benefit payment, she wouldn't object to it anymore either.

It was early August when Cara's National Insurance number arrived. With her pre-settled status and that number, we could now open a bank account for her and apply for the first unemployment benefit. I submitted the maternity benefit application and a one-off payment online, doing whatever I could. Cara acknowledged, with satisfaction, that in September she'd have her own money. Not much, just half the monthly minimum wage, but better than nothing, and she was happy to learn that when the baby was born, she'd get another payment of the same amount. Everything went as expected, and we were soon all back in an "everything will work out in the end" frame of mind. I was working flat-out, Jack was working whenever he could, and by the first week of September, the move was also off the agenda, or at least I didn't hear anything about it. All was quiet; Cara didn't say anything about it.

We planned the last few purchases, the things we still needed, and thought through what was missing. We had nappies and wipes. Jack and Cara had stocked up on those while they were on special offer, back in July. We also had a changing cabinet, although it still needed a little mattress. We had to buy that, along with the baby bath. And a breast pump, bottle steriliser, and breathing monitor. And it turned out the cradle we'd bought on Marketplace in the early spring wasn't up to scratch after all. Cara wanted a baby bay to put next to the bed, so it would be easy to pick up the baby for breastfeeding at night. Jack bought this for her, secondhand. The pushchair they'd bought together in the spring wasn't up to scratch anymore either. The three-in-one travel system had to be replaced with a more modern one. Without a word, Jack bought a new pushchair. A better-looking one. The kind of Cara wanted.

Between shifts, I happily browsed online stores for the missing items, the baby bath, the breast pump, etc. I took screenshots and sent them to Cara so she could see them first. I asked her to choose the ones we should buy. But once when I did this, she rounded on me furiously:

> *"Stop behaving like this is your baby. It's really annoying what you're doing. You know, I'm the mother of this child, I'll buy what's needed!"*

My blood ran cold. But I tried to explain tactfully that she'd be giving birth any moment, and these were things she'd need. By the time she got the money to buy them herself, it would probably be too late. She was unlikely to get any money before the baby was born. She didn't reply to this. But the next week, when I bought something small for the baby and sent her a photo, she wrote back:

> *"Please, only buy things for the baby or me if I don't have to pay you back, because if you buy something*

and I have to give you the money later, there'll never be anything left for me."

I reassured her that she wouldn't have to repay anything. What I bought for the baby was a gift, and paying for gifts isn't a thing. I said all this kindly, and I wouldn't have accepted a penny even if she offered. But she never did. She never even tried. She never paid a penny toward anything, before or after that.

Back in August, I'd bought some baby clothes in the sale. I couldn't resist the temptation. I was expecting my first grandchild after all. Later, a neighbour offered her goddaughter's outgrown clothes, which were like new. Carol wasn't asking much for them, so I was happy to pay. At the time, Cara was thrilled about this. The three of us went together to see the two large sacks of beautiful clothes. When we took them home, Cara tipped them out onto the double bed and marvelled at the tiny baby-grows, vests, and skirts, enthralled. She almost thanked us. Her joy was like a thank-you. That's what I felt at the time.

– "These don't even need washing. They smell so good!" she said, stroking the little onesies.

We said nothing, Jack and I, just smiled. We were too tired to comment. Of course, you should always wash second-hand clothes before putting them on a newborn baby.

Then Cara stuffed the big heap of clothes back into the sacks, took them to the nursery, and put them into the wardrobe just as they were.

In early September, Cara was already very tired. Her belly was weighing her down, the baby was heavy inside, and she complained constantly that the child was moving around too much, getting in the way, and not letting her sleep. One afternoon, we managed to persuade Cara to join us for a walk on the beach. She rarely went out, as there was nowhere she liked to go. The only thing that entertained her, the thing she liked to do, was spending time in her room, lying on the bed, watching TikTok videos. On the beach, Cara admitted to me that she hadn't wanted children, and she'd never wanted lots of children, one at most, but much later in life.

- "I'd like to have lived a little first", she said.
- "You could have been honest about that", I replied. "My son was already in love with you. He'd have waited, and stood by you..."

Based on the past few months, I wasn't so sure about that anymore, but for some reason, I still had to say it. It seemed like the right thing to do.

Cara couldn't take much more and wanted the baby to be born at the end of August. The due date was 26 September, but Cara was hoping labour would start in early August. She was experiencing Braxton-Hicks contractions but didn't know what they were. She didn't understand what was happening and didn't believe me when I told her. She only grasped what these false labour pains were when Lynn, the midwife, explained them to her. Once, when I was very tired, I tried to comfort her by saying maybe she'd have an early birth. But she rounded on me. How could I say such a thing? Did I want her baby to have something wrong with it or die?! "It's still way too early for it to be born!" she shouted. Nothing I said or did was right, so after a while I decided it was better not to say anything. Whatever I said or did, however I looked at her, nothing was any good. I tried to keep a low profile, go unnoticed. So, I went to work. But Cara could reach me there if she wanted to. Sometimes I received messages from her, in the late evening or in the small hours, at one or two in the morning. It seemed like she never slept at night, only in the morning when it was light. One of her messages was about the dog again. It was evening, and I'd just got into work:

> *"It's barking again, I can't stand it. Do something about it. That dog's always barking!"*

I was thirty miles away. The whole thing was nonsense. My dog isn't a quiet breed, but it doesn't bark that much. It's old, and I trained it not to bark unnecessarily, so it only barks if someone's at the door or wants to come into the house. I was exhausted by these conversations and messages, so all I wrote back was:

> "The dogs bark, but the caravan moves on."

A proverb. She didn't understand. But when I explained it to her, she took offence, saying I wasn't taking her seriously and that I was making fun of her and her problems. Clearly, this hadn't been my intention. I even felt a little ashamed. To smooth things over, I asked if everything was alright, apart from the dog, of course. Was she okay? Had she eaten? When did Jack say he'd be home? Then she calmed down. A little attention always calmed her down.

She doesn't get sarcasm, that's okay. She just needs a little attention, I thought. So, I tried to meet her need for attention while remaining invisible. That wasn't easy.

In the first week of September, Cara's waters started leaking. A small quantity of colourless, watery fluid trickled slowly down the inside of her leg. I was just waking up when she went to shower, and she was very happy that something was finally happening. She called Jack home from work. Jack helped her towel-dry and shave after the shower because they were getting ready to leave for the hospital. They called the maternity unit and were told to go in. Cara was having contractions, but they were neither regular nor strong. She was happily getting ready. When I asked about the contractions, she said they were easily bearable and that they came and went. A couple of hours later, they came back from the hospital, a little disappointed. Cara hadn't been admitted. They'd told her to monitor her contractions and only return when they started coming regularly at five-minute intervals, or if a larger quantity of amniotic fluid started flowing, or if she experienced bleeding. I left to work the night shift, and they went to bed. I asked them to write to me if anything happened. After midnight, Cara wrote that there was nothing to report; she was going to lie down and try to sleep.

Tuesday and Wednesday both passed uneventfully. Cara ate and slept. She and Jack went shopping every day. Sometimes she complained of tummy pain, but after a few contractions, she felt better and said she couldn't feel anything. I was on the night shift again on Wednesday, and in the small hours of Thursday, I got a message. Cara wrote that at four in the morning, she'd woken up in a puddle and couldn't get back to sleep. Jack had a new job at a different agency and would have to leave for work soon, at six. I promised to hurry home and take Cara to the hospital, but I said they should call the midwife and the maternity unit first, so they'd know we were on our way.

- "But the midwife won't come here, will she?" asked Cara, worried.
- "I doubt she'd go out to you so early, and there's nothing she needs to do there anyway", I tried to reassure her. "Lynn will just say go to the hospital, but she needs to know what's happening", I added.
- "Okay," Cara replied.

And that's what happened. I went home, drank a coffee, and we set off.

Cara wasn't having any contractions. She happily walked alongside me from the car to the maternity unit entrance, through the big car park, along the full length of the building. We didn't have to stop once or rest for her to catch her breath or breathe through a contraction. We took the lift to the maternity unit, where they were waiting for us. A kind midwife was on duty that day, around forty years old, plump. She must have just started her shift, so she wasn't tired and frazzled yet. There weren't many people waiting to be admitted, so the staff had plenty of time to devote to us. They laid Cara down on a bed and hooked her up to the monitors. They examined Cara and said that her cervix was barely dilated, and they couldn't see any clear signs that her waters had broken. But we should be patient, because they were curious to see whether any contractions appeared on the CTG monitor and, if so, how strong they were. We listened to the baby's heartbeat and waited for Jack, who'd managed to get time off work.

A New Life Is Born - Elsie

The midwife eventually decided that the waters were indeed breaking, because after twenty minutes she made Cara stand up while she squatted down next to the bed and saw the clear fluid trickling down Cara's thigh with her own eyes. But Cara still wasn't admitted.

The midwife said a few very kind, encouraging words and released Cara with instructions to return to the hospital at eight the next morning if she didn't go into labour spontaneously by then. Jack arrived and took Cara home, while I went shopping and lay down to sleep after my night shift. In the afternoon, Cara had stronger contractions, but they didn't become regular, and she was still able to have her supper cheerfully and in comfort. The two of them went upstairs after that, and I tidied up a little downstairs before going to bed myself around midnight. Cara woke me at three in the morning. She stood by my bed and whispered to me to wake up. Her lower back was really hurting, she said, and her lower abdomen too; it was unbearable. She said she'd go to the toilet. I got myself together, brewed a coffee, and waited for her in the kitchen. The poor thing fell asleep on the toilet. I knocked and went in to wake her up. The two of us sat in the kitchen until five, measuring, or rather trying to measure, the contractions. But they only came every 10-20 minutes, and they weren't strong enough to make Cara stand or feel uncomfortable. At around six, Jack got up too and rang the hospital. The duty midwife told him to wait patiently and leave the house only when contractions came every five minutes, because there was no point in going before then. "They're expecting you at eight anyway", I told them. "Let's try to get some rest until then." But Cara didn't want to lie down. She went to the toilet and snacked while watching videos on her phone.

At eight in the morning, we finally went, but we had to wait a good hour and a half before we were admitted. Cara was annoyed, constantly complaining and saying that she didn't feel well.

- "Nobody here's doing anything! Look, everyone else is going in before us. Those two women are already wearing hospital gowns, but they got here after us. Can't you talk to someone? Let's call

Lynn, and maybe she can talk to someone. I can't bear to just sit here and wait!"

The midwife eventually called Cara in and examined her, but said there was still a long way to go; the cervix was only dilated a couple of centimetres. There was even a suggestion that she should go home and wait there until things really got started. When Jack told me this, I got a little annoyed because the protocol is not to wait more than 24-48 hours before inducing labour if the waters have broken. And Cara's waters had been seeping out for nearly five days. I waited for the midwife to return to the corridor to call someone in, and spoke to her. I told her that Cara had been there yesterday, and today she'd come to be admitted and have labour induced. Her waters had broken five days ago. But the midwife rounded on me:

– "And who might you be?"

I raised an eyebrow and introduced myself.

– "I see", she replied. "I know all that. It's all in her red book, and I can read. But you're not allowed to be here if you're not the partner named in the birth plan! The quarantine rules remain in effect, and mothers may have only one person with them. The person named in the birth plan", she told me rudely, and ordered me to leave the building.

I tried to persuade her to at least let me wait in the corridor, but I had to leave the whole building. I was dismayed, but I understood the reasons. Everyone was still afraid of Covid and reluctant to lift the restrictions. We agreed to stay in touch by phone. Jack and Cara told me not to worry, one of them would write every hour to let me know how things were going.

At 11 o'clock, they finally admitted Cara to the maternity ward, but instead of the delivery room or labour ward, she was just told to lie down in an examination cubicle. Between then and three in the afternoon, they looked in on her twice and asked if everything was ok. Then, at four, they finally hooked her up to an oxytocin drip, and a few hours later, she was given an epidural. They both wrote me short messages on how things were going.

I went home and started cleaning. I loaded the baby grows and bedclothes into the washing machine, mopped the floor everywhere, and did the washing up. I also vacuumed and mopped the floor in Jack and Cara's room. I cleaned under their bed, too, and found an estate agent's contract that Cara and Jack had signed barely a few days before. They were looking for a two-bed house or flat within a 30-mile radius. This took me by surprise, because Cara hadn't mentioned the move for a few weeks, and a few days earlier she'd even said they wouldn't look for a flat until she started working – there wouldn't be any point anyway, as they couldn't afford the rent. So, I was surprised to find the contract like this. This proved the exact opposite of what Cara had said, in other words, it exposed a lie, but – if I remember well – I didn't bother myself about it very much. I just put the document on Jack's desk, so it wouldn't get lost. I wasn't interested in anything other than getting the house tidy and getting everything ready, because my grandchild would soon be born. This would be my first grandchild. At last, I was going to be a grandmother! I was so happy, quietly happy, and also worried about them, anxious that everything should go smoothly. As evening drew in, I took the dog to the beach for a walk. The sky was darkening above us, but we were in for a beautiful starlit night. I caught myself praying out loud:

> "Come on, little girl! Come and arrive in safety, security, and peace, my little grandchild. We're all waiting for you here on this earth, you're so loved! Please God, don't let there be any problems, let everything go smoothly!"

I went home and sat at the kitchen table, trying to read, but I didn't really have the patience for anything.

Elsie was born at two in the morning. Jack sent a picture of her and videos of him, the proud father, cutting the umbilical cord. Then Elsie rested on his chest. Yes, Elsie spent the golden hour, the first magical 60 minutes after birth, with her father. This was because in the last hours of labour, Cara developed a fever and fell asleep, exhausted. In these photos, Jack looked happier than maybe he'd ever been.

Jack didn't come home until noon the next day. He waited for Cara and Elsie to be moved from the labour ward to the neonatal ward. I wasn't allowed in because the rules there were even stricter, but early in the morning, I bought Cara her favourite food, which she'd asked me to bring, for breakfast. I took it to the hospital car park, and Jack took the package up to her.

It was four days before Cara and Elsie came home from the hospital, because they both needed intravenous antibiotics. On the second day, Cara wanted to send the baby home with Jack, saying she couldn't sleep because of the baby, and she wasn't able to breastfeed anyway. She wasn't producing milk, and she was exhausted. But Jack, understandably, wasn't allowed to take Elsie home. The baby needed medicine too, and there were more tests to be done.

In a message, Cara asked me to buy a breast pump after all. Perhaps it would stimulate her milk production. I sent her pictures of what was available; she chose one, I bought it, and sent it in with Jack. Before they finally came home, I cleaned the house again thoroughly, and we set up the baby bay alongside the double bed. Everything was clean, fragrant, and pretty. I wanted to decorate the front door as well, but there wasn't time.

When they arrived, Jack wanted to show the baby to me, and to the dog too. He held Elsie up and showed her to me, then set the baby carrier on the floor so the dog could sniff the little girl. But Cara growled at him.

- "Don't provoke the dog. What are you doing? Take that child upstairs! Can you hear me? Do what I say!"

It was a very aggressive tone. I turned my head away, but still glimpsed Jack's face transformed for a moment as he looked at me without a word. Then, he picked up the carrier and set off upstairs. Cara went to bed, and half an hour later, Jack brought the baby down to the kitchen to give her the colostrum, expressed before the birth, from the little syringes waiting in the freezer. Elsie happily sipped and sucked on the syringes. Jack burped her on his shoulder. And he was happy. My son had become a father. And I was a grandmother.

Later that afternoon, we introduced Elsie to her maternal grandparents via video chat. Everyone was overjoyed and sent their heartfelt congratulations. I was making soup, and even down in the kitchen, I could hear Cara's mother telling her to let me help, to accept help – she'd need it – and not to be proud. But the next day, Cara made it clear to me that she'd prefer me not to go upstairs unless she called me, because she wanted to rest and didn't want anyone to disturb her and the baby. I hadn't gone upstairs that much, or that willingly, anyway. Upstairs was their home. I never wanted to intrude on their private space.

Cara came home from the hospital with antibiotics. The intravenous dose had been switched to tablets, and she was supposed to take them for another three days. She was prescribed two different types of pills. There was no written record of whether the infection was caused by Strep B or by the five-day leakage of amniotic fluid, but it must have been massive if they were treating it that way. The next day, when Jack brought down the rubbish, I found the pills in the bin. Jack shrugged. "Cara said she doesn't need them", he explained in one brief sentence, adding no other comments. I didn't either.

In the afternoon, the midwife, Lynn, examined the baby and said she would only come once more the next day. Then they would part company, because her job here was done. From then on, the health visitor and neonatal nurse would visit Cara and Elsie every week until she was seven weeks old, then once a month, and later once every two months. I gave Lynn the little gift package I'd made for her, with a thank-you card and an embroidered felt heart that I'd brought from Hungary. I thanked her for being with us for those long months and for trying to help. Lynn was visibly moved, and she hugged me. She said I should keep my eyes open, be watchful, and be the baby's voice, because I'm her grandmother. If there are any problems, I should get in touch with her immediately. She also said that, in a week, she'd come back to introduce the family support officer, who would be a man. His name was Dan, and his job was to help young parents. I was very grateful to her for arranging this as well.

Somebody would be there to help the young family. We were privileged. This isn't automatically granted to everyone.

Lynn left, and a few hours after she'd gone, Cara asked Jack to take her into town to buy a few things for Elsie. She needs a little hat, and we don't have any burp cloths either; we forgot to buy those. I was happy at the chance to babysit for a while, but Cara immediately retorted that there was no question of that. She wouldn't go anywhere without the baby.

- "But she's barely a few days old!" I reasoned. "I'm happy to look after her, and you'll be able to go shopping in peace."
- "No, no, we're taking her with us!"
- "To the shopping centre? But it's really crowded. She's still so tiny, and it's cold."
- "Don't worry, I can look after her", said Cara.

So, they took Elsie to the shopping centre, with her bald little head uncovered. They didn't come back for two hours. Later, Cara asked Jack why I had to interfere in everything and when I would finally accept that they have a life of their own. Jack told me he agreed that I worry too much. He'd checked on the internet, and everyone says that it's okay to take a newborn baby out into the fresh air. "Maybe that wasn't the accepted wisdom when I was a baby," said Jack. "But that was 30 years ago, and now everyone thinks differently about everything." I accepted this but added that while I didn't have a problem with a newborn being taken outside for some fresh air, they went to a shopping centre with a thousand people in it, when only a few days before, I hadn't been allowed into the hospital and the neonatal ward because of the risk of infection. Jack said he understood, but he couldn't face arguing with Cara about anything. Nor could I, to be honest. So, after that, Cara and Jack went shopping with Elsie for a few hours every day, sometimes to one place, sometimes another, and sometimes just to the local shop, but they took her with them everywhere they went.

Jack stayed at home for two weeks, and apart from that one heated exchange, a deep peace settled on the household. I did what Cara asked, never going upstairs unless she called me. After the birth, Cara smoked as much as she had both before and during the pregnancy, and a few times she asked me to go up to the room and look after Elsie while she popped downstairs for a smoke. "But don't touch the baby", said Cara, "because she's asleep. Only pick her up if she wakes up". Luckily, Elsie woke up a lot. When she did, I rocked her, cuddled her, stroked her thin, silky hair, and took deep breaths of that delicious baby aroma.

I wanted to photograph Elsie, but mostly I could only do so in secret, because Cara didn't approve of my taking pictures of my grandchild. And she absolutely prohibited me from announcing the birth anywhere or posting about it on social media. She wasn't even happy about me sharing pictures of Elsie in the family group, "*because anyone could still copy it from there*", she said. The family group only consisted of the uncles, the aunt, and my aged parents.

Elsie was two weeks old when she first caught a cold. Her nose started running, and she developed a fever. The health visitor came and examined her, but said it was just a virus, not to worry, it would pass. Cara should breastfeed her as much as she can. By then, Cara could breastfeed and was producing copious amounts of milk. She regularly expressed her breast milk, too, and Jack froze it for later use. When Elsie turned three weeks old, Jack went back to work, but with reduced hours. Cara found it very hard to cope with Jack not being at home, and on workdays, she called him hourly and sent messages, imploring him to return. I continued to work full-time, but only at night, so when I got home, it was still me who did all the housework. I slept very little during that time. Cara did nothing except breastfeed. It takes six weeks to recover from labour, I thought, and was happy to help by washing up for her and doing her laundry. I'd already been doing that anyway, so it wasn't a big change; the extra few baby clothes weren't a big deal. I kept the ground floor of the house tidy, but only saw upstairs when I took up clean clothes or when Cara went down to the kitchen for a smoke. And Cara strictly forbade me to do anything up there, although I offered several times to clean up and change the bedclothes. "You don't need to touch a thing, I'll do all that", she said.

- "I don't want you to have more work, and the baby needs to sleep a lot. I'm happy when she finally falls asleep. Don't wake her up by tidying. I'll clean when she's awake", promised Cara.

Jack worked, and when he came home, he looked after Elsie. When he was home, he usually did everything related to the baby. He changed her nappy, bathed her, rocked her if she cried, and got up at night to give her the expressed milk so Cara could rest. Jack cooked for Cara because after a few weeks, she wouldn't eat my cooking. She said she always found dog hairs and human hairs in it. So, on an average day, Jack came home from work, and they went shopping. Jack cooked what Cara wanted to eat, then they spent time with the baby, showered, ate, and went to bed. This meant Jack didn't have the time and energy to clean upstairs.

Jack sometimes seemed very tense, but I just put it down to exhaustion. I had no idea what was going on between them. Jack never complained, and Cara was very quiet. It was only months later, when I had to read the messages Cara had sent Jack, and when I realised what kind of stress those twenty or thirty text messages per day must have caused to my son. Most of the messages were instructions to Jack, what he should bring home or do, and questions about where he was, what he was doing, who he'd talked to, what about, who he was with, and – if he didn't reply straight away – why didn't he write or respond? But there were also plenty of more ominous messages. Cara wanted to move, again, and she was blackmailing Jack again: if it didn't happen, she would divorce him and take Elsie away. It was always the same record: "*I'll leave, and you won't get to know the kid; she won't even know you were her father.*" I knew nothing about any of this. All I knew was that Cara complained to her parents about how we treated her. This led to a row between us when I asked what I hadn't done for her and why she was feeling so bad. I asked her kindly; I had no ill intent behind my questions. I didn't expect gratitude; I simply couldn't understand why she was unhappy. But she didn't like this short, restrained conversation either, and from then on, she became even more distraught, demanding, and grumpy with Jack. Just a few of the several hundred messages:

> 22 September
>
> *Elsie isn't sleeping, so I'll have to take her to the doctor's when you get home.*

26 September

Throw that shitty animal the fuck out. It woke Elsie up. Poor thing, how she cried.

Fucking bastard dog.

And don't take that collar off anymore, or I'll beat it myself, and your mum can be as angry as she likes, I won't care.

28 September

"I don't know what's wrong with you. But you never say a word to me either. You're not like you used to be, and I don't deserve that. I'm sorry. God, I'm with Elsie all day long, I haven't eaten yet. You come home and don't do anything, just mope about. I'm starting to think it's not going to work out between us. I think I'd rather go home to my mother, because at least she'd help me.

But the rest of the time, I don't want to go anywhere without you.

But if you think you need to stay here, go ahead. I'm not staying, even if everything we had goes bad, which I think it already has.

Now I'm the one who's treating you all badly again. All I said was to tell your mother that we're moving out.

No, I want to divorce you, you're not the one for me. Let's forget it, before it really does kill me. It's not fair how you treat me, blaming an innocent woman, making me out to be the bad guy.

I'll ask my mum and dad to come over and help get Elsie's passport and sort out the paperwork so I can get a divorce. Then it's up to you whether you want to see Elsie or not.

It's not nice what you're doing.

And congrats to your mother for wrecking a young family, she should be proud.

Why does she have to wake up a child with that fucking dog?

You and your mother only see what you want to.

Babe

I'm sorry (Crying emojis), I love you

1 October

Please don't go to work all day; I can't take it now.

2 October

I'm a little scared that Elsie can't see. She doesn't react to anything.

3 October

Hey, baby, come home.

I didn't want to be alone for so long.

I'd love to spend some time with you.

4 October

– What's wrong with you? Why won't you even look at me? What did your mum say to you yesterday?

– Nothing, I'm just very tired. I don't sleep much, just 10 minutes at a time.

– That's why I don't want you to work all day, I can't even go to the toilet. I'm happy if I can smoke a cigarette" ...

Meanwhile, because Cara didn't give up and Jack wanted to resolve the situation, their search with the estate agent was still active, and they found a house for themselves, twenty-five miles from where we lived, in a small village. The estate agent contacted Cara and Jack with the offer. The house was being rented out by a private landlord, and if they could find a guarantor, they could take possession without a credit check, deposit, or down payment. Cara and Jack visited the house and signed the contract on the spot because they loved the property. "It's in a nice location, it's perfect," they said. I only found out about all this when they handed me the contract to sign as guarantor. Seven pages of typed paper. They were surprised that I wanted to read it. Jack started begging

- "Mum, don't do this, please sign it!"
- "Once I've read the contract and the terms, I'll sign it without further ado", I replied.

The house wasn't in the best neighbourhood; it was far from the city, a half-hour's drive from Jack's workplace, which I mentioned to Jack. But it wasn't my job to think about it any further. It was their life, what neighbourhood they lived in, that was their decision. The contract was a different matter, especially since they wanted me as a guarantor. The terms and conditions were listed in countless points on the paper. It also stated that the property had to be rented for at least a year and that the contract could not be terminated before a year. Smoking was not allowed in the house, and it had to be maintained; if anything went wrong, they had to have it repaired. And finally, it was clearly and precisely stated that if the tenant was unable to pay or incurred a debt, the guarantor would have to pay it, or it would be collected from the guarantor. I spent half the night reading about the legal consequences online, and by morning, I knew I wasn't going to sign this contract. Unfortunately, no.

I knew what was coming. So, I prepared myself for war on Cara's part, which began almost immediately. I could argue reasonably and kindly, but it didn't matter. In long messages and speeches, I was dragged through the mud for being the kind of person who stands in the way of their happiness, who doesn't help at all, and I was also told that her mother would have signed anything immediately, including this paper, so what's wrong with me? Cara yelled at me. Then she started begging. She promised everything. That she and Jack would come every week, not just once, and that I could visit them anytime. And that I could look after Elsie as much as I wanted, whenever I wanted. She didn't understand. That it wasn't the distance that mattered. And that the problem wasn't that they were moving away, because I wanted that with all my heart, honestly! The problem was that I couldn't afford to pay for another rental property and any repairs on their behalf.

Cara didn't understand that the private landlord could evict them at any time if they violated the terms of the contract, which they would, at least by smoking, and even if they were evicted, they would still have to pay a year's rent. She didn't understand. That I wouldn't let us ruin ourselves. Neither my son nor I. We were already in a pretty difficult financial situation, and we hadn't even recovered from the wedding expenses.

Cara sent long messages to Jack and me separately. She started gently, but later became angry:

> 15 October
>
> "*I can't believe you're letting your mother ruin this, too! You're crying about how far away the house is, but what makes it far away? What do you mean it's far away? I live a thousand kilometres away from my family, and you're crying about 40 kilometres? You know what? Stay with your mother then, nothing will ever be good enough for you or for her, I'm tired of it, I can't take it anymore*
>
> *OK. Stay here, I'll cancel the house, but don't expect anything more from me. From now on, we'll go our separate ways. I'll go and pack, take out the money my mother sent me, and I'll go to London with Elsie. I'll stay there until Elsie's passport is ready, then I'll go home and arrange the divorce from there. What you're doing is a joke. You're a total pussy for wanting to stay with your mother. You're crying because you'll be 23 minutes away from her. Stay with your mother, stay here, in this mess. Every normal man wants to live with his family. Be a man and not a pussy who just wants to stay with his mother.*"

It was a two-day war, at the end of which I wrote a message to Cara about what needed to be changed in the contract for me to sign it. I asked them to send it to the owner, the landlord, to see what his response would be to my ultimatum. I didn't ask for anything else, just that the lease not be fixed for a year, and that if there could be a designated area where the young couple could smoke. Because they were both smokers. The landlord responded quickly. And he said it was impossible to amend the contract in this form, and he was unwilling to change the clause allowing the lease to be terminated at any time. It wasn't worth it for him, so he wouldn't agree to it. – he said. And apparently, he spoke very rudely to them. To Cara and to Jack, too. He suddenly became very rude. So, Cara finally gave up on the house. A few days later, she sent me a message saying she had told her mother what had happened, and that her mother agreed I was right. She now realised that she needed to be more careful in business matters. She didn't say thank you or apologise. But at least she forgave me. Hallelujah. Cara called a truce with me.

But I had no illusions about what she thought of me. And I had already lost faith that she had any goodwill towards me. Everyone else was stupid to her, not just me. Even Lynn, the midwife, whom she liked. When Lynn warned her about how smoking could harm her baby, Lynn, too, was transferred to the „other side". To the side where those existed, who had different opinions about certain things than Cara did, and who weren't afraid to express their opinions. Enemies. Those who held different opinions became Cara's enemies. After her first visit, even the paediatric nurse was nothing more than a stupid bitch, and the health visitor earned the title of „The old whore". Everyone who thinks differently from her is an enemy – this is what Cara thought - and everyone is „too clever". – This is what Cara told me a couple of times. And of course, - Cara explained to me, - she has to listen politely to these people, because that's the proper thing to do, and she has to nod her head to show that she understands what they're saying, but once these people, the „enemies" have finally left, she can send them to hell in long monologues. Because Cara knows how to treat a baby, she is the one who gave birth to this child. She is the mother. No one should explain any nonsense to her! And don't tell her that her child might die just because she smokes. Don't scare her to death and stress her out with this, because her mother smoked with all her children, and none of them died! Cara thought: Everyone just comes to annoy her. They should know that she needs peace and quiet. Because, in fact, when she is upset, it is the most harmful to her and to the baby. After a while, it became painful to listen to Cara's monologues. I've never seen anyone in my entire life so disrespectful as Cara. And somehow it was scary. Intervening or saying anything against her opinion was life-threatening. Another war would have broken out, breaking the fragile truce. And nobody wanted that. I realised that I was walking on eggshells almost all the time. But later, events unfolded in such a way that it was impossible to avoid the conflict.

Ever since she came home from the hospital, Elsie had been sleeping in the big bed between her mother and father, on the mattress, in their bedding, and she hardly ever used the cot. Cara and Jack both smoked, and on top of that, Cara heated the room to thirty degrees so that Elsie wouldn't be cold. We bought a breathing monitor, but Cara didn't put it on the baby, and she got very angry with me when I bought it and gave it to her.

- "Leave me alone, are you just trying to stress me out? Breathing monitor? For what? My child isn't going to die! How can you be like this? You're so negative, I don't understand what's wrong with you?" she shouted at me.

I printed an article in her language, German, for her, which I thought she would understand better than the common language we used. The article explained why a breathing monitor is good and how useful it is, even when babies sleep in their parents' bed. Cara read the article, then rudely told me I didn't trust her child and that the whole thing was nonsense! She didn't use these words; she put it much more harshly. She also complained to Jack, so there was nothing I could do. The breathing monitor was still under warranty, so I took it back to the shop and, thank God, got my money back. But I was worried about Elsie.

Cara changed a lot in a few weeks after giving birth; she became even more withdrawn. From the person we thought she was. Her mood got worse day by day; she didn't even come downstairs, and she didn't leave their room. She didn't bathe or wash; she ate upstairs, and she went downstairs only to the toilet when she needed to pee or smoke. I wrote an email to Lynn when Elsie was six weeks old: three bags of dirty nappies at the top of the stairs, and food scraps and dirty dishes lying in the baby's bed. I couldn't bear to look at it any longer. I would have been happy to clean up, even every day, but Cara wouldn't let me. The two upstairs rooms were covered with laundry and rubbish. I also wrote Lynn about how Cara had changed, becoming apathetic and sad. Lynn replied to my email that same afternoon, saying she would have to report it to social services. She asked if I agreed. I replied that, of course, I did. "Someone just does something!" And Lynn acted pretty quickly. The social worker with the health visitor knocked on the door at eight o'clock the next morning. Jack, Elsie and Cara, all three of them were still asleep upstairs. I woke Jack up, who panicked and asked me not to open the door until he said everything was ready. I told him it might not be a good idea to start cleaning now, but he didn't understand what I meant. He rushed upstairs, gathered what he could, and cleaned up as fast as he could. He took the rubbish bags to the box room and threw the dirty clothes and dishes in there too. The health visitor stood at the door for 10 minutes, then Jack finally told me to let her in.

Of course, the health visitor didn't see the reality of the situation and, in fact, had no idea what was going on. She later told Lynn and wrote in her report to social services that she had found no serious problems with the baby's care. But she did add that the young mother seemed depressed. She didn't use that word; she just described it. She basically outlined Cara's behaviour. That she spends all day locked in their room upstairs, eats upstairs, doesn't like to use the rest of the house, and seems very sad, listless, and pale. And the health visitor suggested to the young parents that I, as the landlord, write a letter saying that I find it very difficult to have them living with me and that I will evict them because I find the situation unbearable. She said that if I wrote such a letter, she could write a request to the city council to allocate a council flat to the three of them as soon as possible. The social worker never spoke to me, not a single word, and apart from letting her in twice, she never even saw me. She didn't ask me anything and knew nothing about me or the nature of my relationship with Cara.

It was difficult for me, but I wrote the letter. I didn't write in it that I was going to put them out on the street, because I couldn't bring myself to do it; it was too cruel, even as a joke. I would never have done such a thing, and I still wouldn't do it today: put my own child and her family out on the street. But I wrote the letter and explained the circumstances. To help. Because that's what they asked me to do. I fundamentally disagreed with the idea because the story was grossly misrepresented. It wasn't that I found it difficult to have them living with me, but that they were living with me the way they were. That was happening. And that something was wrong. But no one seemed to care, except for Lynn, the midwife, who no longer had anything to do with us officially. I hoped for help, for someone to notice what was happening, but I didn't get any help. The health visitor wasn't interested in what the real problem was either. However, through her intervention, Jack and Cara were given a two-bedroom council flat within a week.

The new house

It was neat, not too big and not too small, with a front garden and a back yard.

– "You can plant flowers here too," Cara said with a smile.

While they both enthusiastically described the layout of the rooms, what they would take with them, and where they could place their existing furniture alongside the furnishings they would receive. They had been told they could request furniture from the council at a discounted price and get everything they needed; they just had to write down what they needed.

The house was not far away, a 10–15-minute walk from me, which we were all happy about, I think, but I'm not entirely sure anymore. In any case, Jack and I were happy about it. This will make the move much easier, we thought; we'll easily transport everything in two cars, even the smaller pieces of furniture, and we'll be done with it quickly.

They could move in within two weeks if they wanted to. It could be sooner, the council told them, but then Jack would have to paint the house and lay new flooring in the rooms, because the carpet had to be removed after the previous tenant, and the house needed cosmetic renovation. The council would do the refurbishment for them, but it would take time. Cara immediately replied that no, no, there was no need to wait, and that of course Jack would do everything that needed to be done. Jack was very hands-on anyway, so that couldn't be an obstacle to moving in as soon as possible. As soon as they got the keys, they went to buy laminate flooring and paint. Cara was terribly happy; she was walking on air, having finally come down from her room, and wearing a smile. She tried to be nice. I thought that maybe the health visitor was right. Maybe that was all it took, really, for them to have their own flat, just the two of them, so that Cara could finally feel like an adult and live independently. Maybe everything would go back to how it was when it started, and she would be the person we knew her to be, a cheerful, kind, lively young girl with dreams and plans that she was trying to realise.

- "Imagine, we're getting a refrigerator, a washing machine, and a new stove!", Cara announced, beaming. "And they're bringing two big wardrobes and a chest of drawers for Elsie's room, and even a sofa for the living room!"
- "We're paying for it in instalments, we're not just getting it for free," added Jack, "but the instalments are a ridiculous £20 a month for a couple of years, so it's really like getting it for free. The best thing is that we don't have to run around after it and pay for it all at once; we couldn't afford it anyway."

Jack was happy too. I was sincerely grateful to the health visitor. Although I had no idea what the health visitor wrote in the application, to which she attached my letter, I thought it was worth it, whatever it was!

I was planning to visit my daughter in a few days. I was also glad that everything had been neatly sorted out before I left.

- "When you come back, we'll show you the house!", Cara and Jack told me.
- "All right," I replied, and offered to take whatever she wanted from the kitchen. The new pots and pans we bought together after the wedding, the dishes, cutlery, and anything else she needed!
- "Sure, thanks! But no, thank you. I don't want to take anything from you. I'd rather have everything new", she replied with a smile.

I started packing my suitcase. My daughter Sophia was at the end of her pregnancy, and because of her gestational diabetes, the doctors had planned to induce labour, so we knew exactly when she would be going into the hospital. Both of us, or rather all three of us, including my son-in-law, wanted me to be there for the birth of my first grandson, and it happened to be at the end of the week when Jack was renovating their house. We agreed that I would travel to Sophia's house for the birth and stay with them for three days, and then, when my son-in-law's paternity leave ended, I would return to help them for about two weeks. The timing of the flat allocation was perfect, and everything turned out perfectly. It turned out to be a sound, obvious plan: I would travel to Sophia's, Jack would renovate their future home, and when I returned, I would be able to help them move.

I set off happily and spent three wonderful days in Scandinavia. After a stormy and long night, my little Viking grandchild was born, healthy and strong. That afternoon, a beautiful rainbow appeared over Sophia and Joe's house, stretching across the entire sky. Meanwhile, I was in constant contact with Jack and Cara by phone and video calls. Cara was very interested in what Elsie's cousin was like, how the birth went, and whether everything was okay. She congratulated Sophia warmly in person and flooded their social media photos with hearts. I arrived home happy. The plane had landed late in the evening near the capital, and after midnight, I got off the train in the small rural town where we lived. Jack came to the train station to take me home. Neither Jack nor Cara mentioned during those three days that they had already moved out. Only then and there. When Jack dropped me off at my house, he just ran in for a cigarette and said he was sorry, but that's how it turned out. The last few days had been very busy. Cara wanted to leave as soon as the house was painted. I should just rest now; he would come back the next day, then he would pack up upstairs, and we would talk. He also asked me not to be angry about the mess.

- "How's Elsie? Is everything okay?" - I asked, and my heart was aching a little. I didn't expect to find her awake and see the little girl, but I brought gifts for her and Cara. My big fat black suitcase stood in the middle of the kitchen, full of goodies. I didn't know; I wasn't prepared for them to be gone.

- "Of course, everything is fine," my son replied. - "Cara is very happy, as you can imagine, and I think everything will be fine now; it will all work out nicely."

Jack then quickly hugged me and left. It was one o'clock in the morning. The dog happily ran up and down the flat and followed me wherever I went. I turned on the lights, walked around the house, and went upstairs. In the wardrobe room, there were black bags of rubbish and dirty clothes. In their bedroom, there was rubbish and dirt on the floor, dirty nappies and plates on the bed, and unwashed glasses on the small table. In Elsie's room, where the little girl never stayed, there were all kinds of bags with all kinds of things, piled on top of each other. In the small cradle, there was a bag of mouldy bread, a plate with leftover sausage and dried mustard, and dirt on the floor. Black flies flew confusedly and dizzyingly towards the lamp and the windowpane. I went down to the kitchen. On the counter, under a dirty dishcloth, there were leftovers in a pot, and chicken bones among the unwashed dishes in the sink. Then I felt very tired. I sat down at the kitchen table and, ashamed or not, I cried. And I cried for a while.

I didn't have the strength to do anything else that night except dig out the Raid from under the sink and spray it all over the upstairs rooms. I kept pressing the top of the bottle until it was empty, and even when nothing came out, I kept squeezing the little plastic piece with my fingers. The last drops of the chemical ran down my hands. I took a shower, wrote my daughter a message saying I had arrived safely, and then went to bed. Thankfully, my room downstairs was just as I had left it, and no one had gone in there. I was numb with exhaustion, my body and soul numb. As soon as I lay my head on the pillow, I fell asleep.

The next morning, I started cleaning. I started with the kitchen, and only when I finished did I go upstairs. I swept up a dozen dead flies and opened the windows so that if any of them were still alive, they could go to their doom in the November cold. I washed the doors and mopped the floor. By noon, the whole flat smelled of Domestos. I collected 11 large black bags of rubbish, four bags of clothes, and a bag of twenty pairs of shoes and boots that Cara had left behind. I put Elsie's dirty onesies in the washing machine. Jack arrived just as I was hanging them out to dry. I didn't feel like talking about the mess and disorder, so I didn't say a word. We had a cup of coffee, then Jack took Cara's bags of clothes to his car and came back to talk for a while. He looked around and packed a few more things into the only black bag that was left. He took some pictures off the wall, Elsie's open packet of nappies, and a few other small items. There was a gift box with a little outfit on top of the wardrobe that I had bought for the baby girl after she was born, a red two-piece knitted set with an embroidered teddy bear pattern on the jumper. I don't think Cara liked it; she never opened it or put it on Elsie. Now it lay untouched on the changing table. Jack's eyes lit up when he saw the box.

- "Oh, look, this is still here, left behind. I'll take this!"
- "No way!" I shouted at him and snatched the white box from his hands. "You're not taking this anywhere!"

Jack looked at me in confusion.

- "But why? ... Didn't you buy it for Elsie?"
- "Yes, I did. But you're not taking it away! It's mine, I bought it for her! I'll give it to her when she comes, if it still fits her... if she hasn't outgrown it."

Suddenly, I felt so fed up and tired that I couldn't control myself and burst into tears in the middle of the room. Jack came over to me and hugged me.

- "Mum, ... Mum, what's wrong? Please don't be upset, everything will be fine."

I pulled away from Jack's embrace

- "Nothing will be alright, nothing... Something is very wrong. Son, how could you leave this flat like this? Honestly! There was no mention that you weren't here anymore. I couldn't help you! This isn't what we agreed."

Jack stood in front of me, confused, and I saw uncertainty and some kind of shame on his face. Something I never wanted to see.

- "I know, Mum, I'm sorry, I wanted to clean up, but I didn't have time. I had to finish painting. Cara wanted to leave, and I didn't have time to tidy up and pack."
- "It wasn't your job... I think. You renovated the flat. But that wasn't what we agreed. We agreed you would wait until I came back, and I would help you move. There would have been time for everything, nice and easy. Not black flies... Elsie's room was full of black flies."
- "Yes. I had planned it differently, too. Just as we had agreed. But you know what Cara is like. And she wanted to leave as soon as possible", said Jack.

I couldn't and didn't want to respond. Because no, I didn't know what Cara was like. I had no idea at that time. As for Cara, I still don't know who I'm dealing with or what I'm dealing with. And I didn't understand. Neither her behaviour nor her escape, and especially not her lack of love.

But slowly, I calmed down. Less than two weeks after Jack and Cara moved out, I had settled back into my own house. I enjoyed the silence, finding everything just as I had left it when I went to work and when I came home. I took long walks with the dog every day, corresponded with my daughter, video chatted with the little Viking, watched films, and read a lot. Jack dropped by for coffee at least every other day. We talked about his work, and he sent pictures of Elsie to my phone. I didn't contact Cara. Maybe twice I asked her in a message if she was okay, if everything was fine, and how Elsie was doing, but she only replied in short sentences, writing one or two-word messages, so I didn't push the conversation with her. I figured she would contact me if and when she needed me. I would have loved to see the house they got, but they didn't invite me over, so I didn't go. Jack said I could drop by anytime, but I didn't think it would be a good idea to just show up unannounced. Cara didn't even let me go upstairs in my own house without calling me first, so how could I just go to her house? I really wanted to see Elsie, but Jack was usually working in the mornings, and Cara wouldn't let him bring the little girl over to me. She told Jack it was too cold to take Elsie out this time of year, and that the baby was so unsettled she was afraid of everyone. Besides, she was breastfeeding, Elsie was eating all the time, and there was no telling when she would get hungry, and then she would cry, and obviously, no one wanted that. "She's still too young to be taken away from her mother", Cara concluded.

In mid-November, Cara finally sent me a message saying that if I felt like coming over, she would be happy to see me. Finally! I thought, and I was very happy. I was also happy that the ice might finally be broken, and that it had been worth waiting! I went over one weekday afternoon and took them the gift I had brought them from abroad. I went happily and peacefully, very curious about the house. Cara opened the door with a smile, but as soon as I crossed the threshold, she reproached me for not getting in touch, for not going there before, and for not saying that I wanted to see my grandchild, as she would have been happy to welcome me...The reproach didn't hurt, because somehow I thought that Cara was saying all this because she might have missed me. She then showed me around the house, proudly pointing out what was missing, but adding that all those things had already been taken care of, and that a washing machine and a table for the room would be delivered soon. They had furnished it really nicely, and the house was cosy, warm, and clean. I told Cara this, and I also told her how happy I was to see how much work they had put into the house and how comfortable they felt in it.

Elsie, well, she had grown so much! In just a few weeks, she had become a real chubby baby, happily waving her little hand at me and looking at me with a friendly face, as if she knew me, recognised me. Cara handed her to me, and I rocked her and played with her on the living room sofa. But Cara didn't leave the room; she sat there with us the whole time. She watched TikTok videos on her phone while keeping me in the corner of her eye. She didn't even go out for a cigarette. I wanted to take some photos of Elsie, but I thought Cara wouldn't like that, so I only dared to take three pictures of the little girl when I thought Cara wasn't paying attention.

After half an hour, Cara told me the health visitor would be arriving soon, so if I didn't want to be there when she came, it would be better to leave before she arrived. She added that she would prefer I weren't there, because Elsie usually gets very fussy when the health visitor examines her, and it's quite difficult for her to calm the baby down at such times.

She won't be able to pay attention to me, and she doesn't want me to feel uncomfortable because of that. I understood what she meant, nodded, and started to get ready to leave.

- "But," Cara said kindly, "let me know whenever you want to come over, and we'll discuss a time that suits us both. I'd love to see you, you know."

I nodded again and hugged her. I said goodbye and went home. A week later, I was getting ready to travel to Sophia's and didn't think I would see Elsie again until then. At home, sitting at the kitchen table, I looked at the three photos on my phone for a long time. What a cute, cheerful, chubby little girl, she can already smile, and she smiled at me too, my little granddaughter!

Jack looked at me in bewilderment when he dropped by that evening.

- "You could have waited; I arrived a few minutes after you left! I thought we'd meet there. The health visitor didn't come today. I don't know why Cara is talking nonsense."

I had an idea why, or rather, I knew exactly why, but I didn't want to hurt Jack with it, and I especially didn't want to waste our little time together by saying negative things to him. Instead, I asked him about his work, and we talked about what would happen when I left. When he would come over to feed the dog, when his brother Joe would arrive, how he would give him the keys, when and where they would meet.

We discussed everything in detail, he had a beer, and then Jack went home.

It was mid-November, and the house was starting to get cold, so I turned on the heating and sat down in front of the TV to finish watching my favourite series.

Cara didn't take it very well when anyone dared to mention anything, so I didn't want to tell Jack how my visit had gone and why I had stayed for such a short time. But Jack probably figured out for himself what might have happened. Cara usually slipped up with her lies. She always gave herself away when she wasn't telling the truth. She would either slip up or give away other details. The health visitor didn't come that day, nor was there any mention of her coming. Jack realised that Cara had actually sent me away. The whole visit was quite unpleasant, and in the end, Cara took the baby out of my arms. So I left when I was told to, but I probably would have left on my own very soon anyway. I told Jack that it would be better to do what we had already discussed, namely that Jack or Cara would bring Elsie to me whenever they wanted to. I am happy to look after her here in my own home at any time.

Jack must have said something about this to Cara the next day or even that evening, perhaps he questioned her, perhaps he just asked her what had happened, I don't know. But Cara didn't like being asked questions, especially when she was being questioned. She only liked to exercise control over others. And if someone noticed the contradictions and there was a chance that it would come out that she hadn't told the truth about something, it would completely blow her fuse. Being called to account aroused unbridled hatred in her, and she always lashed out like a cornered wild animal. I had come to know this characteristic of hers very well. The next day, I received another terrible message from her, the following letter:

> *"I would really like to write about how cruel you are... I would post it everywhere for the whole world to see... how you can destroy a person and what you do to an innocent person. Yeah, it was you who attacked a pregnant woman, it was you who threatened innocent people, and it was you who never learned in your life not to stick your nose into everything that's none of your business... you're the only woman in the world who does that.*
>
> *LEARN THIS TOO: LIFE DOESN'T GO THE WAY YOU WANT IT TO, EVERYONE HAS THEIR OWN LIFE, AND STAY OUT OF THINGS THAT ARE NONE OF YOUR BUSINESS! You're the one who writes me messages that don't make sense from start to*

finish. You're the one who wanted to beat me while I was pregnant. SO BE ASHAMED OF YOURSELF! VERY ASHAMED!

You're the one who opens other people's documents because you haven't learned that they're not yours and you shouldn't touch other people's things. You need to learn that too! And I could tell you so much more about what you did to me that I wouldn't be finished by tomorrow! Well, what about you? Can you say a word? No, because you know very well that you treat me like shit and then turn it around and say that I treat you like that, but we both know that you're the one who is doing this! And how can you not be ashamed to ask if you can see my child after what you did to me? You should be grateful that you can see this child, but you're still bossing me around and you're not grateful that you can come here. Another woman would have sent you packing... Yeah, I'll say it. And that line about you treating me like I was your daughter is the best joke of the year.

Then wait until you open your mouth, because all that comes out are stinking lies. You lie so much that it hurts people, you lie to everyone. It's sad how much you lie. I've never seen anyone like you in my life. Not even Fred's mother treats me the way you do... just because you're a Hungarian woman, you think you can do whatever you want with everyone, because I don't know who do you think you are.

And my child will hate you like shit, I'll show her and tell her what you did to me. Just like everyone else knows the truth about what you do to me and what you write and what you plan, and then you play the poor victim. You're a real witch, I tell you. ... You can't even apologise properly because you can't see that it's all your fault! That's why you have so much karma in your life.

> *You treat people badly, that's why no one will hire you, you deserve it and I hope you learn from this. And I'll tell you something, you little liar, I'm definitely not leaving my child alone with a woman like you. If you want to see her, come here, and if not, I don't care... Leave me alone, people like you have no place in my beautiful life! Have a nice life, you lying bitch!"*

Oh, Lord. All of Cara's fears, everything she was terrified of, was in this message, and she used everything she knew against me. The one time I opened her referral for a screening test, which I had to translate anyway, she even blamed me for her own characteristics, her own childhood, and for all the bad things that had happened to her in her life. I had no idea how or why I had earned this immeasurable amount of hatred she had heaped on me that day, as I hadn't complained or whined to Jack too much, in fact, hardly at all. I just tried to set boundaries and said I would rather have and see Elsie at my house. But I didn't say anything bad about Cara, and I certainly didn't say anything that wasn't true. Cara didn't like me, and that was it. That was a fact. I didn't condemn her for it, and it didn't really hurt me. Jack was probably more hurt by Cara's treatment of me than I was. I didn't know how he interpreted what I said, and I certainly didn't know that the two of them had other problems between them. Massive problems. Cara was jealous. She had access to Jack's phone again, reread all the messages, and found messages from women with whom Jack mainly corresponded about the stock market. But his business partners and advisors were all female, and this was a huge problem for Cara.

It was a brutal letter, and I couldn't leave it unanswered, because I knew Cara well and I knew my silence would only add fuel to the fire. Cara would have continued to hate me even more, thinking I was ignoring her. So, I replied, but I wrote her a very short message and only included the facts, only what concerned our shared past. I didn't respond to the insults and absurd accusations; there would have been no point, so I just wrote her a few sentences.

"I never attacked you, and I never hurt you. When you started threatening my son that you would leave him and take his child away, just weeks after your wedding, I asked you to stop this behaviour, but even then, I just shouted at you that we love you. I never wanted to separate you from my son, and everyone knows that. You're talking nonsense, Cara. I'm sorry, really."

The short, factual messages always calmed Cara; they cooled her off, gave her no reason to hate further, and she fell silent.

I found her message deeply pathological because of the projections and fears expressed in it and the references to childhood. But I had no idea how I could help, how I could do anything.

I had a few days left before my trip, and Cara and I didn't speak during that time. I left before we officially made up. That hurt me, but probably not her so much. She later claimed that she didn't remember that I was leaving, that she had forgotten about my trip. Elsie also fell ill again, and Cara's brother Mike came to visit them for a few weeks before leaving the country for good. I didn't know anything about this, but it obviously kept Cara busy and distracted her from me. That's what I thought. The reality was different. Cara turned against Jack again. Two days later, after I received the text above, Jack got his message too. I only saw Jack's message six months later. Cara wanted to get divorced again. This is what she wrote:

> 25 November
>
> *"Let's go for a smoke. I think it would be good to talk everything through now, because I can see that things can't go on like this. We don't really get along, I'm like this and you're like that. There's been too much shit between us, and your mother still can't let it go. That woman never learns; she doesn't see her mistakes, and because of her, this is always between us.*
>
> *You can't understand because you understand her better, even though she's the one causing the trouble. You've never been fair to me, you've never understood how I*

feel because of that evil woman. She was always the poor one and you always felt sorry for her, even though I was the poor innocent woman. But whatever. The way you cling to your mother is what they call a mummy's boy. One would think she was your wife...

You quickly say you're tired when I wake you up, but you don't say anything to your dear mother when you have to go to work, you did the housework, you worked, and you had to go and fix something at hers, it couldn't wait, even though we had a thousand things to do in our house, but you had to help her, well...

Whatever, screw it, be happy with your mum, the woman who ruined everything. She ruined your wife, your relationship, and it's so sad that you still don't see it, but stay with her, if you want her rather than me. I'm tired of you lying about me so much, it's a joke. I don't need people like that.

As far as I'm concerned, this woman will never see my child again in her life. But!! You and I, we'll separate amicably; no court is needed. I'll sign a document stating that I won't leave the country.

And you can see Elsie two or three times a week. What you do with her and who you take her to when she's with you is your business. I just want to know if anything happens to her when she's with you, and if something happens to her, you call me, not your mother, understand? Because I'm her mother and I need to know everything.

You're welcome to stay here while you look for a flat of your own. And it would be better for you to finally tell your mother to fuck off, but whatever.

I won't say anything about you, except that you're letting her ruin your relationship, and that I'm not the right one for you, and you're not the right one for me, and that's all I have to say.

And if I say to bring the child home by 3:30 p.m., I want to see her then. And if you're late, then call me

I hate your mother with all my heart, to be honest"

So, Cara wanted a divorce. Again. I knew nothing about this; Jack never mentioned any problems between them. Since they moved out, I thought everything was fine. I kept my distance, hoping it would help the three of them grow stronger as a family. I didn't drag Jack to my place either; he dropped by for coffee every two or three days and didn't stay too long. I did not call Jack too often; there were days when we didn't even talk. Neither by phone, nor in person. I couldn't understand where this massive hatred and jealousy were coming from. In another message of hers, Cara also claimed that I had wanted to take her child away from her. Never! I never said or even suggested anything like that! I gave her no reason to fear this. I wanted her to get help for her mental health, but not because I wanted to take her child away from her. For God's sake. I raised four children, my own, and I felt old enough to be a real grandmother and nothing more! Someone who has grandchildren visiting, who picks them up from school, and who looks after them while their parents are at work or out having fun. But that's it. I had my life as a mother, and I was able to practise this vocation for many years. Yes, I did suffer from empty nest syndrome, but I quite quickly got over it. I enjoyed the peace and only having to take care of myself. I had lots of great plans for my own future, a bucket list of places I wanted to go, things I wanted to see, read, etc. And I had no plans to start raising children again at any level...

After the summer ups and downs, I talked about Cara with one of my acquaintances, a friend who was a practising psychiatrist. She couldn't help Cara, precisely because she was my friend, and it's an unwritten rule that close acquaintances, almost relatives, cannot be treated by the same psychiatrist. She knows too much; she could be biased. But she couldn't have helped her anyway, because Cara herself didn't think she needed any help.

Ruth, the psychiatrist, listened patiently to me, but she was wise and restrained enough not to confirm my belief in any cobbled-together diagnosis based on internet knowledge. She simply said that help was obviously needed, but warned me against trying to help Cara myself. Ruth warned me that, given my position, I could not be the one to save, treat, or help Cara. I should not even try to help, because whatever I did would almost certainly backfire. I am the mother-in-law. And the mother-in-law is never a positive figure; she cannot be. If she has a bad character, that's why; if she has a good character, that's why, because it is even more painful for the sick psyche that the mother-in-law is just a mother-in-law, not her own mother. Ruth told me interesting things, things I would never have thought of myself. When I mentioned how quickly Cara lost weight after giving birth, and was once again skin and bones, weighing barely forty kilos, Ruth explained to me the possible root of this weight loss: The poor girl, the little girl inside Cara, was trying to return to her former self... When she was a little girl, and she weighed barely forty kilos and wore children's clothes - that was probably the last time she was truly happy. Or that's the point from where she wants to start her life again. Ruth was almost certain that Cara's childhood was when the biggest break occurred (as in most mental illnesses), but unfortunately, there was no way to find out what it was. And there was no hope for treatment until Cara herself initiated it.

Two days before my trip, I cleaned up once more the whole house, put on Joe, my eldest son's favourite bedding, and agreed with him over the phone when he would arrive, where to find things in the house, when to feed the dog, and I left my gym membership card for him on the kitchen counter.

I left and was not entirely at ease. But even in my wildest, worst dreams, I could not have imagined the events that followed. Every boy mum's worst nightmare.

THE SLAP

Sophia and Joseph welcomed me with all the love that a daughter could give. Airport transfer, a warm dinner at a decorated table, a freshly made soft bed, and, most importantly, hugs. And then there was the tiny baby, the little Viking, who was immediately placed into my arms and snuggled in. My grandson. In an instant, I forgot all my sorrows and worries. I could finally breathe. I was on holiday from work, and it was time to relax. And Sophia had planned something for every day. I went there to help her, to look after the baby, babysit, so that she could rest. But she said that the real rest for her was having me there and being able to spend time with me. And she wanted to come with me everywhere, show me everything. That same afternoon, when I arrived, she and my son-in-law took me to the lake near the city, in the middle of the forest. We had cake and coffee in a little forest café by the frozen lake, then we went for a long walk in the pine forest, and I pushed the tiny little Viking in his pram. By evening, we were exhausted, but we happily made plans for the next day over the butter-fried salmon.

I woke up refreshed in the morning and quickly got dressed to go to the living room, from where I could already hear the baby's voice. My grandson was rocking in his Scandinavian swing and demanding breast milk. While Sophia was breastfeeding, I turned on my phone, which I had left on the charger overnight. But I wish I had postponed it, I wish I could have put off this moment! The display showed more than a dozen missed calls, 14 to be exact, with red exclamation marks, and next to them were text messages, every mother's nightmare:

"*Please answer the phone, there's trouble, big trouble with your son, get your son out of there, please, answer the phone or call me back as soon as you get this message! I wish you were here to take Elsie with you and look after her! They've taken your son; get him out of there! Please do something! They're coming back now, I understand. They might take me too*"

Cara also wrote another message, begging:

> *"When this is over, please help us. We must go and ask for help. This can't go on. I just ask you to look after Elsie while we go and get help."...*

Joseph, my son-in-law, came out of the bedroom

- "Do you know what's going on? What happened?" he asked. "I've received a lot of calls and messages."

Sophia searched for her mobile phone on the bed with one hand and glanced at her own display.

- "Me too", said my daughter, "At three in the morning, I had six missed calls from Cara... I think you should call her, Mum!"

By then, I had already written a message to Cara.

"What happened? You can call me now, I'm awake."

But Cara didn't answer. Twenty minutes later, I received a message from her. It was a bit confusing, as her writing usually is.

> *"Everything's fine now. Mike and Jack were just really drunk; they threw up on the carpet, and I was really angry. I cleaned up all night, and I called you so you could talk to Elsie while I was cleaning".*

Elsie wasn't even three months old... Talk to her while Cara cleans up? What? I didn't understand the message.

"What happened?" I wrote back, "Where's Jack?"

"He's asleep upstairs", Cara replied.

- "Something's not right", I turned to Sophia, "this girl is writing nonsense, I have no idea what could have happened?"
- "Mum, she knows you're here with us, she's probably just demanding attention", said Sophia angrily, pouting. "I was sure

this was what she would do... that she would try to ruin your holiday. But I hoped she would wait a few days before starting" ...

- "I don't know, I need to talk to Jack", I replied. "I don't understand what Cara is writing. Especially where to pick up Jack and where *they* are taking him. What on earth could have happened? But she wrote earlier that Jack is fine and everything is okay, he's sleeping upstairs... I don't understand. None of it."

I wrote to Cara:"Please tell Jack to call me when he wakes up."

No reply. We started breakfast. Less than half an hour later, my phone rang. Cara called me via the internet. I picked up my coat and went out onto the terrace. It had snowed overnight, covering the landscape and the distant mountains in a wonderful white blanket. But it was very cold. Even in my socks and fur-lined slippers, my feet were cold, and even though I was wearing a bathrobe under my coat, I could feel the cold air seeping into my bones. I sat down on the edge of the bench in the covered part of the terrace. Cara initiated a video call, which I accepted. Her face appeared on the screen. Looked very quiet and smiling.

- "Are you very angry with me?" she asked.

I didn't understand.

- "Why would I be angry, Cara? Where's Jack? Will you tell me what happened?"

Cara lowered her eyes.

- "They took your son away. Last night. Please get him out of there, because they won't talk to me, and I don't even know who to call."
- "So, he's not at home? You wrote that he was sleeping upstairs! Who took him away? And where did they take him?
- "The police. The police took him away. I told him not to do it, not to call them, but he took my phone and called them."
- "But why? What happened?"

- "I hit him. But I didn't hit him hard; I just slapped him, but he was bleeding a lot. His lip was split, there was a lot of blood, and then he took my phone and called them, the police, and they came. And they took him away."
- "Where did they take him? When? And why? What did they say?"
- "At dawn, I don't know, sometime around when I first wrote to you. I don't know where they took him. They came here three times, to my place, and they came with handcuffs and interrogated me. They wanted to take me away, too. They were going to take me in, but Elsie was here, so they didn't take me. Mike would have looked after her, but he was very drunk. So, they left me at home, but they came three times. I was very scared," Cara stammered. "Please try to find out where he is, where they took him, and when they'll let him out! I didn't want this, I'm very sorry... really."
- "All right. I have to hang up now. You know I'm abroad; I don't know if I'll be able to call from here or who I can reach. But I'll try to find out. I'll call you back as soon as I know anything", I told Cara. I suddenly grew angry and nervous.

I threw open the patio door and went straight to the kitchen

- "The police took Jack away last night," I told Sophia, distraught. Joseph stopped stirring with his spoon.
- "What?", Sophia turned pale and looked at me in horror
- "I don't know, sweetheart. Cara just said that she slapped him, his mouth was bleeding, and Jack took her phone and called the police. Then they came and took him away.
- "But why? Why did they take him away? And where did they take him? If Cara slapped him, why did the police take my brother away?"
- "I'd like to find out that too", I replied, and by then I was shaking with nervousness.

I threw a blanket over myself and went back out onto the terrace. I looked up the city police station's number online, added the country code, and dialled. The line was as clear as if I were at home, within the country's borders.

The police offered no information about the situation. They said they couldn't, but they just confirmed that yes, Jack was with them, still sleeping, and they were waiting for him to wake up, so they could question him again.

- "Look, my son is innocent. I don't know why you took him in, but he certainly didn't do anything to deserve being held in there! I just spoke to my daughter-in-law, and she told me what happened! She said she slapped my son. She also said that his lip was split and there was a lot of blood! My son didn't hit her back, I'm sure of that!"
- "Madam, please calm down. You weren't there; you don't know what happened, or whether your son is innocent. You are abroad, if I understand correctly."
- "Yes. I am abroad, and I was not present at the scene, you are right. But my daughter-in-law told me herself what happened! And I've known my son for 28 years, I raised him, and I know he wouldn't hurt a fly, he's never hit anyone, he's never been in a fight, he's never had any trouble with the police, he's never broken the law! Whatever you accuse him of, please consider this."
- "We will certainly do so. We will consider his clean record. But we have to wait until he wakes up to question him. He has been asleep since we brought him in. We have tried to wake him, but he is unresponsive. When he wakes up, you can talk to him."
- "Thank you. I'll call you again later. And please tell him I was looking for him. When he wakes up, please tell him that I will call him."
- "We will, ma'am. As soon as we have questioned him, he will call you, or you can call him."

I hung up the phone. I was shaking all over and felt as if all my strength had left me. I thought I was going mad. I couldn't believe that this was happening to us. Maybe it was just a bad dream! It had to be. A terrible, bad dream that would soon be over. And I thought of my son. I saw him in front of me, sleeping soundly, and I thought about how much stress he had been under in recent months, working constantly, trying to earn money, and looking after Elsie at night so that Cara could sleep. I thought about how exhausted he must be, since even the police couldn't wake him up, and I consoled myself with the thought that at least he was resting now. How absurd, how grotesque is this?! It occurs to you that it's not so bad the police took your son in for an interview, at least he can rest at the station... I trudged back to the flat. Sophia and Joseph were already in the living room, looking at me expectantly. The concern on Sophia's face was indescribable.

- "Mum, oh mum, I told you... I told you this girl would bring trouble upon you!"
- "That doesn't help much now," Joseph muttered under his breath, which I also sighed to myself.
- "Okay, but tell me, what did they say? What's going on? What exactly happened? How is Jack? They're going to let him out, right? When will they let him go home?", Sophia continued to ask anxiously.
- "They couldn't give me any information. All they said was that they had to question him. But he's still asleep. They tried to wake him, but couldn't, and he's still asleep. It's almost 11 o'clock... He must be exhausted", I replied, trying not to cry.
- "What happens now? ... Mum... What happens now? Mum... You're not going home, are you?", Sophia asked in a choked voice, then immediately added: "If you want to go home, I understand... of course. But you're not, are you? I've been waiting so long for you to be here! And you need a rest too…"
- "I'm not going anywhere. Not yet. I don't know what will happen. I need to talk to Jack. We have to wait until he wakes up. I need to find out exactly what happened. And what will happen next?! I don't know yet..."
- "Okay... ", Sophia sighed.

We listened in deep silence for a few minutes. Joseph pushed a coffee towards me on the table. I hadn't even noticed when he'd made it for me, but it was still warm.

– "Then I think we should get dressed, eat something, and go into town", Sophia said quietly. "Joseph has the day off today, and it'll be easier if we go in today, the three of us with the baby. It's so beautiful, you'll see! There's a Christmas market; the whole town is lit up... I was planning on going in today anyway. And then at least you won't think too much. You can make phone calls in the meantime, and we can wait for Jack to call."

I nodded. Sure, that's fine. There would be no point in sitting at home and just waiting. I got dressed, but I don't usually eat breakfast anyway, and now I really didn't feel like eating, so we left right away. The town was truly beautiful, bathed in light, full of tents, small wooden huts, and stalls around them. The air was filled with the smell of mulled wine and cinnamon buns. A Ferris wheel and all kinds of funny animals, forest gnomes, and large statues of reindeer lined the road. For a short time, I managed to forget everything that had happened that morning, but of course I had my phone in my hand, deep in my coat pocket, so that I could not only hear it but also feel it when it rang, lest I miss the call. It was terribly cold. There was still little snow, and hardly any left in the city, but heavy snowfall was forecast for that night. I thought how beautiful it would be! How beautiful the city would look covered in snow...

Jack didn't call until evening. At one o'clock and three o'clock in the afternoon, I called the police again, but they told me Jack was still asleep; they hadn't been able to wake him or question him yet. "But we let him sleep anyway!" added the officer I spoke to, and I thought I detected a hint of pity in his tone. The police officer couldn't tell me whether Jack would be released after the interrogation, and certainly could not tell when that would be, if at all.

Meanwhile, Cara called me three times, twice asking if I had found out anything, and the same thing I wanted to know, when the police would release Jack. But the third time, I didn't answer the phone. I couldn't talk to her anymore. I felt terribly nauseous. I was angry with her. I wished I could tell her: It's your fault he's there! You put him there! My son, who has always been honest, avoided trouble and never did anything wrong, is now sleeping somewhere in a room, on a cot, like some criminal, in a deep sleep from exhaustion, and God knows how miserable he will feel when he wakes up! And they're going to interrogate him! Maybe not as a victim, but as a suspect! No. I didn't feel like talking to Cara and listening to her whining about getting Jack out of the place she put him in. Suddenly, I could recall all of the rude text messages Cara sent me in the past. My mind was crystal clear. My memory was fully awakened.

We had already arrived home, and the little Viking was getting ready for bed when Jack finally called me. It was already 9 o'clock over there, but only 8 at home. Jack's voice sounded very tired, and he spoke rapidly. He said he had just been released and would have called me earlier, but his phone had run out of battery, and he had walked home because he didn't have a car. He had borrowed a charger from the neighbours, but his phone's battery was still at 2%, so he would call me back later.

- "But which neighbour? Where are you now?" I asked, alarmed.
- "Where else would I be, Mum? I came home", Jack replied, his voice breaking. "Al gave me a charger. I'm here now. At home, in the kitchen... I came home, fed the dog... and Mum, I don't want to go back... I'm not going back to her. She hit me... I never would have thought that. I don't want this... I don't want to live like this... Mum, can I stay here? It's okay if I stay here, right?"

I heard the silence and what sounded like my grown son crying. He was 3,000 miles away from me. And I thought my heart would break.

- "Of course you can stay. Don't ask silly questions. Why wouldn't you stay?"
- "Okay, Mum, I'll call you back. I'll just charge my phone and take a shower. But then I'll call you back."
- "All right," I replied, "I'll wait for your call. I won't go to bed until then."

Jack will pull himself together. He's strong. That's what I thought, I remember it well. He's always been strong, tough as nails, as the poet says. And I wondered why, when I find myself in critical situations, I always remember bits of poetry?...

I waited for Jack to call. Meanwhile, Cara bombarded me with messages.

> *"Do you know anything yet? Did they let him out? Where is he? Did he go home?"*

I didn't feel like answering. Especially since I already knew Jack didn't want to go back to her. I stalled for time, putting off my answer for as long as possible. But I couldn't do it for long, because Cara kept sending me questions one after another. Then she tried to call me. I hesitated before finally picking up the phone.

- "I don't know, the police didn't give me any information, and now they're not answering my calls either. It's late. Maybe they've already let him out."
- "But then where is he?"
- "Probably on his way home."
- "But why isn't he answering his phone? I've been calling him non-stop."
- "I don't know, Cara. Maybe his phone is dead. He'll be in touch, I'm sure. Be patient. I'm doing the same."
- "Well, I can't wait patiently! If I don't know where he is!"

I didn't know what to say to that, but I was glad Cara couldn't see my face or my body language. I shrugged my shoulders. I didn't care how Cara felt. Not anymore. I was angry. I thought she should worry. She had every reason to. And she had herself to blame.

Jack called again about half an hour later.

- "Cara won't leave me alone; she keeps calling."
- "I know, she's calling me too. She wants to know where you are."
- "I must return the phone charger to Al. Then I'll call Cara. Or maybe not. I think I'll go downstairs, I mean down to the house and get my own charger, pack a few things, and then I'll talk to her", said Jack.

- "I think you should rest, just call her on the phone. You can go down to the house tomorrow to pick up your things."
- "You may be right", Jack said, "I don't know what to do. I don't feel like going there."
- "Tell me what happened at the interrogation instead! And what happened?", I suggested
- "Nothing really. At the police station. They just took a statement. They asked why we were arguing and what exactly happened. I told them that Cara asked me to take Mike to see the city because he hadn't seen anything since he'd been staying with us, and Cara said to take him out to have some fun while she put Elsie to bed."
- "Wait, I didn't even know Mike was staying with you", I interrupted.
- "He arrived the day you left."
- "And how long is he staying?"
- "Supposedly for a week or two. Then he'll move back home for good. Back to Europe. He must go, he has no right to stay, no status."
- "Okay, fine. So, what happened? You guys left, Cara stayed home with Elsie, and?"
- "Yes. And we got home around midnight. Cara was angry that we had stayed out so late, she asked where we had been, and she was also angry because Mike was drunk and had vomited on the carpet in the living room. I didn't even know he had vomited because I went straight upstairs to the bedroom, washed up, and went to bed. Elsie was sleeping in the big bed, and I went to bed as usual and wanted to sleep because I had to work the next day, which is today. Cara came up and started arguing. She yelled and asked why Mike was drunk and said what a shitty person I was and that her brother got drunk because of me and that she was going to divorce me because she'd had enough…"
- "Great. And how did that turn into her hitting you?"
- "Well, she told me to get up and get out of the room because she didn't want to sleep next to me anymore, and she regretted marrying me. I laughed and asked her to let me sleep. I laughed, and I think that annoyed her. I closed my eyes and turned towards the wall. Then she started shaking me, saying I wasn't

going to sleep now, but I had to listen to everything she had to say, and that tomorrow I would see what would happen because she was leaving tomorrow. I told her okay, just leave me alone to sleep because I had to go to work tomorrow. And then she hit me. She hit me in the face, slapped me, and split my lip. Then I got up and, because my phone was dead, I grabbed her phone and called the police. Meanwhile, she started screaming at me not to call the police, to stop what I was doing. Elsie was sleeping in bed and started to wake up. I held Cara's arm so she couldn't take the phone away, and I called the police and told them what had happened, that she wouldn't let me sleep, had slapped me, and that my mouth was bleeding. The police said they were coming, and that I should leave the house and wait for them on the street. So, I went out and sat in the car, waiting for the police."

- "I see. I just don't understand how you ended up at the police station. Why did they take you in for questioning? Why didn't they take Cara?"
- "I have no idea. I guess it was because Elsie was there."
- "Elsie could have stayed with you, couldn't she?"
- "I don't know, Mum, I have no idea! The police came out, went into the house, looked around, and told me to wait in the car. I guess they questioned Cara, and then they didn't want me to stay there overnight, so they took me away."
- "And what did Cara tell them?"
- "How should I know?"
- "But still? Cara told me that they went back to her three times that night."
- "Maybe, I don't know. They just asked me if I hit her. I said no. I just held her hand so she couldn't hit me again. While I was on the phone. But it happened so fast! Everything... And the police came right away. A few minutes after I called, they were already there."
- …
- "I didn't know what else to do, Mum. The woman we spoke to on the helpline, you know, the Livefearfree helpline, once said that if she was not only emotionally aggressive but also physically aggressive, then we shouldn't wait for anything, but call the

police. You told me that. And today she hit me. I didn't know what else to do. I've had enough. I don't want to live like this!"

- "Okay, of course you don't, I understand."
- "I'm not going back to her, I've had enough."
- "OK. Everything will work out."
- "But the child is there..."
- "Well, yes."
- "And I don't know what will happen now."
- "We need to find a solicitor."
- "Yes, I think so. I won't be able to do anything else. I don't want to lose Elsie...", Jack's voice faltered again. Throughout our conversation, he was desperate, and although he didn't cry, I sensed he was close to it.
- "Try to calm down", I told him.
- "Yes, I think I'll go to bed soon. I'll decide whether to go down now to get my charger and my things or tomorrow, but I think I'll have a cigarette and go to bed", Jack said. I tried to reassure him with a few more words. And soon we hung up the phone.

Exhausted, I went out to the living room. The little Viking was already sleeping peacefully next to Sophia. I quietly recounted my conversation with Jack, and they listened in horror, but had nothing to add. It was late, so I quickly showered, and we all got ready for bed. It was almost midnight when Cara called. I answered the phone but left the flat so as not to disturb my daughter, son-in-law, and grandchild, who were already asleep. I put on Sophia's coat and my boots and went down to the garden. Cara's voice was happy and carefree.

- "I'm just calling to wish you a good night," she said, "and to tell you that you don't have to worry anymore. I found Jack. He went to see you, and I went to get him. We talked everything through. Everything. And now everything will be fine! We talked through the whole thing, everything!
- "Oh, I see, okay," I replied, trying not to sigh loudly, the sigh that escaped me. A kind of wtf, or "what the hell is going on now?" sigh.
- "Is Jack with you now? Did he go home?

- "Of course. I brought him home," Cara said cheerfully. "He was very broken, very upset, and very tired. But we talked everything through! And now everything is fine. Sleep well!
- "Okay, thank you very much. You guys get some rest, you are too! It's very late here, you know. Thank you for calling", I replied and hung up the phone.

I stood in the dark garden, where only a motion-detector lamp indicated my presence. Around me, the city was shrouded in a deep, dark silence. The night was black, the sky an icy ink blue. My breath formed white wisps of vapour. I looked up at the starless sky and saw the first tiny snowflakes in the lamp's yellow light. They fell like cooling manna on my feverish forehead. I stood there for a long time. I was no longer cold. I searched and searched for the future, wondering what would happen next, how things would turn out. But there were no answers to these questions at the time. And perhaps it was better that I did not see the long year ahead of us. I slowly went into the house and fell into a deep, dreamless sleep.

The next day, Jack called me. He told me that Cara had gone to my house and begged him to come home. She promised him everything, that everything would be different from now on, that she would go to therapy, that she would change, that she would no longer threaten or hurt Jack. She would clean, cook, and be a good wife. So, Jack went home with her. They talked half the night, and Cara made promises. Jack said nothing, just accepted her explanations and promises, and then they went to bed.

But Cara woke up the next day as if nothing had happened, and at breakfast she told Jack she hadn't slept much, that she had been thinking and had come to the conclusion it wasn't really her fault that all this had happened. And that she wasn't going to therapy after all, because it would be pointless, since it wasn't her fault what had happened. If therapy was needed, it would be for both of them, but mostly for Jack, because there was really nothing wrong with her, Cara. Jack listened to the speech, then started packing his things, gathering what he thought he needed, and simply told Cara that if that was the case, he had decided to move back to my house. At least for a while, because he wanted to think things through. He left Cara, who became furious. She began threatening again, sent him messages that if that was the case, she would leave as soon as she could. And that Jack was a piece of shit who chose his mother over her. Jack did not respond to the messages; he only told Cara he would visit his daughter every day.

Jack tried to calm down, got some sleep, and went back to work the next day. He was waiting for his brother Joe, who arrived two days later to take care of the dog and look after the house. Joe knew nothing about what had happened. Cara had called him too on that fateful night, but Joe always turns off his phone at night, and for some reason, he didn't think to call his sister-in-law back later.

Jack visited the little girl, Elsie, every day as he had promised, and tried to keep his conversations with Cara to a minimum, but of course, it was inevitable that they would have to discuss things. Jack said he wasn't going back for the time being; he wanted to think about their future, couldn't decide on their relationship right away, and needed time. Cara seemed to accept this and tried to be nice for a while.

Uncle Joe wanted to see his niece, Elsie, and Jack talked to Cara about taking the little girl for an hour or two the next afternoon when he went to visit Elsie after work to introduce her to her uncle. Cara agreed. But when Jack arrived at the house the next day, Cara and Elsie were not there. Mike was watching television and couldn't tell him where they had gone. Jack called Cara, but she didn't answer. He tried six times and left four messages. Cara replied half an hour later

- *Where are you?*
- *I don't know*
- *Cara, why are you doing this?*
- *Why you?*
- *We agreed that I could see the child from 5 to 7, max 8.*
- *I love you with all my heart. If I had to say that*

- *Cara, listen. If you don't want to see me, Mike is here. Bring the child here and let me know when I can pick her up. I have the right to see our child.*
- *(Crying and laughing smiley)*
- *It's not fair that you're taking her away and denying me access to her.*
- *Ciao*
- *I want to see our child. You're cutting the branch you're sitting on*
- *Thank your mother, dear*
- *It won't put you in a better position*
- *Yes, yes*
- *Listen, you left, you left Elsie's medicine at home, yours too, that's irresponsible. Where are you? When will you be back?*
- *All I'm saying is that you're not a good husband!!! Because what you're doing to me is unacceptable. You can't treat your wife like this, learn that!"*

So, after a few hours of silence, Cara finally spoke to Jack, but she didn't tell him where she had gone, and she had no intention of giving Elsie to him. Jack drove around the neighbourhood and finally found Cara at the only person he knew as Cara's friend, but when he knocked on the door, he wasn't allowed into the house. Jack called the police, who came out, but they didn't care that Cara had disappeared with the child, whose father is Jack, who couldn't find them for hours. The police were not interested in finding out what had really happened or if the child was in any danger. Instead, they told Jack to go home, saying it would be better for him to go home because what he was doing could be considered harassment...

Pardon? – I would have asked, but there was nobody to ask this from:

"Since when is it harassment if a father is worried about his child's safety, wants to exercise his rights, and wants to see the child over whom he has equal 50-50 parental custody rights according to the law?

Since when does it not matter that the mother just disappears with a small child, and since when does it not matter that the child might be at risk? Since when can a mother do anything with her child without the father's knowledge?

Since when does it not matter what the father says? Since when does the father not matter?"

These would have been my questions, but I was not there to ask them, and no one has been there to ask them ever since…

Jack went home that day feeling desperate, not knowing what to say to Joe, his brother. His heart broke at the thought of not being able to show off his daughter, to introduce her. But after Cara's threats, he was glad that at least they were alive, within the country's borders, and that he had found them. Joe didn't fully understand what was going on and thought Jack should have handled the whole situation differently, "since he had taken this woman," Jack should have behaved like a man and not let Cara do whatever she wanted. How could someone just take his own child away and disappear with her? The boys didn't argue, but Joe's comments didn't help Jack much that evening. My two sons are two completely different characters anyway. For example, it could never have happened in real life that a woman would hit Joe; that was obvious to me, but also to Jack. And Joe didn't hide his opinion on this either. He didn't understand Jack; he didn't know about Cara's metamorphosis, and he knew nothing about Jack's life. They talked for a while that evening, but they were on completely different wavelengths, on different pages. Uncle Joe then went off to the gym, leaving Jack alone. I tried to keep his spirits up on the phone, even from a few thousand miles away. And in the meantime, I was on pins and needles. My daughter Sophia and my son-in-law did everything they could to make me feel good, and the little Viking was the cutest baby I had ever held in my arms, but all my thoughts were at home, across the border, where I knew my son was sitting miserably alone in the kitchen, wondering what would happen next, what he would do with his life. It was Hanukkah, and the festive flames flickered merrily in the candlestick. Santa Claus and Christmas were approaching, the sweet holidays when everything is about love and miracles. My daughter and I bought and decorated the Christmas tree, dressed my grandson in cute festive clothes, and took photos of him with his toys. We laughed and had fun, but my phone was constantly on. I kept glancing at the screen every minute, on constant alert, not knowing what would happen next, what message I would receive from anyone. Then the day of my return home arrived, and I cried, and my daughter cried too. We didn't know when we would see each other again, but we agreed to meet in February when Sophia would need me and my help. I was confident that this would happen, and I set off for home with this hope.

And I got home. Again, very late, almost at night. And I found ruins everywhere. Both my sons were waiting for me, emotionally shattered. Joe felt his visit had been pointless; he couldn't help, and there was nothing he could do. Jack wasn't very entertaining company; the whole story had overwhelmed him, but Joe couldn't help him either, because there was nothing he could do at that moment. The situation was tense, and in the last two or three days, they had argued several times a day over all sorts of little things. For example, Joe wanted to cook chicken paprikash, but Jack forgot to buy the meat. After that, he didn't have time to take him to town. Or why didn't he go to the gym with him instead of sitting at home? – Joe wanted to help Jack, but he couldn't. They argued a lot, but they made up every day after that, over a few bottles of beer.

Joe left two days later, and we got caught up in the storm with Jack, not knowing how long it would last or where it would take us. Cara's hatred turned against me, but also against Jack. We didn't know what she was capable of or what game she was playing. Nothing was apparent at that point.

Jack sought advice from Dan, the social worker who was supposed to help young parents, on the midwife's recommendation. Dan expressed his regret that things had turned out this way and advised Jack that if his wife refused to let him see their child, he should find a legal representative and file a lawsuit in court initiate child custody proceedings, in which the mother would be obliged to grant access, and it would be determined which parent would be granted custody of the child. Dan also said that social services do not intervene in such conflicts because they are private family matters, and that if any problems arise, legal assistance is required, which is not within their remit.

PART II – THE ESCALATION

AWAITING TRIAL - CHARGES, TRICKS, DEFENCE

At Dan's suggestion, Jack sought out a solicitor the following week for the child custody case. Jack knew that Cara's goals and plans had probably not changed and that she wanted to leave with Elsie as soon as possible, abroad and permanently, as she had told him this every month for the past six months and threatened that if things did not go her way, she would divorce him and move away. Cara had also stated dozens of times that Elsie would never get to know Jack or know who her father was! A fate inherited. Most certainly. Cara intended her own life for her little girl. But I don't think she was aware of it herself. What was she doing, what patterns was she following, and why was she following them? Cara has repeatedly written in her text messages that Elsie deserves a better father, that Jack is a mummy's boy, that he has no will of his own, and that he is a nobody. In the months that followed, Jack was listed in her phone as "Cripple".

Yes, Cara called Jack "cripple" several times in conversations and text messages. I saw and heard it myself, too.

Perhaps it was precisely because I saw and heard everything that Cara started to call me a witch. Sometimes she called me an evil dwarf. Most of the time, I was simply "that woman". The woman Jack did everything for, the woman Jack talked to instead of spending time with, and paid attention to. The woman who ruined her life and tore their relationship apart. The woman who never accepted her, who never wanted them to be happy together. In a matter of months, I became the enemy, a sharp turn from the best mother-in-law to the worst, an evil witch. I couldn't really come to terms with that. But there was no way to change the situation. So, I thought it would be best to keep a low profile. I wanted to remain unnoticed, as if I wasn't even there, as if I didn't exist. But because of Elsie, I couldn't do that completely.

And from time to time, I received messages from Cara. Or Jack received messages from her about me. I suspect he didn't show me everything, but what he did show me was enough.

Jack visited Elsie every day, and in addition to those visits, whenever she could, Cara called him dozens of times and sent him dozens of messages. She put him under tremendous pressure. Me too, but I didn't realise it at the time. I continued to work a lot.

During this time, Cara also wrote a message to her solicitor, which she forwarded to Jack, expressing her intention to reconcile. In this email, Cara emphasised in several paragraphs that there was nothing wrong with Jack, that he was the best husband and the most wonderful father, and that she believed their relationship could still be repaired; he just needed to get rid of me. It was an instructive message, as it also included a sentence saying that they should forget about the slap and the incident of domestic violence and not talk about it anywhere, because it was completely unnecessary. No one would believe Jack anyway, because she, Cara, was just a very young and weak woman, and no one would think that she could have hurt anyone; she had never done anything like that before. Cara wrote the following exactly:

> *"It's ok. If my husband claims that I slapped him, I don't care if he does; nobody will believe him, as I am a young woman who has never done such things..."*

It's like a hidden but clearly audible confession. Of course, this letter to her solicitor never appeared in court...

Months later, when the Johnny Depp – Amber Heard trial appeared online, and I was watching, this sentence echoed in my mind. *"Nobody will believe him."* - It was indescribably shocking that Cara used almost the same words, the same tactic, as Amber.

Flying monkeys? And/or fake profiles on social media?

I had no idea what this expression "Flying monkeys" meant until mid-December, when Jack came home from the gym one evening and shoved his phone under my nose, showing me the messages he had just received from a certain William. William introduced himself politely and addressed Jack as an intelligent man. He explained that he knew Cara from a council-run baby group, that he himself was married with three children, and that he had not approached her with any ulterior motives but had simply struck up a conversation with her the other day as one parent to another. After a brief introduction, William went on at length about Cara's virtues, what an enthusiastic mother she was, how charming she was, how young she still was, but how hard she tried to care for and raise Elsie well, and how successful she was, given how beautiful a baby Elsie was. He then went on at even greater length about Jack having left Cara alone with this little baby, and how unmanly this behaviour was, since a man should be strong and stick it out through thick and thin. After all, he too was suffering greatly, but it would never occur to him to leave his wife and three children! He gently but firmly urged Jack to think about what he had done and was doing, and to consider rekindling his relationship with Cara, because Cara and Elsie were his family, and Cara was a beautiful young woman who was now terribly broken and didn't know what to do, etc., etc. A random message from a random person. Jack couldn't remember ever seeing William at the baby group, where Cara had only been willing to go with him since Elsie was born.

There was also a certain Aurelia, who was either a flying monkey or a fake profile, who tagged Jack on social media before Christmas and started messaging him, chatting with him, then "suddenly realised" who Jack was, i.e. that Jack was Cara's ex, and Aurelia, of course, claimed to be Cara's friend, who knew their story very well. She called Jack all sorts of names, saying he was a shameless person who was capable of leaving his young wife and baby, and now he was flirting with her on the internet, another woman, whom he didn't even know personally! In a long message, she explained what a worthless person Jack was for not going back to his wife, who cried herself to sleep every night and was suffering terribly, even though she had done everything to make Jack happy, had given birth to his child, taken care of him, created a home for him, and so on. Aurelia also went on at length about Cara's virtues, especially her beauty and youth.

Jack replied to both strangers briefly and restrainedly, letting them know that what they were writing about was his private life, and that as outsiders, they could have little understanding of it if they only knew one side of the story. He was not in the habit of discussing his problems with strangers, and he certainly did not seek advice from people he did not know, so he did not wish to continue corresponding with them. He wrote something to that effect. Aurelia disappeared into the depths; William made another attempt to put Cara in a favourable light, suggesting he would like to meet Jack in person, sit down somewhere for a coffee or a beer, and talk man to man. He would be happy to advise on navigating such family crises. Jack was inclined to meet William, but the meeting never took place because William disappeared like a grey donkey in the fog, from one moment to the next, as if he had never been a member of the online community.

At first, I thought William might be a real person, but I had my doubts about Aurelia's existence. Cara had no friends. She had only one friend with whom she kept in touch and sometimes hung out, the mother of a little boy, a few months older than Elsie, from the baby group. But the picture on Aurelia's Facebook profile was not that of the young woman. And the style of Aurelia's text was suspiciously similar to Cara's, so I didn't rule out the possibility that Cara had created a fake Facebook profile for herself and written to Jack herself. What's more, there were small errors in the English message and, interestingly, a German word had somehow found its way into the text...

Once, back in the summer, before Elsie was born, when Cara blocked me everywhere – that was her habit when she got angry with someone, she would simply block them on social media – when this happened to me for the first time, I searched for Cara's name and was shocked to find that she had four Facebook accounts. She had created them at different times, but she used them alternately, and all four accounts were still active. She also had at least three email addresses. I know this because when she asked me to arrange her unemployment benefits and maternity allowance, I needed her email address, but for some reason, she didn't want to use her old emails and created a new one instead. She said herself, "I already have two, but now I'll have a third."

William and Aurelia. We don't know and will never know who they really were. They never appeared in Jack's life again, not even in a single word.

There was another real person who was a flying monkey, the health visitor herself, who, from the beginning, was biased and only willing to talk to Cara about anything related to Elsie. Kelly disapproved of Jack leaving Cara alone and made no secret of her opinion. She demonstratively brought food parcels, clothes, and children's toys to the "poor little girl" and her „poor little mother" who had been abandoned by her husband, while she had no idea how much money Cara was getting from the state and how much she was squeezing out of Jack for this and that, mostly cigarettes and fast food takeaways. In all her reports on Elsie, Kelly, the health visitor, wrote that she did not doubt that Cara was a good mother, as she took wonderful care of the baby, who was visibly plump and healthy, and that there was an extremely strong bond between them. It was clear that she spent a lot of time with her..." It is unfortunate that this young woman has to cope with everything on her own and certainly needs support in a few areas because of this, but she is still very young, so this is natural," Kelly, the Health Visitor, wrote in her reports...

We heard nothing more about the police or the interrogation. Jack had not received the transcript and had no idea whether the case was closed or still under investigation. Jack wrote a letter requesting information and urging the case to be reinvestigated. There was a message on his phone that could serve as evidence; he had forgotten to show it to the police during the interrogation and wanted to present it afterward. The message was from Cara, saying how sorry she was for what had happened, that it should not have happened, and that Jack should come back to her, that everything would be different from now on... But the police didn't say a word; they never called Jack, and they didn't send him a decision. They didn't even respond to his request. It was as if the whole thing had never happened. It was all very strange. It still is today.

THE FIRST HEARING

A week before Christmas, Jack finally found a solicitor of the three he called who agreed to take the case. Ann, the young solicitor, was kind, soft-spoken, and seemed very understanding. Because domestic violence was involved in the case, she urgently filed a petition with the court to initiate child custody proceedings. What Jack didn't expect, and no one else did either, was that Cara had given false testimony to the police, and the moment she found out that Jack had filed a lawsuit against her for custody of Elsie, she went to the organisation called Women's Aid and to the council's social services department, and lied about Jack to both of them. Massive lies. Cara claimed that Jack had always been violent towards her, that he had never worked properly, had not given her any money, had not taken care of them, had not cared about her or their child at all... When the court asked the child welfare agency to investigate, Cara lied and said that Jack was a drug addict and an alcoholic, and that he had sexually abused Elsie... The court hearing was scheduled almost immediately, with the first hearing set for 26 January, three weeks later.

Sexual abuse of a six-week-old baby. "Silver bullet," my psychiatrist friend Ruth said later. Sexual abuse is the unmissable charge that women can easily win any lawsuit with, in any court. No evidence is needed. At least, women don't need evidence right away; women just drop those two words, and everyone immediately condemns the person who has been pinned with this charge.

I didn't know, we didn't know where we stood when this accusation was made. I asked Jack for an explanation, but he just stared ahead, deadpan, unable to speak. "I have no idea," he stammered. Sexual abuse, and against a six-week-old baby at that. What's going on?

A few days later, Jack wanted to talk to me one morning.

- "I think I know now what Cara meant. And I'm sorry to tell you this, it's really embarrassing," Jack said, blushing to his ears.

I sat down on the kitchen chair.

- "That's how it was, and that's all she can mean when she says sexual abuse against Elsie: when Elsie was six weeks old, I really wanted to be with Cara because we hadn't had sex for months, and I missed it a lot, and I thought now we could have finally... I'm sorry, Mum, but this is really awkward. How can I talk about this in front of you? ... Well, anyway... So, I asked Cara if it would be possible or something, but she said she didn't feel ready for it yet, and she said that I should do it for myself if I missed sex so much, and that she would be happy to watch. She'll watch the whole thing. That's what Cara said, and she laughed and also said she'd even record it on video. I told her that there's no way I'm going to let her do that, so she got offended and went to the kitchen to smoke. Then I went down after her about 10 minutes later, and she asked me with a grin, "So, are you done? Was it good?" I don't even remember what I answered; I felt so stupid. Even then.
- "Fantastic. Great." I muttered under my breath and thought that if there's one thing parents don't want to hear stories about, it's their children's sex lives. And vice versa, obviously, no child is curious about their parents' sex life. I also thought, damn it, how grotesque is this whole situation we've gotten ourselves into because of Cara?!
- "But how does Elsie, a six-week-old baby, fit into this? How did this affect the baby as abuse?" I asked Jack.
- "Well, she was there in the room, in her cot next to the bed. I don't know what difference it makes, because even if I had done anything to myself, Elsie was asleep, and she was only six weeks old. That's why Cara went downstairs to smoke, because she had just fed her, and Elsie had fallen asleep.
- "Jesus Christ, and Cara thinks that's sexual abuse?"
- "Yes, I asked her on the phone yesterday how she came up with that and what she meant when she said that to her solicitor, and Cara replied that she was referring to this incident."
- "But son, millions of people used to have sex next to their sleeping babies, in the same room!"

- "Well, I know that too, or at least I think that's the case, but that's what she meant, and she thinks it's an abuse. Because the child was there. And even though she was asleep, she was present."
- "Why? And later, did you never have sex in the presence of the child, or in the same room?"
- "Of course, we did."
- "And that wasn't a problem?"
- "I don't know. Maybe it was. God only knows. The judge will decide..."

Jack drank his coffee, blushed, with red ears, and I felt like I had fallen into the middle of some kind of nauseating tragicomedy, completely independent of my will and intentions. I found it utterly distasteful that Cara would bring up this story and air bedroom secrets that were nobody else's business, especially not in polite company! Religion and sex are absolutely private matters for everyone, but Cara brings this up just to accuse Jack of something. Unbelievable! It's repulsive and devoid of any sense of decency. That's when I realised that Cara was more vulgar than I had ever thought, downright vulgar. And from that moment on, I felt nauseous just thinking about it. I could no longer control my feelings.

Regardless, Jack continued to visit Cara every day to see Elsie. When Jack had a day off, Cara would sometimes ask him to look after the little girl in the morning while she ate, cleaned up, or went shopping. But Jack didn't want to spend too much time at Cara's house in her presence. He constantly felt that Cara was provoking him and didn't know what to expect from her. He was happy to look after Elsie and would have taken her for walks or brought her to his place, but Cara wouldn't let the child out of the house, and she never took her out for fresh air either. The day before the Court Hearing, the following exchange took place:

"Please come over, because I want to eat."
"Good morning! Ok. I'll be there soon."

Jack went over and stayed there while Cara ate and cleaned up. Then, because he had things to do, he had to go somewhere and couldn't stay there for more than an hour to look after Elsie, so he left. After leaving, Jack received the following messages from Cara:

> *"Fuck your mother, you cripple, I'll ruin your life tomorrow, just you wait! I can't trust you with this kid for an hour, you bastard, are you fucking your mother or what, that you can't stay for a fucking hour because of that cripple."*

I hadn't seen these messages at the time; only months later did Jack show them to me.

The hearing was scheduled online because regular court proceedings had not yet resumed after the pandemic. But Cara did not appear at the first hearing because she allegedly could not log in to the online platform. Thus, the hearing had to be postponed. Of course, Jack still had to pay the six-hundred-pound legal fee even though the hearing was postponed. Due to the urgency of the case, the second hearing was scheduled for two weeks later, the 8th of February, and the judge instructed Cara's legal representative that if Cara was unable to log in to the online platform from her own home, she should go to the law office and log in to the hearing from there, otherwise the hearing would be held without her.

A few days after the first hearing, Cara unexpectedly showed Jack a pregnancy test. She also sent Jack and me ultrasound images and a video in a message. It was about a twin pregnancy. Cara did text me the following:

> *"How would you feel if you had four grandchildren next year?"* - she wrote to me, adding a smiley face. And continued: *"Guess what, I'm pregnant. I took three pregnancy tests, and they all came back positive! I must have gotten pregnant before Jack left, before he moved back home to you, right before we had that fight. I went to the doctor last week, and now it's official. It's twins! Girls! Are you happy, Grandma?"*

I sat staring at my phone screen for a few moments. I had no idea how to react. Finally, I remember congratulating her and just writing, "I hope everything will be alright."

Jack was distraught, wondering what to do next. He didn't want to move back in; he'd had enough. He wanted to wait and see how the lawsuit turned out before deciding. But within a few days, things fell into place. Jack logged into the email account he and Cara had shared on a whim. And lo and behold, he found an invoice from Amazon in Cara's name. "Fake positive pregnancy tests" was in the invoice's subject line... Jack didn't immediately ask Cara what this meant; he waited instead. He asked Cara about the ultrasound images and offered to take her for another, so he could be present to see the babies. He tried to arrange a time with Cara that suited her and decided which provider to choose. But Cara rejected every suggestion with some excuse or other. This was more than suspicious, but Jack didn't want to argue or flush the rabbit out of the bush just yet. He waited to see how Cara would get out of this situation. But in the meantime, he wrote to his solicitor about what had happened and informed him about the false pregnancy tests.

Women's Aid arranged free legal representation for Cara, with a free solicitor, paid for by taxpayers' money. It didn't cost Cara a penny to attend the hearings or consult with her solicitor. As she was living on benefits and not employed, and because she had a child, she was entitled to completely free legal aid. This was in addition to all her other benefits.

Jack's relationship with Cara deteriorated during this time. Cara may have noticed that Jack did not believe she was pregnant again, and a few days later, Jack's phone was flooded with pictures of bloody panties and bloody sheets to prove that Cara had lost the babies and no longer believed she was pregnant. Jack played along, telling Cara how sorry he was for what had happened. Jack did not tell Cara that, as a healthcare worker, he had some idea of what a spontaneous miscarriage entailed and that at 10-11 weeks of pregnancy, it was not only indicated by bloody panties, but also by more serious, almost unbearable pain and the visible presence of fully developed dead foetuses... Jack listened, stayed silent, as if he had accepted the massive lie as fact.

Even though he had moved away from Cara, Jack still visited Elsie every day after work, in the afternoon or late in the evening. Most of the time, he bathed her and put her to bed. Despite Cara's provocations and arguments at each visit, Jack persisted in seeing Elsie. By the end of

January and beginning of February, things had deteriorated significantly, mainly because, contrary to Cara's expectations, Jack did not move back in with her after learning of her "pregnancy". Even when Cara tried to be nice to him, and even when she lied to him about being pregnant, Jack did not want to move back in with her; there were too many reasons not to do so, Jack said. Mainly the accusations, the lies, the rudeness. And the threats. When Jack came home from Elsie's, he received various sweet messages from Cara at night:

> *"I'll ruin your life, you'll see! – Cara repeated - I'm leaving this f*cking country with Elsie, you have two weeks left, and after that you'll never see her again! Don't come here anymore, I don't want to see you. I'm in a new relationship, and that man is a hundred times better than you!"*

On certain days, Jack received not only threats but also demands and insults in these messages:

> *"The child has no formula, no baby food, and I have less and less milk. We're out of nappies and wipes. I have nothing to eat. The gas and electricity bills need to be paid. Do something! What kind of person are you that you don't take care of your family?"*

It was like a vicious circle, a downward spiral. Cara sought to get Jack back, but she tried to do so through lies and threats, which only made it harder for her to achieve her goal.

Or maybe I'm wrong, and Cara didn't really want Jack back. If she couldn't use him the way she wanted to, then she'd rather break up with him and leave him, as she started saying after the wedding, and wanted to divorce Jack every month.

I didn't know which was true. Maybe Cara didn't know herself either. She couldn't decide what she wanted. Jack wasn't good for her the way he was, but he was better than nothing. Until then, it would have been good for Jack to stay with her until she could get rid of him and go abroad with their little girl.

At this time, Cara also made a report to Social Services; Jack learned of it months later when he requested a GDPR. Cara reported Jack to the Social Services. She said that she did not want to allow Jack into her house anymore, because Jack was regularly violent, harassing her, shouting at her in front of the baby, and she was scared, so she needed help from the social workers. Cara literally wanted someone to supervise Jack's visiting time; she systematically wanted to remove Jack from Elsie's life, and she wanted to remove both of us.

Cara had already banned me from seeing Elsie, my granddaughter, at the beginning of December. She told Jack and me not to approach them, or she would call the police. Cara said and believed that I ruined her marriage, and if it had been up to me, this child would never have been born, because when she was pregnant, I wanted to beat her up, and I caused her a lot of stress with that and with everything else. Cara sent me private text messages on several occasions, telling me I should be ashamed of myself and declaring that I didn't deserve to see my grandchild and that I shouldn't even dare to go near her house! – She said and wrote these words directly to me. It was very difficult for me to accept this, and it did cause significant distress. But I didn't know what to do. I listened, stayed silent, and didn't respond to the insults.

At the same time, there were days, maybe twice, between December and February, when Cara called me and initiated a video call, showing me how Elsie was playing next to her on the bed. Cara never told me in advance that she was going to call me. On one occasion, I was at work on the day shift and, fortunately, I was able to step out onto the terrace to speak with my granddaughter by phone for about three minutes.

In mid-January, before the trial, Cara even invited me over to her place.

> *"I know you want to see your granddaughter. I'm not really angry with you. I already told Jack on New Year's Eve that you are welcome to come over, so if you feel like it, drop by."*

This was not true; Jack would have certainly told me that I had been invited to see my grandchild, and I wouldn't have missed a single opportunity to see my granddaughter, so of course, I did not say a word of complaint, and I took advantage of the opportunity and went to visit Elsie. Which resulted in an interesting situation. I went to Cara's house at the appointed time and knocked on the door. Cara called out for me to come in. I walked through the door, and Cara was standing in the middle of the living room with Elsie in her arms. The little girl saw me and smiled at me from afar. She looked happy, either because she recognised me or just because she was glad that someone had come. I stepped closer and started talking to her, but I had only said a few words when Elsie's face suddenly changed, as if she had suddenly felt pain. She screamed and began to cry bitterly. I didn't understand any of it. She greeted me with such joy, almost laughing, and then her face suddenly contorted, and she began to cry. Cara rocked her and smiled.

- "I'm sorry, she's been like this lately. She can't stand strangers and is afraid of everyone she doesn't know."
- "A few moments ago, she was smiling at me", I responded
- "You see, that's how it is", said Cara, with a strange expression on her face, as she rocked Elsie more and more vigorously to calm her down.

The baby calmed down within a few minutes, and Cara turned her back on me and kept rocking Elsie as she looked out the window. I stepped closer and started talking to Elsie again, who was now looking at me intently over her mother's shoulder. She was very attentive, but she didn't smile at me again that day. I stayed for a few more minutes, then I said goodbye and headed home.

And I wish I hadn't remembered the story my grandmother once told me. That during the Second World War, when she and her sisters were hiding from German soldiers in a cellar, and the Russians entered Budapest, who were not much different from the Nazis in their treatment of women, the only way they could get the Russian soldiers to leave them alone in the cellar was if a child started crying. It was common knowledge that Russian soldiers couldn't stand the sound of children crying. So, as my grandmother told me, whenever a Russian soldier came near her and her siblings, she would pinch my one-and-a-half-year-old mother's thigh hard to make the baby cry... I wish I hadn't remembered this story while seeking an explanation for Elsie's unusual reaction... Because from then on, I couldn't get the thought out of my head. I tried to remember whether Cara could have done something like that, but I couldn't. I didn't pay attention to her, especially not her hands, when I entered the room. I was so happy to see my grandchild, and I was so happy that she was happy to see me that I only paid attention to her smiling little face, nothing else. I couldn't remember; I wasn't, and I couldn't be sure this had happened, but I could easily imagine it. I was sure Cara could do this, pinching Elsie. Just to hurt me, to cause me pain. Especially because of the things she said after the episode.

> *"That's how she is with strangers these days... she's afraid of everyone she doesn't know..."*

Elsie is my granddaughter. She knew my voice, my face, I was no stranger to her! I loved her from the moment she was born, even before that. I hugged her whenever I could, whenever I was allowed to, and every baby can sense exactly who loves them and how much! Babies still have that special ability to gauge this. You can't fool babies!

THE SECOND AND THIRD HEARINGS

On the 7th of February, Cara called Jack over to look after Elsie while she went into town to run some errands. It later transpired that she had gone to meet her solicitor and to complain to Women's Aid again. But the problem wasn't just that she asked Jack to babysit so she could go and lie about him and badmouth him to others, detailing what a terrible father he was, how evil he was, and what he had done to her, but everything that happened after that.

I hadn't seen Elsie for weeks at that time. Jack offered to let me come over when he was there, secretly, through the back garden, so that the neighbours wouldn't see me. Let me spend some time with my granddaughter. I went happily. I slipped into the house without a sound; no one saw me. I picked Elsie up from her high chair, rocked her, hugged her, and tried to make the five-month-old girl smile. Meanwhile, Jack watched the street anxiously from behind the drawn curtains. The whole time. Barely half an hour after I arrived, Cara called Jack to ask if everything was okay. Jack replied that, of course, it was, Elsie would be asleep soon, to which Cara said that was great because she would be home in about an hour. And that it was fine, Jack should put her to sleep, because Elsie was surely not hungry, as she had fed her shortly before leaving to town. They agreed on this and hung up peacefully. Jack and I were relieved that there was still some time left, and Jack finally moved away from the window and stopped watching the street. He only jumped back when he heard the sound of a car engine. Barely 10 minutes later, a taxi stopped in front of the house, and Cara was already coming up the stairs. I grabbed my coat and shoes and ran barefoot out the kitchen door into the back garden, but it was too late. I suspected that Cara had seen my back and heard my footsteps, as well as the door slamming behind me. I was very scared. I crouched down next to the wall of the house. I still had time and energy to think that if Cara looked out of the kitchen window, at least she wouldn't see me running across the garden. And then I heard them start arguing. Cara yelled at Jack. She yelled very badly, but that wasn't what hurt the most. What hurt was that I had gotten my son into trouble... I slowly and carefully escaped from Cara's garden and went home. Jack also came home a half an hour later.

A few hours after the incident, Cara sent Jack a terrible voice message. The problem with voice messages is that they are even more honest and more revealing than text messages. Voice messages cannot be edited, repetitions cannot be deleted, and every emotion is clear from the emphasis and tone of voice. Due to the slap incident and later the sexual abuse allegations, Jack decided in early January to record Cara's calls, so whenever Cara spoke, he recorded and saved their conversations on his phone. He told Cara this, if only so that she could not later accuse him of recording her voice without her consent.

Jack was pale, but he handed me his phone so I could listen to Cara's message. Cara was shouting into Jack's voicemail while Elsie was next to her. I could hear the little girl playing, and later, as her mother's voice grew increasingly excited and angry, I heard Elsie begin to whimper and cry. The following text arrived in four messages, each lasting one and a half minutes, which I am copying here without any changes:

> *"All you care about is that woman! You don't care about your child. All you care about is your mother, your mother, your mother, your mother, and your mother. Because I don't know what your mother did to you, but she's the only one who matters to you. I don't know, I honestly don't know what your mother did to you or for you. I don't know. But you're even exploiting this innocent little child because of that woman. It's a joke that a man can be like this in this world, I'm telling you, I've never seen anything like this. And you shouldn't be proud of that. You should be ashamed of yourself for that. You should be very ashamed of yourself. My whole family laughs at you, and everyone says you're a real mama's boy. A real mama's boy, and that's what you are because of what you do for that woman... It's a joke, a joke, a joke, a joke, and a joke. And for this and this and this and this and this too. It's unbelievable, man, you should be very ashamed of yourself. Be very ashamed of yourself, you perverted animal."*
>
> *You say that I don't, that I don't love my mother. Oh, my love, no one in this world loves their mother the way you love your mother. That every fucking person thinks you're having sex with your mother. Do you understand? Because you're such a fucking mommy's boy! Because do you understand? I believe she wants to see her grandchild; I believe that you understand. But then you have to be a fucking man and be there for your child instead of running back to your mother. My mother this, my mother that, this and that. Are you people normal? I don't know, I don't know what your problem is. Because*

> *I think you're the only cripples in the whole world. I'm telling you, I've never seen such a crippled family in my life as you and your mother. Even Fred and his mother were better than you two. I'm telling you, there's no one else on earth like you two, and you should be ashamed of yourselves.*
>
> *And then you get angry, and she goes out the back door. Oh, Jack, I tell you, you should be beaten, you should be beaten. You're not the only one who should be beaten, you're not the only one who should be beaten, how can you use your own child, man, how can you be such a crippled mother and son, be a little honest, how can you use your own child for a woman like that, fuck her, she ruined your family, you understand, she ruined everything, Everything. And you still do everything you can to make her happy. I don't know. You deserve a better father. I swear on my life, you need a better father, because this one, this one, fuck his mother, I'm telling you..."*

My heart ached terribly for Jack. For myself, too, but less so. By then, I had immersed myself in psychiatric disorders, and it was obvious to me that Cara was not mentally well. This voicemail only made it more obvious that something was wrong. I couldn't remember exactly which condition the repetition of words and phrases within a sentence belonged to, but I remembered it was a sign of something. Cara repeated the same words five or six times within a single sentence, speaking with a desperate anger I had never heard before in my life. Cara was ill, and the fact that I had visited my granddaughter without her knowledge had clearly triggered her condition. Not just a little.

But Jack didn't know any of this; he hadn't read up on psychiatric conditions, and I had never told him anything about Cara. So, I had no idea how it would affect him, how listening to such a voice message would affect him. The content of the message obviously didn't shock him that much, as it was complete nonsense, utter gibberish. But together with the intonation and style, the whole recording was chillingly frightening to listen to. I saved it for myself so that I would never forget. Not that it could ever be forgotten. I also saved it because it was clearly an emotionally abusive message – as evidence. And I saved this message in the hope that, if someone could listen to it one day, they might finally come up with a diagnosis to treat Cara.

A few hours later, after the voicemail, Jack received a written message as well. Cara had calmed down, and her thoughts had become clearer. There was no longer any anger in her; the text was measured, cold, sarcastic, and testified to a determined resolve.

> *"I've never seen anything like this before. How can you do something like this? Really. But I'm grateful that you showed me right now so that I can say everything, tell everything to everybody, and ruin your fucking miserable life. And I'm now going into a relationship. You're fucked. Let Elsie grow up with a decent father and never call you dad because you're a pile of shit. Thank your lovely wife for all this, because your mother, she really is your wife. You stupid dickhead. Go give your mother your 10-centimetre dick. I can't wait for tomorrow. I'm going to laugh my head off, oh my God. I'll make a video and send it to you so you can see how happy I am."*

Cara's style became increasingly crude, increasingly vulgar, almost unbearably primitive. Was this her true self? If so, then what were those first few months of their relationship? Just an act? Because if it was just an act, then she deserves an Oscar. But the most appalling thing was, and still is, that Cara could and still can play that other role to the outside world. In front of the health visitor and the paediatrician, and in shops, she is demure, kind, and polite. A delicate, gentle creature. And she always smiles at everyone. The Cara we knew, she keeps for herself, behind closed doors, and just for us. Perfect duplicity, masterful manipulation. I thought it was terrifying. To go to court like that. I felt that the time ahead of us would not be child's play; it would not be fun and laughter. And that we had to be prepared for anything. But can you really be prepared for anything?

Cara registered for the second hearing on the online platform. She sat before the monitor, the baby Elsie in her lap, playing with her openly as the judge spoke. She laughed loudly, entertaining the little girl. No sooner had it begun than, after about 10 minutes, the judge adjourned the hearing because infants were not allowed in the courtroom. He asked Cara to arrange childcare for the next hearing and set a new date for 14 February, Valentine's Day. Jack had to pay the solicitor's fee of another £600, even though not a single word had been said in the case and nothing of substance had happened at the hearing. The next day, the solicitor sent a message stating that he felt sorry for Jack and, in light of the circumstances, would waive £100 of his fee.

February 14th arrived, the day of lovers and love, Valentine's Day. On the evening before the trial, Cara wrote another message to Jack, which, lest we lose our way and become sentimental or hopeful, was once again filled with thick hatred.

> *"I'm glad this whole thing will be over tomorrow! You'll get what you deserve, you'll see, I'll destroy you tomorrow! I'll finally be rid of you, and you'll see, I'll be home, back in Europe in two weeks! Everyone says it will be so! You will never see Elsie again!"*

At the hearing, Cara upheld the charges. Jack was an alcoholic, a drug addict, and had sexually abused his own daughter when she was six weeks old. Cara was able to do this, - made false accusations, - without any evidence. No one asked Jack whether he considered these charges to be true, whether he objected to them, or whether he had anything to add. His solicitor denied them on his behalf. But the denial proved futile. At this third, but technically first, successful and conclusive hearing, Jack was immediately banned from visiting his daughter, and he was ordered to undergo the most rigorous alcohol and drug testing, which was to be paid for jointly by the parties. Cara's free legal aid covered her share, so she didn't pay a penny out of her own pocket for the test, but Jack had to pay £400 for the unfounded allegations. And it cost him another £600 for legal representation.

So, Jack was unable to see Elsie for an indefinite period, banned from seeing her from one day to the next. He could no longer go near the little girl he had looked after unsupervised the day before, and whom he had regularly babysat whenever Cara wanted him to. Yesterday, Jack was not a threat to Elsie; today, he was. It did not occur to the judge that if Cara considered Jack to be an evil, rude, uncaring father who had sexually abused the baby, how dare she entrust the baby to him for hours on end, and on what grounds and for what reasons did she allow him into her house at all? It did not occur to anyone that if Jack was as depraved as Cara portrayed him to be, why was Cara still harassing and begging Jack to move back in with her? Perhaps because no one knew exactly what was going on. Even Jack's solicitor, despite being paid hundreds of pounds, failed to guide the judge with a few well-chosen words on what questions to ask. She did not ask Cara's solicitor any questions before the judge. Why? Perhaps she didn't have time. Everything happened incredibly quickly; the hearings lasted barely an hour, and the court hearings here had a completely different schedule than the hearings you see in films. Here, the parties may not speak; only the solicitor may speak on their behalf, and even then, only when the judge asks. The judge asks questions based on the submitted claims, does not deviate from them, and, as if not even thinking, ignores the contradictions, as if he does not even notice them.

A lot awaited us. Terrible weeks and months.

UNDER TESTS AND PRESSURE

The drug test was completed relatively quickly, within a month. Blood, urine, and hair samples were collected from Jack for testing. Before the test, Jack was not allowed to cut or dye his hair; he had been warned in advance and strictly instructed. At the time of sampling, Jack's photograph and fingerprints were taken. Part of the official investigation was certainly that he was treated like a drug addict and alcoholic. The presumption of innocence did not even arise. Not here either. Although the test and sampling were conducted politely, it should not be forgotten that Jack was treated like a criminal throughout. The drug test came back negative, and the alcohol test showed that Jack was an average drinker, consuming 2 x 2 pints of beer or the equivalent amount of alcohol per week.

The negative test did not matter. According to the court order, Jack was not allowed to see Elsie or go near her until the next hearing. He was permitted to see her for only one hour per week, under supervision, at a public institution operated by the child welfare services. The social worker sat in the room throughout the one-hour visit, taking notes and minutes on Jack and Elsie. The reports were then collected and submitted to the court a week before the next hearing. Four social workers observed and examined Jack and Elsie's relationship, yielding eight such reports. The weekly one-hour visit costs £40, with each parent paying £20. After the judge set the next hearing for three months, Jack could see Elsie only once a week.

Hoovering

But after a month and a half, Cara and Jack decided, out of the blue, to try to patch up their relationship... Cara also reached out to me, wishing me a happy birthday and sending me a picture of Elsie. I didn't know what was behind this, but I didn't have the energy to find out either. I asked Jack, but he didn't give me a clear answer, so I stopped asking questions. The solicitor kept sending unpaid bills. I took out a loan, paid half the solicitor's fees with it, and we also paid the rest with our credit cards. Jack worked as hard as he could so that we could slowly, very slowly, pay back the money we had spent. There was a few-month-old baby, they were both young, maybe they could really fix what had gone wrong, maybe this nightmare would end. That's what I thought. Maybe we could start all over again, really! Despite everything that had happened and been said up to that point. I wanted to hope so, but I couldn't always keep that hope alive. I have this problem with my brain; I usually remember words and sentences well. Sometimes, even entire dialogues remain in my head. Not numbers and names, but entire dialogues. And I remembered every single word Cara had said to Jack and to me.

During this period, in the last week of March, Cara even wrote to me, apologizing for the way she had treated me and for everything that had happened.

> *"We both made a lot of mistakes, Jack and I, - Cara said, - but now everything will be different because we've both learned from it."*

For my part, I didn't think they had both made mistakes, but I kept quiet about that. I focused on the second half of the sentence and read "sorry" as an apology.

They decided to try again, and I had no say in the matter anyway. And then, after one of the official visitation times, the three of them, Jack, Elsie, and Cara, just showed up. They simply walked into my house as if nothing had happened. As if the past six months had never existed. As if no nasty accusations and comments had been made, as if we weren't waiting for the next court hearing. As if Jack could see his own child without strict supervision. It was the end of March. The three of them showed up, Cara handed Elsie to me, and smiled.

- "Here, here's your granddaughter! Take care of her! I've had enough. It's time for us to have some fun, relax, and you always wanted this anyway. Now you'll get it, and we can live a little! Right? - Cara looked at Jack and snuggled up to him. - "But shhh!" - Cara looked at me very seriously. No one can find out about this, you understand, because we could be in big trouble! You hear me? You can't tell anyone I'm bringing Elsie to the father when he's not even allowed to see her! Don't tell anyone, because they could take the child away from us! You won't tell it to anyone, will you?

As they say, I didn't even know which way was up. Again. I didn't even know what was going on. This girl, Cara, was standing before me, looking completely confused and babbling nonsense. Again. What should I say? Do I have to answer anything? Should I have let her in at all? Shouldn't I have sent her away? Should I tell Jack that until the matter is settled, they can't come to my house, even if they want to make up? The problem is that I couldn't even formulate these questions in my mind at the time. I was completely paralysed, as if I were in shock. I just stood there. Cara held the baby and handed her over to me, and Elsie started crying, frightened of me, as she hardly knew me by then. She was tired that day. But it did not matter, she is my sweet little granddaughter! I took her from Cara and held her in my arms. I started rocking her, and she quietened, then slowly lifted her gaze to my face, peacefully and attentively. She was already six months old. I didn't even notice that Cara and Jack had gone upstairs to their old room. I didn't pay any attention to them. I didn't know, and I didn't want to spoil the moment when, finally, finally, Elsie was in my arms, I could hold her, talk to her, and be – who knows for how long? – her grandmother. A happy grandmother.

They came over regularly after that day, every single day, Elsie and Cara. When Jack wasn't working or had just come home, Cara would arrive with the baby, and they would all spend the rest of the day at my house. After a brief conversation and/or meal, the parents, Cara and Jack, would go up to their old room and stay there until evening, or until Elsie became tired and had to be taken home. After a few days, I realised that while I was playing with the little girl downstairs in the living room or outside in the garden, the young couple upstairs was not just talking, eating, and watching films. I closed the doors so Elsie and I wouldn't hear them. One day, when they came downstairs laughing and joking, Cara asked me why I was sitting behind closed doors with the baby. I found the question incredibly rude, humiliating, and somehow repulsive. I considered the act itself to be repulsive. They had their own flat. They had their own time to be intimate. I wouldn't have brought it up myself, but when Cara asked me several times and also sent me a WhatsApp message asking whether what they were doing bothered me, I tried to explain the problem to her. I asked them if they wanted to be together like that, or do it somewhere else, in a different way, but not over my head and their little girl's. Jack may have understood, but Cara didn't, and she was terribly offended. She got so offended that she called me a bigoted old woman. And jealous. And again: the destroyer of their lives, the source of all their unhappiness. She sent me messages telling me to accept that they were still married, and when they were together, when they had sex, that was their business. "That's right," I wrote back, "which is why I don't need to be there when that happens!" But that was just adding fuel to the fire – Cara- still didn't get the sarcasm. I forgot that she doesn't understand it. Or rather, she doesn't want to understand it. Today, I also think this kind of reaction annoyed her because it interfered with her plans. Maybe she wanted to provoke me by having sex over my head. Or would she really be that shameless? Honestly, only God knows the answer to that. And psychiatrists, perhaps.

So, three or four weeks passed in relative peace, but no more than that. By Easter, there was tension in the air again. And not just because of me, not just because I asked them to have sex somewhere else, not in my house, in broad daylight, while Elsie was awake and we were both there. But rather because Cara had started controlling Jack again, where he went, when, with whom? She wanted to know everything. She suspected him of cheating on her. When he didn't answer his phone on time, he must have been with another woman. When he went to work and couldn't take her and the little girl somewhere, he must have been spending time with other people, and those other people could only be women, of course. She called Jack ten to twenty times a day, constantly wanting to talk to him, sending him dozens of messages, and she didn't understand why Jack wasn't moving back in with her, why he was still living with me, in my house, since his family wasn't there. And now that everything was fine, the two of them had sorted everything out between themselves, according to Cara, Jack could really move back into her house...

"Of course, you always answer your mother's phone calls! If she gives you the slightest hint, you always rush to do what she asks! You can't spend time with me, you haven't been able to clean the floor and lay the carpet on the stairs for weeks", Cara began her complaints and harassments, belittling Jack again. *"You're a mummy's boy, you're incapable of changing! Elsie really deserves better; she needs a better father! All grown men live separately. All normal men are attached to their wives, not to their mothers!"*

Cara no longer called Jack "Cripple" on her phone, but she called him "Shit". That's how he appeared in her call log and messages. She was careless enough to send Jack a screenshot of one of their conversations. Jack's name was replaced with "Shit" in capital letters.

Jack didn't even notice this. I still remember the feeling I had when I saw it. SHIT. It was there, in big capital letters, where my son's name should have been. I showed it to Jack. He looked at me in shock. I remember Jack's face too. There was such a vulnerable, disappointed look in his eyes. In his phone, Cara was still listed under "My Wife," surrounded by smiling, heart-shaped emojis.

Cara declared that Jack was unable to change, but it was obvious to me that Cara hadn't changed at all either. She tried to convince us, and perhaps herself, that she had, but she didn't succeed. In reality, Cara remained herself. If things didn't go the way she wanted them to, if she couldn't control them, she couldn't tolerate the situation for long and reverted to her rude, aggressive self, the person who was full of anger, disappointment, and perhaps even fear. And she started blackmailing Jack again and threatening him and trying to manipulate him, playing with him and everything. With every means possible. Especially with the little child. Who is my grandchild…

At the next hearing, they both had to present what they accused the other of and prove it. Cara had no evidence for anything. The tests were negative. It turned out that Jack had never been a drug addict or an alcoholic. Jack received impeccable references from the child welfare observers. Four officials stated that Jack is a sensitive father who is attentive to his child and her needs; that Elsie is happy and cheerful when with him; that their time together is meaningful; and that their loving relationship is clearly visible. The father's behaviour showed no signs of endangering the child's well-being or physical and mental development in any way; on the contrary, the father treated the little girl in a manner appropriate to her age and engaged her in age-appropriate play activities that were conducive to her development. There was no evidence of sexual abuse. Although the quality of the relationship had to be reported in detail to the court and described in a statement explaining what Cara understood by sexual abuse and why the act itself did not qualify as such, there was no evidence of rudeness or aggression, and the evidence section remained empty alongside Cara's accusation. Neglect and indifference could not be discussed either, as Jack provided for all of Elsie's needs. He bought clothes, formula, and nappies for Elsie from the moment she was born and continued to do so even after he moved out of Cara's home. He paid the utility bills long after they stopped living together. Cara had no evidence to support any of her claims. Jack had a rebuttal to each of her claims and proved his own. The slap, the neglect of the small child, the dirty flat, the dirty clothes, the constant blackmail, the threats in messages and phone calls, and the lack of a vast amount of money spent. Screenshots of messages, letters, photographs, bank statements, and fake pregnancy tests. A long list of financial, emotional, psychological, and physical abuse, and evidence of it.

The fourth hearing

Fact-finding hearing. This would have been the next step, as the trial and the case progressed. Cara's accusations are unfounded. As for Jack's, it would have been proven that there were good reasons for everyone to think that the mother was unstable, immature, unfit to raise a child, or only fit to do so to a limited extent. Cara, probably on her solicitor's advice, sought a settlement this time, as she had no other choice.

The next hearing was scheduled for the 5th of May. The charges against the father proved to be false. The charges were dropped. The charges against the mother were never investigated. Because the parties are seeking an agreement. That was the final sentence, which also meant that there was no need for a fact-finding hearing. But the mother, Cara, had filed a separate request at this hearing, the judge informed Jack and his solicitor, to leave the country with Elsie and return permanently to her country of origin. The news came as a shock to Jack. After all, Cara had been trying to convince him for the past month and a half that she wanted to start over and that the plan was to repair their relationship...

In the court order, the judge granted the father three visits a week, each lasting four hours, without supervision. The father was free to take the child wherever he wanted on Monday, Wednesday, and Friday afternoons from 1:30 to 5:30 p.m. The father's solicitor requested that the little girl be allowed to stay overnight with her father, but the mother's solicitor refused because Elsie was still young and her mother was still breastfeeding her...

Cara had not had any milk for three months. But she shamelessly claimed before her solicitor and the court, with a straight face, that she was breastfeeding, and no one checked whether she was telling the truth. The mother requested permission to go home to her parents for a two-week holiday. The court granted this request if she presented her plane tickets and gave her exact address. The court then set the next hearing for September and ordered a detailed guardianship investigation into the parents' financial, material, and moral background and circumstances. The mother had to submit a statement explaining why she wanted to leave the country permanently with her child and why the move would be in the child's best interests. In response to this statement, the father also had to write a statement explaining why he did not consent to his child moving abroad and why, in his opinion, it would not be in the child's best interests.

So, from the fifth of May, my granddaughter was able to come three times a week and spend time with his father, and sometimes with me too. This was a joy, as was Jack's acquittal of the false charges. But justice was not fully served. In fact, it was far from it. There were no consequences for Cara's false accusations against Jack. Cara was held accountable for nothing, and Jack received no compensation. Because the judge did not see clearly in the case and the mother filed a relocation request, the judge ordered the involvement of child protective services. The false accusations not only caused us serious financial harm but also left our future completely uncertain. It was terrible because we lived in constant fear, under a level of stress that was difficult to tolerate. When will the child protective services come? What will they investigate, what will they ask, what will they think? How should we talk, what should we say, and what should we not say? What will happen to Elsie? If Cara takes her on holiday, will she return her? If the court finally releases Cara after the September hearing and allows her to leave the country, how and when will we see the little girl? And how should we live, how should we behave, so that until everything is settled and resolved, there can be at least some peace? What should we say and what should we not say, what can we write down so that neither Cara, nor the court, nor any authority can use it against us? How should we talk to Cara, who deceived Jack and misled the court in the case? How should we behave? We had no idea. One thing was certain: we had not yet managed to escape from hell. We could only continue to suffer in it.

What next?

We already knew; we had learned because we had been warned not to say anything derogatory about the mother. My daughter Sophia said:

- "Mum, she (Cara) is protected now. She is a young woman who has given birth, and the child is still small. Even if the mother has mood swings, everyone will assume that it's because she has just given birth and is still very young. No one can see how you live and what you are going through, and probably no one really cares what Cara does to you. She is now a young mother, and society as a whole will only see that, and everyone will defend her!"

Great. Nice prognosis. But Sophia was probably right. Again.

Because the official aid organisations said almost exactly the same thing. Justice for Fathers, which protects fathers' rights, and Family Needs Fathers took a similar stance. PAIN, an aid organisation set up to defend falsely accused people, warned us outright that although we had been treated unjustly and abused, the best thing to do was to practise the so-called "reverse" psychology and put the child's interests first, writing about it everywhere. The child needs both parents. This is a fact, and we must insist on it, repeat it, and we cannot say or ask for more than that. Shared custody, in equal proportions, is all we can ask for – and that is all Jack can get, even in the best-case scenario, with the most positive outcome. Because the child is too young and no one will award custody to the father anyway, they said. If it is proven that the mother is mentally ill, then perhaps the outcome could be different, the court's decision could be different, but let us be aware that we cannot say that the mother is mentally ill, nor can we suggest it. Even if there were tangible evidence of this, no one would look at it or listen to it, and believe me, - the advisor of PAIN said - with such an argument, you would only be seen as malicious, ill-intentioned people who want to take the child away from the mother. It is up to the judge to realise that something is wrong with the mother. And no, our solicitor cannot request a psychological examination either, because, on the one hand, it is extremely expensive and, unless the judge orders it, we have to pay for it out of our own pocket, but, on the other hand, we will probably not even get that far, because if the judge does not come up with the idea himself, he will not agree to such an examination... Great. We were at a dead end, in the deepest pit of hell, and no one knew how to get out of it; no one could help us.

The whole system proved to be broken. The justice system is totally flawed and inconsistent.

Jack could have been sent to prison without consequence for perjury, placed in pre-trial detention, and charged with drug use, alcoholism, and sexual abuse. He could have been blackmailed, threatened, and humiliated with impunity, harassed daily with 30 phone calls and 50 abusive messages, woken up in the middle of the night at any time, and sexually exploited. Jack could have all his money taken from his pocket, which was almost natural anyway, since he was the breadwinner, the man, the father – "Just pay up! And pay for everything. You are the man; you must just pay!" – And I? As a grandmother, I could be emotionally abused with impunity and without consequences, I could be scolded for no reason, and I could be insulted. Child wise: Elsie could be neglected, kept in dirty clothes and dirty nappies, so that her sore bottom did not heal for months. She could be kept in a baby seat in a semi-sitting position until she was six months old, with no developmental, intellectual, emotional, or mental stimulation, so that the little girl did not begin to sit up or crawl until nine months. After they started coming to me, I spent long hours every day for weeks exercising her, lying her on her stomach, putting a play mat under her, and talking and singing to her. Elsie couldn't even roll over onto her side at 8-9 months old. These are facts, and I'm not saying this to show off; I just want to say that I was really worried about it. And I consciously began to develop her so that she would finally move out of her supine position, when she just looked at me and everyone else desperately with her big eyes, and wanted to be held all the time so she could see something of the world. When Elsie first heard the birds singing in the garden, she looked so delighted, her face was so full of wonder, that I almost cried. When she first saw the flowers in the garden, she reached out her little hands towards them, her face alight with a smile, and the beauty of it was beyond words! Until she was seven months old, Elsie received no vitamin D or other dietary supplements. Her mother sometimes breastfed her, sometimes bottle-fed her, and from the age of six months, she gave her whatever she ate, chewed up. Elsie's nails were never cut, except when her father cut them; her hair was never washed, except when her father washed it, and at six months old, her head was covered with such thick dandruff that it took a month to get rid of it. The baby only received her mandatory vaccinations when her father took her there. But according to the health visitor, everything was fine because the child was gaining weight nicely. The health visitor had no doubts about the child's development and well-being. "The mother takes good care of the baby," she continued to write this in her notes, "she just needs support because she is still very young." Yes, with Elsie and us, anything could be done with impunity. The authorities were completely uninterested and completely blindly biased towards the mother.

Today, I know, and Jack knows, that it was a huge mistake to seek an agreement, to accept Cara's offer to settle, to believe that she wanted to repair their relationship. It was a huge mistake not to go straight to a fact-finding hearing, where the truth could have come out. Because only there could the whole truth have come out.

Without a fact-finding hearing, even though we could prove everything, no one was interested in the evidence. Nor in our statements. They didn't even listen to Jack. Or to me. Should we listen or shout? Listening and staying silent were not options because Jack didn't want to lose his daughter. But when we shouted, they told us to be quiet and cautious. When we spoke quietly, wrote down our doubts, and presented photographs and text messages, it didn't matter what we said or what the photographs showed. The only question was why we were writing, taking screenshots, and taking photographs. And the conclusion: we are obviously malicious, we are not tolerant enough towards the young mother, who, according to the health visitor, has nothing wrong with her; she just needs support. And we obviously took the photos to gather evidence against the mother... According to one police officer, the domestic violence Jack suffered is "perfectly normal" in a man's life, "there are much more serious cases than this", and "that little girl (meaning Cara) just needs to grow up" – the police officer said this to us verbatim. "She just needs to grow up." That's not how we experienced the slaps, the threats, the verbal abuse, and the daily harassment. The emotional and psychological terror completely exhausted us; we had no reserves left, and we barely had the strength to get through each day. But above all, this was about a small child whose life, well-being, and safety were our top priority. Should we apologise for that? Certainly not! No one wanted to take the child away from her mother. Never. None of us wanted anything like that. Jack and I just wanted to know that Elsie was safe. As her father, Jack just wanted the same rights as her mother, even though they no longer lived together, and he wanted to avoid spending the next decade and a half in fear that his daughter would be taken away from him and sent abroad. Whether we had come even a centimetre closer to what we wanted – and the peace that would come with it – was still unclear, still unknown. We had to wait another three months for the next hearing, about which all we knew for sure was that it might not be the last...

The day after the hearing, Cara called Jack in despair to say that Elsie had eaten cigarettes; it was not known how many because it was not known how many were in the packet, but now some were missing, and they had managed to get some out of the child's mouth, but possibly not all of them. Of course, it wasn't Cara's fault, but her sister-in-law, Elenor's, whom Cara had entrusted with looking after the little girl while she went to the toilet... It was Elenor who wasn't paying attention, who didn't notice the cigarettes left on the table, or that Elsie was eating them. Of course, it wasn't Cara's fault, but Elenor's. Everything was always someone else's fault, never hers. Jack took Elsie to the emergency room with Cara that afternoon, where she was observed and released because, thankfully, she had no symptoms that would indicate poisoning.

Elsie leaves

On 10 May, five days after the hearing, Cara announced that she had bought plane tickets and would be travelling to her parents' house with Elsie on the 18th of May for two weeks, as the court had allowed her to do so. Jack had just started seeing his little girl on his own and was really enjoying spending time with her, without Cara's presence or supervision... Jack spent time with Elsie on his own, but most of the time they took me with them, or I was with them when they were together, which, of course, I was very happy about. We took long walks on the beach, bought Elsie a paddling pool because it suddenly turned into a real summer, played with her in the grass, fed her, put her down for her afternoon nap, loved her, and enjoyed every moment with her. But barely two weeks had passed since the semi-consolidated period when Cara announced that she was leaving with the baby. It frustrated us, it came as a shock, and we were upset about it for many reasons. Jack and I both were.

I asked Cara three times at the end of April, before I enrolled Elsie in baby ballet, whether she would like to go and whether we should enroll our little girl. Baby ballet is not like a regular ballet class, where babies who can't even walk yet are taught to dance. This group is more sensory, where babies' senses and motor skills are developed through music and a variety of materials. Babies really enjoy this activity, and I found Elsie to be a very musical baby, so I was sure she would love it. Elsie, as I said, was already behind in her development. Cara kept her in a baby seat in front of the TV in a semi-sitting position but lying on her back and giving her all kinds of snacks to keep her quiet – this is what Cara said, in her own words. Elsie had no opportunity to move; she hardly ever spent any time on her tummy because, again in Cara's own words, "Elsie hates being on her tummy". Elsie weighed 10 kilos at 7 months, even though she was born weighing just under 3 kilos. She was a cute, chubby baby, peaceful, very quiet, and happy with every activity and new stimulus. I was sure that baby ballet would do her good and that she would enjoy it. Cara agreed, even seeming happy about the opportunity.

"Of course, thank you very much, let's go!" - she wrote three times in response to my messages. So, I confidently paid the course fee in advance for a month and a half.

The first session was the week after the Court Hearing. I sat to one side of the room while Cara joined the class with Elsie, holding her in her lap. Elsie laughed and smiled throughout, rocking herself to the music, welcoming the conductor's approach with abandon and happiness. I took lots of photos and videos. Cara clearly liked the place too. I was happy to have finally done something for my granddaughter that made her mother happy, too. We left with high hopes, cheerfully thanked the conductor for the lesson, and told her we would see her next week!

But we couldn't go the following week because Cara said Elsie was too tired that day, and she was sure the little girl wouldn't feel like participating in the class.

- "We'll take her when we come back," said Cara, "we won't be here next week anyway, you know, because we're going away, so there's no point in going tomorrow. Besides, the baby is still too young for ballet. I'll take her when she can walk, that's when my parents took me when I was a child. Elsie is still too young for this."

My heart sank. And not because I had paid for nothing. But because I knew that by the time we could take the little girl again, this group would be over, and the summer break would begin at the course. Elsie had just started something she really enjoyed, and then she would immediately lose the chance to participate... And Cara didn't even understand what the whole class was about! That it wasn't ballet and why it would be so good for Elsie. She didn't even care how much fun the little girl was having! It hurt my heart terribly, but there was nothing I could do.

Cara bought the plane tickets for 18 May. It was hard not to think that she had deliberately arranged it so that Jack would have as little contact with Elsie as possible, because Cara knew very well that in the first days of June, when she returned, we would be leaving to celebrate my father's 80th birthday abroad and we would be away for ten days... Jack and Cara had agreed that Cara would take Elsie to visit her family at the same time we were visiting ours. They agreed that this would be the best solution. But Cara suddenly changed her mind and bought the tickets two weeks earlier, so we won't see Elsie for four weeks. And four weeks is a long time in the life of such a small baby, she might even forget her father during that time... Jack was terribly upset. He asked that, since Cara had already organised her trip, when the two of them came back, Elsie should come with us, even if only for a few days, so that Jack could introduce her to her great-grandfather! But Cara immediately rejected this idea:

- "This child is still very young; she still needs her mother! She wouldn't sleep at your place, you wouldn't be able to feed her properly, she would cry the whole time, you can't do this to this little child!" said Cara.

Elsie was nine months old and loved being with Jack. She slept peacefully in our home every afternoon, with Jack rocking her to sleep, and Elsie never cried, not even for a minute. Jack and I played with her every day. I exercised her and bought her a baby walker so she could move around freely and spin around. We also provided her with tummy time, and she was already lifting her chest, attempting to crawl, and learning to sit up from a side position. Elsie loved being with us from the very beginning. She got to know the dog and the cats, and there were lots of toys. We never turned on the TV for her. We talked to her, sang to her, and took her out into the garden. Dad played aeroplane with her and sat her on his shoulders, we took her to the sea and showed her the big blue water, and she could hardly contain her excitement, waving her little arms at the waves and laughing. Elsie laughed a lot, loudly, and then she started babbling. I'm sure nothing would have happened if we had taken her with us for three or four days; Jack would have watched over her like the apple of his eye. But Cara obviously didn't want that and didn't give in to Jack's pleas. It broke my heart to think that this beautiful time was coming to an end, even if only temporarily. I also thought of my father, who was eagerly awaiting his first great-grandchild and asked for pictures of her every week - he wouldn't see her on his birthday, even though we had promised him he would. And who knows if he would ever see her? If so, when? Dad, Grandpa is 80 years old, and his heart isn't in good shape... But I didn't know what to do. I didn't even try to talk to Cara. By then, I was the enemy again, she hated me again, and she still thought I was the reason Jack wasn't moving back in with her. She sent Jack brutal messages about it even then:

> *"Your mum is to blame for everything! If you could just not talk to her for a month and not say anything to her, everything would be different between us, you know that!"*

Jack didn't mention these messages or show them to me until weeks or months later, before the next court hearing. So, I didn't know that Cara was writing things like that about me. But I didn't need to know about them to feel her lack of love - it was almost palpable. If I wrote to her about anything, asked about Elsie or how she was doing, Cara would reply hours later, in short sentences, half-words, or not at all, depending on her mood. I hadn't seen her since the baby ballet session. Jack collected Elsie on the contact days, and he also took her back. I wouldn't say that Cara's rejection didn't hurt me, but I was very tired, somehow worn out by this relationship, and I continued to work a lot. I didn't have time to deal with my feelings. With what I was feeling and how much it did hurt or upset me. I didn't care anymore.

May 17th arrived, and in the afternoon, Cara asked Jack to drive them to the airport the next day if he didn't want her and Elsie to take a two-hour bus ride... Of course, she didn't put it that way; she had no intention of asking Jack in a normal way. In her own way, she resorted to manipulation again. She asked Jack if he would take them to the airport. She added that if he didn't take them, they would take the bus. Elsie was small and couldn't even walk or stand up yet. How would Cara manage with a suitcase and a small child? Jack agreed to take them, of course. But on the 18th, at dawn, Cara realised she had left her passport at the currency exchange the day before, so she had to wait for it to open and hope it had been set aside and was still there. I secretly hoped that it wouldn't be there and she wouldn't be able to leave. Perhaps God will forgive me for this. It hurt my heart that Elsie was leaving, that I wouldn't see her for two weeks and then for another two weeks, and I couldn't even be sure she would come back, because I knew Cara's intentions, her ultimate goal, just as well as the court did: Cara had just applied for permission to move abroad, back home for good. And I wasn't at all sure she wouldn't try to do so as soon as she was out of the country. I thought she would be tempted to do so, and in that case, Jack would have to go to the Hague court, and it would take months for someone to bring Elsie back. But unfortunately, the passport was found the next morning, taken to the currency exchange, and returned to Cara. Jack took them to the airport, and they caught the plane at the last minute. Before they left, they turned in front of the house because Jack ran in for something. I had just come home from somewhere, so I walked past the car. I saw Elsie in her car seat, napping. I saw Cara, too. She noticed me. She didn't even say hello; she just turned her head away.

The plane took off with them, and Jack called me, his voice breaking on the phone. "I miss Elsie already," he said.

Summer in full swing
My homeland – My homeland

The sky is black, with red and purple streaks clawing at the clouds – it will be windy tomorrow, I remembered my grandmother's wisdom. If the sky turns red after dusk, strong winds and storms can be expected the next day. That's what the old woman said, but she wasn't always right. Maybe she won't be right this time either. We came home for the holidays. The trees no longer rustle around us; the roads are full of potholes. But that doesn't matter, nothing really matters anymore, all that matters is that it's summer, warm, real summer. My homeland. My homeland, please give comfort to your children!

It was a dark night on the plains in the middle of the Carpathian Basin, and it was past midnight when we finally arrived home. A black June night. I watch my son sleeping soundly, who drove us halfway across Europe and fell asleep almost immediately after dinner when we arrived at our accommodation, lying on the bed fully clothed.

I watched him wring his hands in his sleep. The grown-up child, the mature man, whom I haven't seen crying in decades, and who isn't crying now either. He's just wringing his hands. While he sleeps. I wouldn't wish that feeling on any mother. I sit down on the edge of his bed and place my hand on his forehead. His skin is hot and clammy. He tries to rest in a restless sleep. His eyelashes flutter, but he doesn't wake up at my touch. - God, please heal us! – I pray. – God, please comfort my child, give him peace!

And God tried to heal us, and our homeland would have given us comfort, striving with all its might. The turquoise mirror of the lake Balaton in Tihany, the lavender fields, the grandparents' garden, the vine arbour, the fountain on Margaret Island in Budapest, and the cobblestones of the street. Friends, siblings, melodies. Colours and lights. All memories. And all magic.

But the daily phone calls continued. So did the messages. They came by the dozen from Cara. Promises. That Cara would bring Elsie to Budapest, since it was only a few hours' drive from Austria. But then, when she didn't bring her, she messaged that Jack should go to her instead. It would be easier for him, Jack. If he really loved the little girl, if he wanted to see her, then he could do that much for her! Then, when they came over with her parents but did not yet know when, she would let him know. Jack was constantly on standby, wondering where he might have to go and when. He kept hoping he might see Elsie and have the chance to introduce her to her grandfather and great-grandfather. It was one of the cruellest things I had ever witnessed. Keeping someone's hopes up, constantly reassuring them, and then taking it all away.

Sophia understood the situation perfectly, as she always did, and she was terribly angry with Cara. She saw right through her, as if looking through a windowpane.

- "All this woman cares about is destroying you! She doesn't want you to have a moment of peace; she doesn't want you to be able to relax for a single moment! She doesn't want you to breathe without her! Turn off your phone! At least for one day!" – his sister begged Jack.

- "How could I turn it off?" Jack asked resignedly. "She has the child. She may call at any time regarding Elsie if there's a problem. Or anything else that might be related to Elsie.
- "I think you have Stockholm syndrome," replied Sophia, "you need therapy. You too. You won't be able to do this for long. You can't live like this.

The ten days passed too quickly, and we set off on our journey back. The farewell wasn't as long or as painful this time. Not least because we were going to see Elsie the next day.

The little girl looked at us reservedly and didn't approach us for the first half hour. Jack's face betrayed his fright.

- "She doesn't recognise me..." Jack muttered, sitting cross-legged on the carpet opposite Elsie. "See, she's not even smiling, she's afraid of me! She doesn't know who I am, she doesn't remember me!" he added desperately.
- "Of course she does! Just give her time! She'll remember everything soon! She's only nine months old; it takes her longer to remember things!" - I tried to comfort Jack, and I had no idea where I was getting such nonsense from, I mean, that it would take a baby longer to recall memories?! But the idea seemed logical. If Elsie hadn't seen her father in the last four weeks of her nine months of life, then obviously it would be harder for her to remember where she knew him from...
- "Play with her like you usually do!" I suggested. "Say the same words you usually say to her!" Jack then stretched out his arms towards Elsie.
- "Come here, sweetie pie, come to Daddy," he said softly, and waited for Elsie to think about the familiar words, then slowly get up on all fours and crawl towards him.

Then Jack picked her up and lifted her high into the air, sitting her on his shoulders. And then the ice finally broke. Elsie laughed out loud. And from then on, she didn't want to get down from her father's lap and arms.

At the beginning of June, Cara was required to submit a statement with her application, in which she had to substantiate, with facts, why it would be in Elsie's best interests for Elsie to move abroad with her. Jack had to challenge this statement in a so-called counterstatement, in which he had to refute everything point by point and write down why it would be much more in the child's best interests to remain in the country where she was born. Cara was usually 10-14 days late in submitting the official documents to the court. And no one ever held it against her. Her solicitor usually justified the delay by saying that Cara did not speak English, so everything she wrote or said in official matters had to be translated. Cara had an interpreter and translator at every hearing, free of charge, or rather, financed by Legal Aid, i.e., taxpayers' money. Cara claimed she understood only German, which was nothing more than a blatant lie. She and Jack spoke Hungarian, and Cara spoke It fluently, as it was her native language, but she couldn't write it correctly. Jack didn't have an interpreter, and he couldn't have afforded to pay for a translator out of his own pocket. He was not eligible for Legal Aid because he did not live on benefits or unemployment assistance; he had worked all his life, honestly. Anyone who works and earns at least the minimum wage is not eligible for free legal aid... There are no income-based discounts either. Anyone who works regularly and lives without benefits must pay for legal representation out of their own pocket, covering 100% of the private solicitor's fees. It sounds unbelievable, but it's true. This is the reality. It is distorted and unfair.

In mid-June, Jack finally received Cara's statement from her solicitor so that he could refute it. It was not an easy task because the statement itself contained numerous falsehoods. Sneaky lies. The four-page document was full of half-truths that made Jack's hair stand on end, and mine too.

For example, Cara claimed that she intended to live with her mother, who had a five-bedroom house. Which may well have been true. Jack had never seen his mother-in-law's house and did not assume Cara would lie about it. However, we knew, because Cara herself had told us, that six people already lived in that house. Cara's three brothers, her eldest brother's new partner, and her parents. So, it would have been quite difficult for any reasonable person to imagine that Cara and Elsie would have separate rooms and bathrooms in that house.

Cara also stated that if she moved back home, she would start working immediately, and her mother would care for the child, Elsie, until she was three years old and started nursery. It seemed unlikely that an active grandmother in her forties, who worked shifts at a hospital, would give up her job so her daughter could earn money while supporting two other sons under 18. Cara also claimed that the welfare system in that country was much more favourable than in the UK. This was relatively easy to refute, as each country's welfare service maintains a website that lists the available benefits in detail. All we had to do was compare the two. The best part, however, was the paragraph in which Cara explained that she saw herself as a nurse in the future. She copied Jack's job description, his schedule, and the way he loved and cared for people... She even added that this was what she had always wanted to do. Meanwhile, we both knew that Cara found Jack's job disgusting and had repeatedly said that she would never be able to clean an adult person's bottom and change diapers. She was even disgusted by Elsie's nappies.

Mirroring.

Oh, yeah.

A complete and perfect example of what the literature refers to as this. That's what I thought, and I despaired. If Cara really is narcissistic, no one will ever notice or be able to treat it. The justice system in the UK knows very little about this condition, is not aware of it at all, and narcissistic behaviour or abuse is mostly impossible to prove in court proceedings.

Cara's statement also included details of which paediatrician and dentist Elsie would be registered with after the move. Jack then realised that

Cara had used her time off, her holiday, to get everything sorted out so she could take the documents confirming Elsie's placement to the court hearing in September.

Jack quickly prepared his rebuttal and submitted it to his solicitor within a few days. The case was delayed; Jack was not at fault, and he could only hope the investigations would be completed on time. We could only wait for the ordered guardianship review thereafter, because the guardianship authority also wanted to consider whether to permit the child to leave the country, so they wanted to see both the statement and the counterstatement.

The rebuttal was also sent to Cara, translated into German. The text must have been powerful, because Cara made a huge scene the following week. She didn't want to give Elsie to Jack; she threatened to call the police, she repeated over and over again that she would have Jack sent to prison, and then we'll see. She provoked and harassed Jack, and on one occasion, when Jack went to pick up Elsie, she pushed him down the stairs leading to the front door and even tried to hit him. That day, she threw their framed wedding photo on the floor, smashing it to pieces, and threw her wedding ring out the window onto the street. Jack came home pale as death. He said he would have liked to call the police, but he didn't dare, for fear of what had happened last November would happen again. That the police would take him away again and question him in custody, instead of taking Cara, who abused him.

At the same time, Cara was looking for Elsie's Healthy Start Voucher card so she could buy cigarettes. And this is no joke; there is a message she sent to Jack on Messenger

> *"Do you know where that card is? You know, the Healthy Start card. Could you check if it's in your car? I really need it so I can at least buy cigarettes..."*

The card wasn't in Jack's car, and he couldn't find it at home, either in the house or in his trouser pockets.

Cara then accused Jack of taking and hiding the voucher issued in Elsie's name and told her social worker that Jack had stolen it from her... The social worker reported Jack to the police and launched an investigation to have the police search for the card. The police did their job, and within a few weeks it turned out that all the money on the card had been spent in the region where Cara's sister-in-law, Elenor, lived... Elenor admitted in her messages to Cara that she had the card and, as agreed, she would pay her back the money she had spent in instalments. The false accusation was thus lifted from Jack's shoulders once again, but Jack was still very upset by the whole incident. He was upset that his daughter's money had been stolen and that he had been suspected of the theft. But there was nothing he could do. The social worker did not know Jack, had never spoken to him, and had perhaps seen him twice in passing. None of this prevented her from reporting Jack and, in her report to child protective services, stating that she suspected him of theft because, in her opinion, Jack was the only person who had access to the card and knew the PIN. When the truth came out, the social worker still did not feel that she should apologise to Jack or say anything that could be construed as an apology. On the contrary. She continued her verbal abuse, at least according to Cara, who claimed that the social worker regularly asked her about the status of their relationship and, when Cara provided her with information, the social worker made comments about Jack, such as that he was manipulative and exercised too much control over Cara's life.

"Listen, he comes here and doesn't talk about anything else but asks questions about you. I think he's into you (horny for you)" Cara wrote in a message to Jack with a laughing smiley at the end of the sentence.

It had already occurred to me that the social worker might be overstepping her authority and that her suspicions and unjustified accusations should be addressed, but I had no idea how to do so. Everything was so sneaky and underhanded; everything happened behind closed doors! And I didn't know anyone; I wasn't familiar with the procedures for reporting someone. Every day was so busy. Either we were both working, or we were with Elsie; I couldn't find the time to defend ourselves. Moreover, I only learned about this episode weeks later. Jack never complained to me; he didn't tell me much because he wanted to save me and was already tired of the whole story. Things only came out when he was already in despair.

At the end of the month, barely a week later, Cara changed her tactics, or I don't know what happened to her. She calmed down completely and wrote to Jack that she accepted it was over between them and understood there was no going back for her. She wrote that she regretted what had happened and begged Jack to try to remain friends. She promised that she would do everything she could to make that happen. She tried to be funny and provocative at the same time, telling Jack that friendship could include many things, and if he needed sex, he should just let her know, not be shy; she would be happy to oblige. At the same time, she assured him she had a new partner and suggested Jack find one, too, so they could both start a new life. But a few days later, she invited Jack to dinner. When Jack declined, she sent him tearful, heartfelt messages saying she would always love him, that he should know it, and that Jack was the only man in her life she truly loved. Even though she had a new partner, it wasn't the same, and she couldn't even sleep with him because of that. Hoovering, Level X, God knows how many times, and again. Cara had definitely shifted into high gear. I didn't know anything about this either; I only found out months later what had happened on those hot June days in 2022. At the end of the month, Cara begged for a goodbye sex, just one last time, when she could still hug Jack like she used to.

"*Just sleep with me one more time*", she begged Jack in her messages.

THE WAITING PERIOD

Jack and Cara tried to repair their relationship again, but it didn't work out this time either. Cara managed to be nice for 7-10 days, then she always reverted to a fury-like creature, always having problems with everyone, and never pleased with anything. And it all started over and over again.

> *"Where are you going, what are you doing, who are you meeting, when are you coming back, why don't you move back home, Mummy's boy?"*

I suggested to Jack a few times that when she asked him, "*Why don't you move back?*", he should explain to Cara that this was exactly why he wouldn't! Because of her questions and constant control. And not because of me. Not because I exist or because I would talk him out of moving back. But I don't think Jack ever told Cara the truth to her face. He manoeuvred. He avoided conflict. He found Cara's tantrums repulsive, but he might also have been afraid of her.

I hated the expression "mummy's boy" terribly, mainly because I felt it was infinitely unfair. Jack, the mummy's boy, was the most independent and self-sufficient of my four children. He was the first one who didn't need me or my help. In fact, at 16, he was already lending me money from his own pocket money, money he had earned himself. He was the one who cleaned his own room at 7 and baked pancakes for his friends at 9. He washed up after himself. He had his own ways and his own plans, but I never had to worry about him. Even when he officially became an adult and we lived together, Jack took care of himself. He did his own laundry, bought his own food, cooked for himself, and sometimes offered me some. He didn't live in a "mama hotel", as they say, but was perfectly self-sufficient. The fact that he lived under the same roof as his brother and sometimes with me to save money did not mean that he was dependent on me or relied on me for anything. This is difficult to see and understand, especially for those who don't want to. Jack didn't let anyone interfere in his life, and Cara was one of the results of that. I would have loved to tell Cara that, too. I wish Jack had been a mummy's boy! Then you definitely wouldn't have come here, you wouldn't have come into our lives! ... But when I first thought of what I would say and how I would say it to Cara, I realised that I couldn't really love her anymore. So, I kept quiet, saying nothing to anyone.

Love. Like in 1 Corinthians 13 in the Bible. Who can practise everything that is written there? "Love believes all things, hopes all things, endures all things, does not take account of evil." – This is simply a Mission

Impossible. Even though the phrase kept coming to mind, I found it increasingly difficult to apply this law to Cara and to our relationship. And only conscious thinking helped. My head. My will. Because my heart protested, and emotions arose in it that I had never thought were there...

What I asked Cara not to do less than a year ago, she did exactly that. She systematically destroyed our whole life. Especially Jack's. She turned my son inside out, and he no longer knew who he was. Jack tried to save what could be saved, not to lose his daughter, so he tried to comply and remain on good terms with Cara, whose only goal was to find a new father for Elsie and move out of the country; she never made a secret of it. A dark mistress who played with a man's soul as if it were a marionette puppet. She made Jack submit to her, only to throw him far away, pull him, let him go, because that's where she found the most joy in this game. Perhaps her goal was never anything other than the game itself. I saw through her, so I became her enemy. To outsiders, Cara was a poor little girl who craved love. A young, fragile woman. But I knew that when she did receive love, and not just any love, but love in any form, she received it with disgust, wanted to get rid of it, and found the greatest pleasure in humiliating the one who gave her love. She humiliated them by rejecting it. Because either it wasn't enough, or she didn't need that type of love. "I'm leaving, I don't feel well, we're not really suited to each other" – these words came at the moment when most love was being given. And the donor was desperate. What was he doing wrong? How could he give more? Why was he never enough? And when Cara saw Jack desperate, she was happy, truly happy. For a few moments, she was honestly, fully happy. Is this game the so-called love? It certainly isn't! This "game" was frightening on Cara's part and, after a while, repulsive.

I tried to talk to Jack. I talked with him frequently; I made him speak, and I spoke with him. For some reason, he didn't see the situation clearly. He explained to me clearly that he was only trying to manoeuvre. He could no longer love Cara, but he kept trying. Maybe one day he would be able to love Cara in a way that made her happy, and she would love him back in a way that was good for him, too. So that it would be good for everyone.

So, Jack, as I understood it, tried to find common ground, as if he were in a negotiation, trying to engage Cara in a dialogue about her and his own feelings. And when this clearly failed, time and time again, Jack increasingly lashed out: Who needs me? Who will ever love me? No one will ever need me, and I don't think I'll ever be able to love anyone after this...

I didn't know what to do, so I prayed silently. And thoughts like this came to mind: There is no dialogue with fascists. But I couldn't say that to Jack. He wouldn't have understood the parallel, and I didn't understand it either; I just felt it. That's what Cara was doing to him, and to me, was nothing more than a kind of emotional fascism. As terrible as that sounds. And dialogue with fascists is impossible. They only understand force and power. Force and power would have been achieved by treating her as invisible and ignoring her. By cutting off all contact with her. "No contact" would have been the only way to free us from the constant abuse. But there was no chance of no contact. Because of Elsie. Whose biological mother was Cara.

Mummy's boy... I've been thinking about this a lot lately.

I first heard this expression when Cara introduced it to me, much to my misfortune. I had no idea that a documentary series had been made about this problem in the United States. Later, I watched a few episodes.

I found the concepts to be quite confusing. There are certainly men like most of those featured in the series, who could easily be classified as having a psychological problem. These are men who cannot detach from their mothers, who remain overly emotionally attached to them, and/or whose mothers do not allow them to detach and keep them tied to them by any means necessary. However, the series and its enthusiastic supporters of the Mummy's Boy theory somehow overlooked the fact that mother-son relationships can exist without separation difficulties and still involve a strong emotional bond. In some cultures, it is still known and accepted that such relationships exist, but in the West, all mother-son relationships are now stigmatised and condemned as too strong bonds. Children should grow up, stand on their own two feet, and leave their families, as this proves they have reached adulthood.

With complete independence from everyone. In the Western world, in so-called advanced cultures, this has become the guiding principle, the example to follow.

A few decades ago, people still lived in large, multi-generational families, where everyone had their own role and tasks. And these families were perfectly functioning small units within society. No one would have thought of calling Aunt Mariska's son Józsi a mummy's boy because Aunt Mariska cooked for him and ironed his shirt before they went to church, and Józsi milked the cow and brought her a jug of milk every morning... Józsi was not a mummy's boy, even if he asked Aunt Mariska for advice on anything or hoped for help in looking after her children.

When these small communities broke up in the middle of the twentieth century, certain forms of contact remained: Sunday lunches, card parties, working together in each other's houses, and free childcare provided by grandparents. I also remember my parents' relationship with my grandparents. Daily phone calls, discussing any problems that arose, sharing any joys. It was natural. There was no question that my father loved my grandmother and shared his thoughts with her, asking her opinion on his decisions. No one condemned him for this or stigmatised him. It didn't even occur to anyone.

But today, you must break away from your parents as soon as possible, and living under the same roof with them is considered downright abnormal. The consequences are clear: Parents will end up in a nursing home and can consider themselves lucky if someone from their family sits by their deathbed, rather than just a tired nurse checking in every hour to see if they are still breathing.

In certain cultures (and religions), respect (and love) for mothers from sons is still natural and almost obligatory. There are prayers in which men first ask God to bless their mothers. In that religion and in those cultures, no one would think of calling men Mummy's boys, and not just because of their prayers. In that culture, what Cara did to Jack is called haram. And haram has consequences; it does not go unnoticed.

It would be good to distinguish between a mother-son bond based on simple love and respect and a truly pathological mother-son relationship of the "we can't live without each other" type. But that seems difficult. It is difficult for many people. Even for the editors of the American series.

Cara came from a different family and grew up in a different generation. She was not religious and knew nothing about other cultures. I could even say that she knew neither God nor man.

Tícia - The beginning of a new relationship

Jack was struggling, and this only made him increasingly unstable. Like a boat tossed about on the sea. I tried to calm him down and encourage him, not just any old way, but every single day. Again, and again.

- "What do you mean, who would want you? How could anyone not want you?! Do you know how many decent women there are, outside in the world, kind, good-hearted, good women who would give half their lives to be loved by a man the way you loved Cara?"
- "I think you're wrong, mum. All women are like that. All women are like Cara. I don't think there's much difference between them."
- "How could all women be like that?" and I listed the names of those friends and colleagues Jack knew. "None of them is like that! They never were! And there are lots of lovely girls out there, you just have to look for them!"
- "They wouldn't want me", he responded, and I felt that every day we ended up in the same place. That no one would want him, but he couldn't trust anyone anymore, either. "It's okay," he added, "I'll be fine on my own. I'll travel, play the stock market, and retire early. You can be happy on your own...You do the same and can be happy. Can't you?"
- "Yes. You can be happy on your own. But you're still young, and you're not the type of person who should be alone! I'm sure

you'll find someone who will love you the way you deserve to be loved! You just have to look for them. You just have to wait."

These words always comforted Jack to some extent. And he was able to carry on with his daily life. And then Tícia, whom Jack had met at work, appeared on the horizon. They worked together as care assistants in the care home, often on the same shifts.

The British girl entered Jack's life with cool elegance and stayed there for a good three months. Then she went to university, which would have taken up all her time anyway, but Tícia's reason for breaking up with him was ultimately that she couldn't stand Cara constantly calling Jack, and when she wasn't calling, she was texting him, and Jack was constantly glued to his phone reading her messages. Jack couldn't explain to Tícia that he had to read every message in case something had happened to Elsie – sooner or later, everyone concluded that this was impossible to understand or accept.

– "No divorced woman calls her ex-husband thirty times a day because of their child!" said Tícia, and I completely agreed with her.

I understood Jack too – he tried to manoeuvre his way out of it and couldn't get out of this behaviour, even if he wanted to. He was afraid of Cara; he didn't want to make her angry with him (or with Elsie), and only those who knew Cara understood this defensive behaviour. This young woman was completely unpredictable when things didn't go her way. She slammed her phone, shook Elsie, and banged her own head against the wall. She clattered the dishes, shouted, and threatened. No one knew about these things; no one had ever seen them, except Jack. And me. If we had tried to tell anyone, no one would have believed us. "Come on! That charming, fragile young girl? With her gentle face and doe-brown eyes, there's no way she would behave like that!"

Some messages survived:

> *"I'm about to scream! I want to go far, far away from here, without a phone, without anything."*

"I'm about to hang myself!"

"I know you're with your bloody mother, pick up that bloody phone or I'll f@ck your arse!"

Behind closed doors and in her private messages, Cara was rude and endlessly vulgar, downright crude.

Throughout their relationship, Jack tried to keep Ticia a secret from Cara. But Cara continued to probe Jack's social media accounts, and although she no longer knew the passwords, she read the comments and posts wherever she could. Ticia agreed with Jack that they would not make their relationship public, but she regularly liked Jack's posts and commented on his photos. This was more than suspicious. Cara didn't need any more evidence. One late summer afternoon, she sent Tícia a private message asking her what the relationship between Jack and her was. She also asked if they were sexually involved.

This was too much even for Jack, not to mention Tícia. Jack's solicitor called Cara's solicitor and asked her to warn her client about what she was and was not entitled to do, but this only slowed Cara down for a short time. In fact, it didn't slow her down at all; it just redirected her mental efforts. From then on, Cara wrote to me, trying to get information from me and sending me tearful emojis about how badly Jack had treated her, how he was already in a new relationship, how he had cheated on her, and how she would not survive this because she still loved Jack and would die if she saw him happy with someone else. But she wishes him well...

For many long months, I was Cara's number one enemy, the main obstacle to Cara's happiness, the head witch herself, but now she had a more serious and pressing problem than me, so she forgot about it for a moment. Or rather, she was willing to put it aside.

Cara mercilessly reviled Ticia, even though she didn't know her. "*This woman is just a whore who will leave Jack anyway, an ugly bitch who needs half a kilo of paint on her face to look like anything,*" she messaged me

She wrote things like this to me, and I didn't know what to do with these messages. It was difficult to read them, but I had no intention of showing them to Jack. If that was Cara's goal, it didn't work. If the plan was for me to hate Ticia, too, and curse her along with Cara, that didn't work either. If she just wanted to complain or cry to me, that was so unlike her that I didn't even consider it. She had asked me a few times before not to talk Jack out of it – for some reason, she always thought I had a say in my son's love life – but I don't think she meant that with all this abuse, I would go to Jack and say: Listen, son, Cara was much better suited to you, leave this woman, because Cara loves you, go back to her... I wouldn't have done that even if I thought so. But I didn't think so. Cara had tormented us; we were covered in wounds that were slowly festering. And I'm no saint, I had to accept that, I can't endure everything with unbroken love.

Strange as it may seem, I agreed with Cara that Tícia would leave Jack anyway; it was only a matter of time for me, too. Tícia was going to university, she was young, and I was sure she wanted to live. Jack was looking for a long-term relationship again, as always. They came from different worlds anyway. Tícia came from a strong middle-class British family, whose grandparents also lived in Great Britain, while Jack was a poor immigrant who might have been interesting and exotic for a while, but was unlikely to be a good match in any sense. I didn't trust Tícia, even though Jack kept insisting how well they got along – and they clearly did get along very well – but when Tícia still hadn't introduced Jack to her parents weeks later, I was sure that, harmony or not, this girl wasn't ready for a long-term relationship. I didn't want to upset Jack, but I did drop a few hints about the future and how Ticia's life would be very different when she went to university, but to no avail. Jack didn't get the message; he was living in a dream world and refused to be disabused of it. I was worried about the disappointment and heartbreak Jack would experience, but at the same time, I was infinitely grateful to Ticia for at least bringing Jack out of the paralysed, apathetic state he was in when they found each other. Because of her, Jack no longer thought that no one would ever want him. At least, he didn't think so for as long as their relationship lasted.

Elsie continued to come to us three times a week for four hours at a time, and it stayed that way all summer. She was with Jack on Mondays, Wednesdays, and Fridays from 2:30 to 6:30. Sometimes she came more than once, because when Cara had things to do, she would drop her little girl off at her father's for an hour or two. In July and August, it happened several times a week that Cara would call Jack after 10 p.m. to say she couldn't get Elsie to sleep, so Jack would take the baby for a few laps around the buildings by his car and then put her to bed at his place... Jack adored Elsie and was happy to help with anything and everything, anytime.

Cara clearly didn't care much about Elsie and treated her like a little girl treats her doll. When she felt like it, she would dress her up nicely, buy her funny and cheerful little clothes, put them on her, put a hairband with a bow on her little bald head, and put sandals on her feet. But she didn't cut her nails, she didn't bathe her, and she couldn't wash her hair either, and the best part was that she could justify it: She won't force the child, *"if she doesn't want to bathe, she won't bathe,"* and *„she cries a lot when washing her hair, she can't stand it, so I won't force her"* said Cara. Elsie had thick dandruff all over her head when she started coming to us regularly, which took three oil treatments over several weeks to get rid of. Elsie often came over dirty, in dirty clothes, with dried saliva and food residue on her neck, especially after long weekends when she was with her mother from Friday afternoon to early Monday afternoon. On those days, we always started the day with a bath. The little girl loved to bathe! Elsie's body often had purple marks, scratches, and abrasions, so I started taking photos after a while because they didn't look like typical toddler injuries. But I never sent the pictures to anyone, except before the child welfare investigation, and even then, only because the fingerprint-like purple marks on Elsie's arms and thighs were bothering me.

Elsie ate well; she loved fruit, vegetables, and everything else. She was a chubby baby, a kind of "solid delight," who always smiled when her tummy was full. But according to Cara, *"this child will never have a normal, beautiful figure and shape, she's as fat as a piglet"*... And *"she's getting worse and worse, she's unbearable, she would deserve to grow up in an orphanage instead"*.... These words and comments did hurt me a lot. But I did not say a word. Cara was „something else," and I've got it already. When he went to pick up Elsie, Jack always asked what she had eaten and when she would be hungry. Cara's answer was always:

"Why are you asking stupid questions? You'll notice when she's hungry," and *"She'll sleep when she's sleepy, you'll notice that too, because she falls asleep wherever she is,"* - Cara said and laughed. She laughed at how little Jack understood about small children when he asked her such questions. She probably thought Jack had little understanding, but that wasn't the case. Jack only asked about Elsie's daily routine.

I found it discouraging that the little girl had no daily routine, even though she was almost a year old.

Elsie was becoming increasingly adorable to us. She loved summer, water, the garden, and wanted to be outside whenever she could. She was already crawling on all fours without any problems, sitting up on her own and sitting confidently, and starting to eat and drink independently. Four hours is not very long, especially for a toddler under one year old who still sleeps once or twice a day. Elsie usually arrived at our house exhausted, often falling asleep in my arms or Jack's arms as soon as she arrived. But sometimes we could take her to the beach or into town, and we played a lot in the garden. Elsie also got to meet her cousin in mid-July, because my daughter Sophia came to visit us for two weeks with the little Viking. We had a wonderful time together.

Meanwhile, Cara kept trying to control Jack and the time he spent with Elsie. She always wanted to know where they were, what they were doing, and who they were with. She even watched our house to see if both our cars were parked there, because I kept getting messages from her in an imperative tone:

> *"Let his father be with the child. Why do you always have to be there with them when they're together?"*
> *"Elsie isn't going to you when I give her to Jack. She's not your child; I'm going to forbid you from seeing her."*

Cara started new relationships, but she was still very jealous of Jack. Tícia had only just appeared on the scene and wasn't even in a relationship with Jack when we celebrated my daughter Sophia's birthday. For her birthday, we had balloons to go with the cake, and they were in the window of the room facing the street because the little Viking and Sophia were staying there during their visit. As soon as the balloons went up in the window, Jack got a message from Cara. That same evening:

> *"How lovely of you to buy her balloons already! Who is that princess? Can I know her name?"*

Sophia watched a parenting series on Netflix, and the little Viking watched Peppa Pig cartoons every morning. Jack still had a joint subscription to this service with his ex-wife, so Cara saw the list of recently watched films and, of course, she had a message about that too:

> *"Did you get together with a mother of small children so that someone in your house could watch cartoons all the time? And films about parenting?"*

Cara was stalking Jack, but I wasn't even familiar with this word at that time, nor with the fact that Jack could report Cara to the Police for this behaviour. Jack wrote to his solicitor again, who wrote another letter to Cara's solicitor, asking her to tell her client to be a little more restrained in her communications. Cara's messages then became less frequent for a while. But they did not stop completely and permanently. We were being watched by Cara, who apparently had nothing else to do but know everything about us.

After a while, I got really fed up with the coercive control and the way Cara treated Elsie. I was afraid that Cara was serious about banning me from seeing my granddaughter, so I sought out legal advice and found a solicitor who wanted to arrange for me, as her grandmother, to have half a day or a few hours every week to spend with Elsie. However, before I could request this from the court, I had to mediate with Cara. I wouldn't have minded talking in front of a third party, but I suspected Cara wouldn't even respond to the mediator's letter. I was right, so I wasn't surprised. Cara completely ignored the mediator's official letter. So, I got the necessary certification and could have gone to court for visitation rights, but on my solicitor's advice, I didn't, because he thought it would irritate the court if two separate lawsuits were filed at the same time for the same child. Today, I'm not sure if my solicitor was right, but at the time, I didn't want to ruin Jack's chances in any way. Instead of mediation, I wrote a letter to Cara about our relationship, what it had been like in the past, and what I thought the future held. I wrote that I would support her in her work and further education if she decided to work or study, and I asked her not to take Elsie out of the country. It was a beautiful letter. My solicitor was quite moved by it and thought it was the right thing to do, so I sent it to Cara. There was no immediate response to the letter, but instead, Cara wrote a letter to Jack and me about love. She wrote about what she wanted and still wants, how we should love each other, and how sorry she is that everything has fallen apart, but – she added at the end of the letter – Jack and I are actually to blame for everything. Although she made many mistakes, we didn't love her well enough and were never really good to her... We didn't know what to say to this letter either.

It was Cara's birthday in mid-August. Although she did not respond to the offer of mediation, I tried to maintain a human relationship with her. I replied to her messages and asked her from time to time if she was okay. I thought about her often, even when she didn't write for a few days. Was she okay? Was she more balanced now? Now that Elsie was spending time with her father regularly, Cara had some free time. Was she able to relax and feel better about herself? Cara turned 21 that year. The 21st birthday is a big deal; in Anglo-Saxon countries, it marks the transition to adulthood. I often thought about what the policeman had said to Jack: "This girl just needs to grow up." If the policeman was right, then Cara would become more mature, and each birthday would bring her closer to adulthood. I wanted to let her know that I was thinking of her. I bought her a greeting card and a £30 gift card so she could buy herself something nice. I don't remember her reacting at the time. Later, she told the child welfare officer that she appreciated it, and the officer included this comment in the official report.

The court date was approaching.

We requested the information concerning Elsie from the social services department. This request is made as part of an official procedure, based on the principle that everyone has the right to know what the authorities have on file about them. Jack made a SAR request. It took a few weeks to receive the records, the GDPR. More than fifty pages he received. These included the social workers' notes and Jack's letters. We learned that Elsie had not been placed in a child protection programme or under supervision. This was both bitter and sweet. On the one hand, it is good that there are no serious problems and that no social worker is assigned to specifically monitor the child's welfare, as this suggests that at least one of the two parents is somewhat competent in performing their parental duties. On the other hand, the lack of supervision also meant that the social services did not take any of Jack's reports seriously. However, we learned that they had visited the mother several times, talked to her several times – and only to her – and based on these conversations, they concluded that the relationship between the mother and father was toxic. In this regard, the social workers also wrote that, as social workers, they believed it was in the child's best interests for the parents to remain separate and not continue living in the same household. This was painful to read, even though I agreed with it... And I was deeply saddened that Jack was not interviewed at all before this decision and declaration were made. Because this fact clearly implied that social services believed that the relationship was toxic primarily because of Jack. They only listened to Cara, and she said whatever she wanted... She could lie without restraint, saying whatever she wanted. The principle of "hearing both sides" was unknown to social services; at least they did not practise it.

Jack wanted to request the same information from the police, but it would likely be a much more complicated procedure, and the police file would not be ready by the hearing date, so we decided to postpone filing the request.

We waited for the guardianship interview. The guardianship investigation was scheduled for 12 weeks because the guardianship service needed to collect a wide range of background information on both parents. Mainly about the father's parental capacity and the mother's financial situation. I have no idea how they planned to measure parental capacity, but on the recommendation of one of the aid organisations, Jack took two online infant-care courses, just to be on the safe side. We waited for the child welfare services to visit us all summer long, thinking they would also conduct an environmental study and, if they wanted to assess the father's capacity, come and see how he treated the child when they were together in their own home... But no one came, no one knocked on the door, and no one called Jack until mid-August. Then someone called, and in a phone conversation lasting barely an hour, the child welfare services settled the investigation! Based on a phone conversation. It could have been anyone on the other end of the line. And they could have said anything. But even if they were 100% certain of Jack's identity, it remains incomprehensible how they could have formed an opinion about him from a single phone call.

They did the same with the mother. No environmental assessment, no one was interested in the circumstances in which the little child whose fate they were deciding lived. Yet the mother had cleared away the twenty bags of rubbish that had accumulated in her back garden, cleaned the flat until it sparkled, and furnished a separate room for the child in the first two weeks of August. An interpreter was provided for the mother's telephone interview at the taxpayers' expense, just as during the court hearings, so that the mother could better understand the questions asked and give accurate answers. However, it was not possible to ascertain the mother's financial situation, as another telephone conversation would have been required, and the interpreter was unavailable that day... Thus, it did not come to light that the mother lives solely on benefits, for which she regularly asks the father for additional support, amounting to £200-300 per month. It did not come to light that the parent deemed responsible was entirely financially dependent on the other parent for the child's care.

Six days before the hearing, the guardian finally put together his report and sent it to the court and the solicitors, who forwarded it to their clients. If the clients had any objections to the report, they could have challenged it in a petition within five days. Five days later, the day of the possible final hearing arrived, and no one wanted to postpone it.

The report contained the following important findings:

The guardianship authority did not support the mother's move abroad because it would have infringed on the father's rights. Due to the child's young age, the guardianship authority recommended that the child be placed with the mother and have regular contact with the father. The mother was instructed to care for the child, and the father was instructed to respect the mother. During the telephone interview, the mother complained that the father and his family did not treat her with sufficient respect and understanding. They were also overly critical of her...

The child welfare service did not investigate Elsie's injuries and requested reports from the health visitor and social services, who both considered that the mother was raising the child perfectly and that her injuries were age-appropriate and unavoidable...

The report also stated that child protective services did not conduct an environmental study because neither parent requested that it investigate the other parent's living circumstances. Furthermore, the parents had no doubts about the other parent's mental state, so no questions were asked in this regard, and no recommendations for further investigation were made.

With this report, the guardianship authority closed the investigation referred to as Section 7, which should be – and usually is – one of the most thorough screenings in the legal process of determining parental custody rights. I had no comment on this. Neither Jack had any comments. He was in shock.

THE FIFTH HEARING

The day of the hearing arrived. Cara sought a settlement, so the fact-finding hearing was ultimately cancelled. We later learned that this was at her solicitor's advice. Because Cara couldn't have won. All her accusations were based on lies, and she couldn't prove anything. She could have been labelled a malicious parent for her unfounded accusations and repeated rudeness, and she could have lost her parental custody rights. It is a pity that Jack did not know this, and it is also unfortunate that his lawyer did not advise him to insist on the fact-finding hearings, for he could have gained much from them... But the lawyer was also afraid. In this mother- and woman-centred society, it was impossible to know what the judge was thinking or what decision he might make. In the United Kingdom, even Johnny Depp failed to win his case, and, what's more, without legal support, we were unable to pursue another fact-finding hearing because we had no financial reserves left. Private legal services had already consumed all our money, and we didn't believe we could afford another hearing. The fact-finding hearing would have cost an additional £2,000-£3,000. So, Jack agreed to the settlement Cara offered: "Just let's get this over with!" said Cara, and asked Jack what he wanted to agree on. Then she drew up the agreement, and they went before the judge. Cara gave up on moving abroad with Elsie and decided to stay in the country, but she would travel abroad several times a year for 1-2 weeks at a time. Jack could spend almost half the time with Elsie; the little girl could sleep over at his place, and next year she could even go on holiday with him. They were nice promises, and I was curious to see which ones would come true and whether the judge would even allow such an agreement. I wished the judge would at least be suspicious and notice the contradictions: how did a violent, careless, drug-addicted husband suddenly become a partner who could be trusted with the child without supervision, even overnight? How could serious charges be withdrawn with a shrug of the shoulders in the space of a few months, with a simple "*oh, I didn't mean it after all*"? And how could a judge accept this without saying a word, without asking any questions? I would have liked at least a warning for Cara's false accusations, but most of all, I would have liked the judge to question whether something was wrong with the young lady and to order a detailed psychological examination of both parents, if needed, before making a decision! But none of this happened. Nothing like that happened at all. I suppose it was because the judge had had enough of two penniless immigrants in his country, in his court, talking nonsense and arguing over the life of a small child. They are both still very young, she may have thought to herself, it's good to put an end to this, it's a waste of money, especially taxpayers' money! It's not worth it for anyone.

The trial finally became a Final Hearing, lasted six hours, and the case was closed. The court made its final decision, and while it did so, I looked after Elsie. This court decision was supposed to last for 16 years, provided that the parents cooperated and there were no major changes in their lives. After the hearing, Jack's barrister congratulated him, said goodbye, but with a grimace on her face, stated, "Cara is a' big player'," and warned Jack to be careful in the future. Child custody cases do not usually return to court once a final decision has been made regarding the placement of children, but remain in effect until the children reach adulthood and everyone lives happily ever after. Within a few weeks, it became clear that this would not be the case for Jack and Cara. Jack's barrister was right. Cara was a big player.

PART III – THE COLLAPSE

LIES & CONFUSION

Cara was planning to travel with the little girl, Elsie, after the hearing to visit her parents again. The court allowed her two weeks, which was part of the settlement she had recommended, and the trip took place two weeks after the final hearing, when the decision was made.

The child was awarded to the mother, and Cara was granted a "live with" order. She had the final say on everything concerning the child, including who would be her family doctor and where she would go to school and nursery. Cara was also allowed to keep the little girl's passport and health record book. No one cared that she did not speak the country's language and therefore could not handle any of the matters entrusted to her. Not then, and not now. The servants of the law surely thought that the mother would learn English and then she would know what to do... How things would be until then, that was not their concern.

The father retained and exercised his parental rights and maintained contact with the child. The judge ruled that he could see the child three times per week, for at least eight hours per day, with increasing frequency of overnight stays. One month after the hearing, the father was allowed to spend one day and one night a week with his child; two months later, two days and two nights a week; and six months later, three days and three nights a week. Thus, on Mondays, Wednesdays, and Fridays, the little girl could be with Jack, and from the age of 20 months, her father could take her on holiday for no longer than two weeks. A prohibited steps order was also issued, stating that Elsie could not be moved abroad. The mother was entitled to take the child on holiday for up to two weeks, but the court order did not specify how many times a year she or the father could travel with the little girl.

Cara requested to leave immediately after the hearing, so the father was obliged to hand over Elsie's passport. Cara was required to present her return tickets before the trip and to specify exactly where she would be staying with the child during those two weeks. Street, house number, town name.

Regardless, Jack was not at ease. Cara behaved in a completely unpredictable manner; it was impossible to know what she was planning, what she was thinking, how she would act the next day, or whether she would do the exact opposite of what she had promised the day before. She was very angry with Jack because of Tícia's presence, sometimes accusing him in angry messages, sometimes trying to win Jack back. There were still no guarantees, especially not that Cara would come back with the little girl or that her family's influence would make her decide to stay abroad. If she travels abroad with court permission and her father's consent, the police will not take any action even if she does not return. The police will only take action if Cara leaves without her father's consent. In all other cases, only the Hague court can decide, and that process can take months, even if there is a final child custody order.

Jack and I celebrated Elsie's first birthday together, and Cara insisted that we celebrate together, so we went on a strange and forced outing to the zoo together, followed by pizza. The occasion was peaceful and lasted only a few hours. We all focused on the child to make sure she was happy. There were no loud arguments, emotional blackmail, or word games. Nothing that day. Finally. And three days later, Cara left.

After leaving the UK, it took her two days to contact us. She didn't write to say they had arrived safely and everything was fine; instead, she sent me a rather bizarre message about her doubts and concerns.

She repeated many times what she had said and written before: that she didn't believe us when we said that, when the little girl was with Jack or me, she didn't cry or look for her. She thought we were lying, or if she really didn't cry and didn't miss her mother, it could only be because I was secretly breastfeeding the child...That was Cara's conclusion. That I was breastfeeding my own granddaughter.

Wtf? – the good old Brit would say.

I thought about it for a few days. And I concluded that I was probably the cause of the problem, or at least part of it, because before they left, I told Cara how cute Elsie was, how many words she already knew, how many words she understood, that she knew what a dog, a cat and a bird, and I happily told her that she even knows the word boob. When her father is half-naked in the garden in the heat of summer, she points to his upper body and says "boobies", and what a clever little girl she is, because when she's in my arms at that moment, she immediately glances at my chest and pulls at my T-shirt and says "boobies" to me too... Well, I shouldn't have done that! Obviously, it was a mistake to mention the word "boobies" at all – I should have stuck to words like "dog", "kitty" and "bird"... but who knew, who would have thought that this could cause a problem?

I read the message six times, if not more, to make sure I was seeing what was written before I replied

> *"This may be disgusting, but I am just wondering, you're not giving her your boob, are you? Because you told me before we left. And now I keep thinking that you're giving it to her."* This is what Cara wrote me, continuing to share her concerns. *"If you are doing that, please stop because Elsie won't realise that someone has breasts unless they show them to her."*

I didn't know whether to cry or laugh, or maybe do both at the same time? A few months earlier, I read an article in a group on a social networking site on cultural anthropology, which has always interested me, and it talked about how, in certain cultures, it is still common practice for family members, especially younger or older female relatives, to help young mothers feed their newborns and babies by breastfeeding them. I was quite surprised by this, so I researched how it was possible and shared my thoughts with my daughter. Sophia even joked with me that if she ever has a baby, this will come in handy! We had a good laugh about it. But thank God I never mentioned this article to Cara, nor did I tell her what I thought about it. So now I had no idea how Cara arrived at all this. Where did she get this idea? We live in a Western, civilised European country where this is not a practice or a custom. I am 55 years old. My grandchildren are the greatest joy in my life; you could say they are my greatest source of happiness. However, it would never have occurred to me to feed them any other way than with a bottle or a small spoon... After a few minutes, I replied to Cara:

"Of course I wouldn't give it to her! I never said anything like that! Why would I give Elsie my breast? How could you even think such a thing? It's really disgusting that you think that about me... I'm Elsie's grandmother. How could you think that about me?"

Cara wrote a rather unusual apology and, with great difficulty, returned to the subject several times, but ultimately we dropped it.

> *"I don't think that about you. I just asked you not to give it to her, okay? I'm truly sorry if I hurt your feelings. Elsie cried to my mother today, and I told her off for giving Elsie her breast, and she said the same as you that I shouldn't say things like that to her, that she should give her granddaughter her breast. She also said that I'm sick in the head. I should go get myself checked out."*

"I think you're just misunderstanding things, Cara. But I don't know why", I responded, and I tried to comfort her. "How are you, by the way? Is the weather nice there?"

> *"Everything's fine, yeah, it's raining."* Cara responded, but she continued: *"I'll never know because she doesn't talk... But I think a mother knows her child so well that*

> *she can tell that Elsie doesn't touch her boobs unless someone tells her to or shows her, because Elsie was looked after by a woman for hours and didn't touch anyone's boobs because she didn't know that anyone else had them except me, because that's how she grew up with me! Interestingly, she touched yours... She never touched my mum's until she told her to! I just don't know if it would be too harsh to give it to her, and I'm not saying this to hurt you; we just need to talk about it. And I'm sorry to say this, honestly, I just don't want anyone else to give her the boob, but part of me also knows that you won't give it to her because you'd have to be pretty sick to give your child's boob to someone else. I'm stupid for now...*

"Elsie doesn't cry when she's being put to sleep at our house; she falls asleep easily in her father's arms or mine, we just have to rock her and sing to her. She falls asleep easily; she doesn't need anything else. She never cries." I wrote this to Cara to reassure her, as my final word. She didn't reply. The next day, Cara raised another matter that was more important to her. It was about not leaving Elsie alone in her room when she was staying with us, because Cara was sure that if we had done so, some demon would possess Elsie. She attached a video from some unknown channel to her message the next day, which I didn't even watch because I don't believe that demons possess little children when they are left alone in a room to sleep. I didn't reply much to Cara's message, just saying OK.

"Elsie never sleeps alone; there is always someone nearby." That was all I wrote to her, and I was quietly glad she had dropped the "*grandmother breastfeeding her grandchild*" topic.

But six months later, the same breastfeeding issue arose again, and this time, Cara spoke with Jack about it, and the narrative was completely different. Cara told Jack that she caught her own mother trying to breastfeed Elsie and that she had a big fight with her about it. According to Cara, her mother was very embarrassed and defended herself by saying that she was just curious to see if the little girl would accept her breast.

Jack told me the story indignantly on the day Cara told him, and he was completely upset by it. He was only partially aware of the background and did not know or remember what Cara had written to me in her messages six months earlier – completely contradictory things – including that her mother had told her there was something wrong with her head and suggested she see a doctor...

So confusing. And we will never know the truth. Nor will we know where or how the idea entered Cara's mind that either of her grandmothers would breastfeed Elsie. Just because I mentioned to her once in conversation that, among many other words, Elsie already knew the word "boob"? And why? Why was she so preoccupied with this question that she came up with various narratives about it? God only knows. Somehow, I found the whole story, Cara's way of thinking, as it was, morbid. What's more, when this first came up as an accusation against me, Cara hadn't been breastfeeding for months. Elsie already had four teeth, ate everything, and Cara had lost significant weight; her milk had dried up. She complained about this several times. Cara did give her breast to her daughter for comfort, but Elsie was already weaning and knew other techniques to help her fall asleep. Was the thought that someone else would feed her baby born out of fear, or out of sadness that she could no longer breastfeed? What was the reason she even thought of such a thing? Only a psychologist could answer that question.

Ruth, my friend, who is a psychiatrist, gave me an answer again and explained clearly how she thought this idea had developed in Cara's mind:

"Cara subconsciously knows and feels that you are nurturing Elsie – even if not with breast milk, but you are nurturing and developing her and giving her something that she would like to give her, but perhaps she cannot or is not yet able to give her. The little girl is visibly developing and blossoming when she is with you," said Ruth, and added that she believed Cara was jealous of this.

According to Ruth, I should neither take this seriously nor take it literally. Perhaps I should have taken Cara's accusation about breastfeeding figuratively, but it was difficult to do so because Cara gave specific examples, based on things I myself had told her, and they were very physical examples. The word "boob" was mentioned, and the finger was pointed.

Apart from this episode, Cara was in a good mood and remained on relatively good terms with me during this time, sending me a photo of Elsie every other day, along with a few sentences about where they were and how they were spending their time.

Until 22 September, everything went well, but then Cara went silent. She didn't write or send any photos. I asked if everything was okay, but Cara didn't reply; in fact, she didn't even read my messages. She, who was constantly on her phone, had suddenly disappeared from the internet. Of course, I was terrified and started to worry. Cara didn't write anything for three whole days. When she finally got in touch, she said her phone had broken because Elsie had been pressing buttons all over the place and had dropped it, so she had to take it in for repair. I didn't quite believe her. On the fourth day, Cara admitted that Elsie had been ill.

"Elsie was quite ill, but now she's fine. Don't worry", Cara wrote. But she added that the little girl had had a high fever and had to go to see the doctor...

First Breach of the Court Order

Cara was supposed to return with Elsie on the 26th, but instead of reassuring messages saying they were already on the plane, Jack received phone calls that morning. Cara called and told him, in a flustered voice, that they were already at the airport, but Elsie's passport had been left in Cara's stepfather's car, so – surprise, surprise – they weren't being allowed on the plane. Jack was devastated and angry. Cara called me too, and I immediately set about finding another flight for them. There was a flight that afternoon, and the ticket only cost 50 euros. I even offered to pay for it, just so they could board that plane. But Cara refused – what was I thinking? She wasn't going to wait at the airport until the afternoon. Elsie was sick and cranky, and her stepfather had already left to pick them up. They would come home on one of the upcoming days, and she would look for tickets as soon as she got back to her mother's flat. I sent her screenshots of various flights all afternoon. None of them was suitable because they were either too early, too late, or too expensive. Besides,

> *"I haven't had any money left either,"* Cara messaged me, *"if it's important to Jack that we get home as soon as possible, then he should pay for the tickets."*

"Of course." I thought bitterly.

Finally, four days later, they managed to board an early-morning flight.

Cara then begged Jack not to take her back to court over this incident. "Everyone makes mistakes!" she said, and she was sorry she had left her passport in her stepfather's car, but "it could happen to anyone!" Jack was quietly furious:

"No, it doesn't happen to anyone!" he muttered to himself, but in the end, he didn't report the matter to the court.

Other, bigger problems arose. Upon her return, Elsie was really sick. She lost about two kilos in two weeks and had a severe fungal infection on her bottom. The day after they arrived, Jack took the little girl to the doctor. Elsie was given antibiotics and Nystatin because her mouth was also full of fungus, and the doctor prescribed a special cream for her bottom.

The next day, when Jack went to pick her up, Elsie happily climbed into her father's arms. Now that she was over a year old, it didn't even occur to him that she might not recognise him after a two-week holiday. She happily came to us at the time ordered by the court. She slept well and ate well with us, and it took four weeks for the sores on her little bottom to disappear, only to return occasionally when she caught a virus and her immune system broke down. At those times, she was always given antibiotics, which caused her fungal infection to reappear again and again. I started giving her Sambucol, elderberry syrup, to strengthen her immune system. She grimaced at it at first, but later grew to like the sour syrup.

I found a music-and-sensory group, and we began taking her to a children's community program. Elsie thoroughly enjoyed the sessions and made rapid progress, but she remained behind for her age, particularly in gross motor skills. At 15 months, she was not yet walking, but she was crawling on all fours and standing beside tables and chairs. She gradually began to regain weight.

We contacted the health visitor, but she remained extremely hostile toward Jack and responded only in a condescending, patronising manner, if she deigned to respond at all. Jack took Elsie for her vaccinations because Cara still didn't speak English, and Jack wanted to know if the little girl was developing well. He also wanted to be present for her one-year check-up, but the health visitor refused, stating that the father could attend the examinations only if the mother consented. Which was absolutely untrue and unfair. Jack had and still has parental custody, but the health visitor chose to ignore this fact for some reason. She said that the fungal infection, which was very difficult to cure and kept coming back, was "a quite common problem", meaning that it was a fairly widespread and common problem. She explained Elsie's repeated illnesses by saying that children nowadays have weaker immune systems due to the coronavirus. ... I didn't argue with the health visitor – she wouldn't have listened to me anyway, as I'm "just the grandmother" and I have no right to speak about my grandchild – even though I had good reason to. But soon, other, new, and more serious problems arose.

In the middle of the whirlwind

It was late October when Cara sent a message to both Jack and me one afternoon. The message included an ultrasound scan showing that Cara was 17 weeks pregnant. She claimed that the baby could only be Jack's because she had no other partner at the time of conception. (Which was not true, because she's had. She also shared their photo on social media and with Jack.) Cara wrote that she had gone for the ultrasound scan with her new boyfriend, because she thought she was only 7-8 weeks pregnant and that the baby was from her new partner. The sonographer's measurements revealed that her pregnancy was much further along, so the foetus was probably not conceived in her new relationship. I reacted to Cara's message as I usually did. I sat beside my kitchen table, staring at the phone screen, paralysed, frozen, muttering to myself that this couldn't be true! This is impossible, it can't be! The sound of Jack's footsteps rushing down the stairs startled me out of my stupor. He stopped in the middle of the kitchen and looked at me, pale as death.

- "Did you get it too? What did Cara send me? Her message," he asked, stammering. I nodded.
- "But I don't believe it! Do you hear me, Mum? This child isn't mine; I didn't want to give this woman another child. I don't want it!"
- "It seems you're a little bit late thinking about that, son," I replied softly
- "But I don't want it! I won't accept it, and I don't want it! I don't want this child!"
- "It's too late for that now," I said, and suddenly felt very tired. "If the child is yours, then it will be your responsibility to take care of it. And whether it's yours or not will be revealed as soon as it's born."

I leaned on the kitchen table and buried my face in my hands.

"I can't believe it, damn it, this can't be happening! This can't be happening, or if it is, it can't be happening to us!" I muttered to myself. Everything was just falling into place, things were just calming down, we could finally relax, and then this...

Jack searched for a cigarette on the kitchen counter, and when he found it, he lit it with a trembling hand on the gas stove.

- "But I didn't want this! What am I going to tell Ticia now? I must tell her. I can't keep it from her because she'll find out sooner or later. What will she say?"
- "Well, that's a good question. But that will come out too. You shouldn't rush to tell her, though. Cara weighs forty kilos; she

may not even be able to carry this baby to term, and it may not even be your child. I would wait before telling anyone the news."

That's what I advised Jack to do. Of course, he didn't take my advice. The next day, he told Tícia what had happened, which was too much for her, and she broke up with Jack almost as soon as she heard the news. I was almost certain that this would happen. For some time, I had felt that Ticia was just looking for an excuse to break up with Jack – their relationship had become very strained in recent weeks – and she couldn't have found a more perfect excuse. It suited her perfectly.

Jack was completely devastated. For days, weeks, he wandered around the house like a ghost, like a shadow. The gay guys at work tried to cheer him up, but I couldn't do anything to calm him down. He made suicidal statements, couldn't sleep at night, couldn't get up in the morning, "Why did I even wake up?" He kept saying, and I was really worried about him. He began to hate Cara immensely, which worried me too, because I thought he already had no feelings for her.

Jack told Cara that he would not simply accept that he was the child's father, that a DNA test would be necessary if he wanted to be the father of this child, who had been conceived against his will, and that he had not yet decided, but that Cara should not count on his support at all. Jack was surprisingly firm, clear, and direct, perhaps for the first time in his life, and this shocked Cara.

"Jack doesn't want this child," she wrote to me with a sad smiley, and I felt a strong temptation to ask her: - Why, what did you expect? - But I didn't do that. Instead, I wrote

"I'm sorry, he told me that too."

Cara was 17 weeks pregnant. I did the math: Cara got pregnant at the end of June, when she was already in another relationship and was begging Jack for a goodbye sex. Who knew whose baby it was? Who knew if she had realised, she was pregnant earlier and just kept quiet about it, kept it a secret? Who knew how much of this whole story was intentional? I was inclined to think that, like everything else in Cara's life, this pregnancy was just part of the manipulation she had always practised over us. Especially over Jack. I found it hard to imagine that she hadn't realised she was pregnant for more than three months. We live in the 21st century, for God's sake!

My son was not in a good state of mind, to put it mildly, but he was tenacious and tough. He was composed. Still. And determined. At least he knew exactly what he wanted and what he didn't want. He wanted to live in peace, not in a war zone, under constant control. He decided not to move back in with Cara, even if she was pregnant, even if she was expecting his child, and even if the child was born and Cara could pretend for months that she had changed.

With Tícia's departure, Jack found himself in a vacuum, floating there. He lived from visit to visit, being himself when Elsie came to see him and going to work in between. For Jack, work had always been like therapy, so in addition to his main job, he took on many shifts at an agency.

Elsie slept at our place for the first time in the second week of October. We were worried about how it would go, but Elsie slept through the night on her first visit, woke up smiling, and played happily with her toys. Later, we established a good routine for the little girl. In the afternoons, we played with her a lot, mostly outside, where she got tired. Then we fed her dinner, bathed her, and took her to her room, where she could play a little more before we took out her books and read to her. When we turned on the music box, she knew it was time to go to bed. There she drank her milk from her bottle. The music box was a fantastic, wonderful little device! In addition to classic lullabies and classical music, it also had recordings of so-called white noise, the sound of water flowing, rain, crickets chirping, and birds chirping, "noises" that have been scientifically proven to have a calming effect on the human nervous system. Elsie loved the sound of owls hooting and the rustle of leaves in the trees most of all. She always fell asleep very easily and quickly. Either Jack or I slept next to her on a mattress laid out next to her cot.

We looked forward to Mondays and later Wednesdays, when we could spend a full 24 hours with the little girl. Jack took her to the playhouse, shopping, to the park, and to the petting zoo—we took her everywhere with us. Elsie was a very reserved, fearful little girl, and at first, she often burst into tears when she saw new places and new faces. She was completely unsocialised. Cara took her to a nearby playground at most, where she hardly interacted with anyone. It took a few weeks for Elsie to become completely confident, greeting even strangers and new faces with a smile.

Cara constantly threatened and tried to keep Elsie with her, not to hand her over. Or she handed her over, but not on time. We wanted to start baby ballet again, but Cara found out we'd been taking Elsie there and never handed her over on time, so we always missed the classes. However, Cara didn't know about the music and sensory group, which started later, so we were able to go there every week. Jack also started taking Elsie swimming, and she loved splashing around. She ate well and slept through the night. She became a lively, happy little toddler. She loved dogs and cats, and said her first words at 14 months: doggy, kitty, Nana, and Daddy.

Cara's pregnancy was progressing, and because she asked me to, I took her to the GP and midwife for her appointments. Cara hoped Jack would move back in with her because of her pregnancy, and she was delighted that Jack and Tícia had broken up. She didn't realise that Tícia had left because of her and that Jack hated her twice as much because of it. Cara used me to get information about Jack, who had completely cut her out of his life by then. I knew Cara was using me and only asking me to drive her around so she could stay in touch with Jack through me. I played along. This was partly because we couldn't be sure that the baby she was carrying wasn't Jack's, in which case, as I told Jack, it would be our duty to take care of her, and partly because I am a nurse and a woman myself. As a nurse, I had learned, and it was also my principle, that we should not leave a pregnant woman alone. Besides, Cara had my grandchild, whom I did not want to lose sight of. And probably also because I still loved her, in some measure. I have no idea why. I had no reason to love her anymore. But I still did. And when she complained that she no longer had any trousers that fit her, I happily rushed out to buy her maternity trousers, vitamins, and sweets... Someone will explain this, my behaviour too, if they know how. Why did I still love and feel sorry for someone who had treated my son and me so cruelly, more than anyone else ever had?

From September onwards, Cara regularly asked Jack and me for money. She sent two or three messages a month saying that Elsie had run out of formula and nappies and that she had no money, and that they were both starving. Jack paid child support, but even with all the benefits and Jack's support, Cara never had enough money to last until the end of the month. Jack regularly did her shopping and cared for Elsie. Cara's social worker sued Jack for family allowance, the child benefit, the meagre £83 a month that had been paid into Jack's account for a few months, because Cara was not entitled to it, but no money was enough for Cara.

Dark winter nights reloaded

In December, Elsie finally started walking, and her first steps were touching; there was no happier little child on earth at that moment! By then, she could clap her hands, and it became her habit to laugh and clap her hands whenever something made her happy. Her face took on a proud little expression as she clapped and laughed. I think she considered it a real milestone that she could now change position just like the grown-ups do! And from the moment she stood up and started walking, Elsie never crawled on all fours again, even when she was tired. She loved to walk on the street, on the beach, and she hardly ever asked to be carried in her father's arms, wanting to practise walking with all her might. Elsie began to grow into a very conscious, intelligent, clever, and very well-organised little child who followed systematic patterns and behaviours. She enjoyed the routine, knowing what was going to happen next: playing after lunch, taking a bath in the evening, and happily curling up in her bed, hugging her music box, which projected colourful stars onto her room's ceiling along with white noise. Elsie loved books and stories, began to imitate words, and talked more and more. She arranged her toys in rows, knew where everything was and where it belonged, and loved to keep things tidy around her. When I did the washing up, she joined me; when I swept the floor, she asked for the broom and tried to help. She paid close attention to everything and observed everything carefully. She became increasingly skilled at handling objects, and her fine motor skills developed rapidly.

Rats moved into Cara's house, into the children's room, in December. She sent pictures and a video of the rodents emerging from under the floor and asked me to help because they were scratching the boards and the wall, and she was terribly afraid of falling asleep. She wrote that she was keeping Elsie beside her in bed so nothing would happen to her. I referred Cara to her social worker, telling her that he would help, and recommended a commercially available rat poison that she could safely place in the room. Cara said the rats came from the neighbouring house, that the neighbours were responsible for the situation, and that it was definitely not the rubbish piled up in her garden next to the kitchen that was keeping the rats there. The health visitor said that this was not a problem, that rats were everywhere, that they were commonplace in the neighbourhood, and that many families struggled with similar problems in winter... I did not comment on this, only to myself. And I cursed the day we moved to this place. Not because of the rats. But I was sure professionals in the capital would have a different opinion and approach to this issue. But I didn't know what to do. It was no use when Lynn, the midwife, told me to be my grandchild's voice and if I noticed anything that wasn't right, to speak up and speak for her. There was nowhere to talk, no one to tell. I'm just the grandmother, and I have no rights whatsoever in matters concerning my grandchild, as the officials told me and as Cara has repeatedly made clear to me. I had no right to speak up.

I tried to pay attention to Elsie and focus all my energy on making sure that when she was spending time with her father and me, my granddaughter was happy and got everything she needed.

Christmas was approaching, and Jack and I planned to visit my older son, Joe, who lived not too far away, two counties away, with Elsie. Cara tried to prevent this, making threats and trying to distract him with questions about how he would hand Elsie over to Jack and for how long, but thankfully, the court order specified the Christmas visitation times in detail, so Jack only had to remind Cara what she was supposed to do. Cara was afraid of the court and feared that if their case went back to court, she would lose Elsie. Cara, with some difficulty, had been complying with the court order since September. And so, we arrived at Uncle Joe's, where he was finally able to meet his niece, almost exactly a year after he had planned to do so when he came to visit us in vain.

Uncle Joe and his new fiancée, Aunt Camilla, were expecting their first child and welcomed Elsie with boundless love. We spent a wonderful afternoon and evening together, compensating ourselves for not being able to go home to my elderly father for the holidays...

For Christmas, Cara bought me gifts, perfume, and other fragrances, and I paid for the 4D ultrasound.

After the 4D ultrasound and the strange conversation that followed, Cara and I did not meet in person again, but we exchanged short messages on chat. I asked her how she was, if she needed any help, when she was going for her check-ups, and if everything was okay. Cara replied when she had time and always wrote when she needed £40-50.

Cara entrusted Elsie to Jack more and more because she was tired, and they discussed officially changing the visitation schedule so that Elsie could sleep at Jack's for an extra day and Jack could take on childcare duties one Sunday every two weeks. They tried to reach an agreement: Jack wrote to his solicitor; Cara wrote to hers. They were ready to petition the court to change the child-custody arrangement as part of their parenting plan. It seemed that there was complete consensus between them.

But then, at thirty weeks pregnant, Cara decided she wanted to go home to her parents with Elsie for a while. She said it would be for two weeks. But Jack did not agree to this because he did not think it was safe for Cara, who was in an advanced stage of pregnancy, to take Elsie with her on a seven-hour train-and-plane journey with her belly. He also didn't agree because Cara had mentioned to him a few times before that she didn't want to give birth to her second child here, in this country. Jack thought it likely that if Cara left, she would not return until the baby was born, because she would not be able to board the return flight after a certain point, as most airlines would not allow her to travel. It wouldn't be Cara's fault that she couldn't come back, and she would have a good reason for why she "had" to stay there; no one would blame her for it. If that happened, Jack wouldn't see Elsie for a long time, two or three months. Knowing this, Jack couldn't agree to Cara's trip. This, of course, led to another minor war. Jack offered Cara alternatives, such as saying he would be happy to look after Elsie so that Cara could travel home without any worries, but Cara did not agree, so Jack turned to his solicitor for advice on what to do. The solicitor wrote a letter warning Cara of the court order and urging her to ensure the father retained parental custody and access rights. I received another lovely message from Cara, because, of course, she thought I was behind everything:

> "*You know what, I hope you never dare to look me in the eye again and never come near me! You persuaded your son to go to court, which is really sad. Shame on you for doing this again! Maybe you weren't happy when you were young, and I hope that what is happening to me now will happen to your daughter too, so that you will realise that this is not humane.*
>
> *I will not teach Elsie to be bad, she will see for herself what kind of people you are, and as soon as she can talk, it will be easier for me, because then you will not be able to lie that she is in a bad place with me, or lie that you do not sleep with her, which is disgusting, it is disgusting that you sleep with her. And the other thousand lies you talk about me! I'll tell you one thing, you know what, 1. if your son takes me back to court, then know that you've ruined this again, just like you ruined everything before 2. In the worst-case scenario, I will win, because I am no longer stupid enough to make a deal with your son. I will see this through until I can go home with my children, because I don't think I will stay here after all this. 3. And it will be easier for me to go home because now I have two children and I am alone with them.*
>
> *Don't write to me anymore, and don't try to mess with me. I hope one day you come to your senses and realise that what you're doing is evil. That this child will grow up with court, court, court, because that's what you're like! Delete my number, but if I hear even once that I'm*

> *to blame because I'm going to fight now, then you'll get to know me properly, especially you."*

Great. There was no mention of court, only between them, and even then, only in relation to an agreement, but that's not a problem. Jack saw through her plans and what she was playing at, how she was trying to outsmart him, but Cara didn't even think Jack was capable of seeing through her. She assumed that I had warned Jack, so once again, I was to blame for everything; I was the disgusting one and the liar. We were cursed again (this time, my poor daughter too) and threatened that if we dared to say anything bad about her, she would leave and take the children with her, and that now, this time, she would win, she would be able to leave. " We would get to know her properly," she said, especially me. Well, thank you. I already knew her well enough. It made me sad enough to get to know her and realise that nothing had changed, probably nothing will ever change.

After that, we talked even less, even on chat. Cara's mental state probably deteriorated as her second pregnancy progressed, just as it had with her first, when she was pregnant with Elsie. At the end of January and beginning of February, she even made comments to Jack that she wished this child would just die in her womb... "*Because nobody wants this child,*" Cara said. And if it is born and Jack is not the baby's father, she will not keep it; she will send it to Austria because she does not want to take care of it. "*I will love it, but I don't want to take care of it. My mother will raise it. I want to live now. I won't even breastfeed it. I've had enough! And Elsie, too. Elsie is so bad, I can't stand her. She hits my stomach; it'll be a miracle if the baby survives. But even if it's born, Elsie might kill it. If this child is yours, you'd better know now that you're going to raise it, because I don't want it!*" she wrote to Jack.

It was awful to hear, see, and read these messages.

I tried to remain invisible, but every two or three days, I asked Cara on chat if she needed anything. She responded according to her mood at the time, or sometimes didn't respond at all. She kept sending Jack messages saying they were starving, so Jack went shopping for them regularly.

Cara once asked me to buy her chicken, tomatoes, and bread, promising to give me the money back, as usual. How lucky that I didn't delete her number as she asked me to, right?

Cara regularly passed Elsie on to Jack at the weekends because she was tired and couldn't cope with her. Elsie was becoming more and more confident, climbing on everything, a real little toddler who was interested in everything in the world. She needed a lot of attention. There was still no baby gate on the stairs in Cara's house, and they were very steep, so on sleepless nights, Jack and I had a terrible obsession that Elsie would fall them one day... Jack wrote to social services, asking for the health visitor's help. In his letter, he wrote that he would be happy to buy a baby gate for the stairs and pay for someone to install it, but no one responded to his request. After the third letter, the health visitor finally promised to take action, but nothing happened for months.

Cara's strange behaviour

Around this time, Jack received a strange message from Cara, which Jack forwarded to me, and I kept and saved the screenshot on my phone. Cara sometimes asked how Elsie had slept and whether she had cried a lot. Jack always reassured her that Elsie had slept happily, never cried, and slept through the night without any problems. But for some reason, Cara never believed it. In this screenshot of her saved message, she advised Jack on how to help Elsie fall asleep quickly and how to calm her down if she cried before falling asleep or didn't want to go to sleep. The message read: "*If she doesn't want to fall asleep, stroke her down there, down below; she really likes that. She always asks me to take off her nappy and stroke her down there. She falls asleep quickly then.*" Jack showed me the message, shocked. He just replied that Elsie was already asleep, that she always fell asleep easily, and had never needed such comforting. I saved the message without knowing that Jack would one day need it very much.

At the bottom of the vortex

In February, Cara's gas and electricity were cut off because she hadn't paid her bills. She had accumulated considerable debt, which she claimed she was unaware of. The social worker in charge of council housing arranged for her debt to be written off or suspended, and Cara was given a pay-as-you-go meter. She couldn't even pay that, so she went without heat and electricity for days. Even though she regularly left Elsie with Jack when she wanted to sleep, rest, or go shopping, on the days when there was no heating in the house, she didn't ask Jack to take the little girl to his place until the situation was resolved. Instead, she sent photos of Elsie sleeping in a coat and hat in the cold room...

I knew her, but I no longer understood Cara, and perhaps I no longer wanted to understand her. She was alone, bored, and for me, the whole situation was incomprehensible, unimaginable, perhaps because I had never been bored in my life. Cara may have also been lonely, I understood that, but I didn't understand why she was bombarding Jack with every means possible to get him to move back in with her and restart their relationship.

"Now we're going to have two children!" – Cara kept saying.

But Jack had made it clear to her months ago that it was over between them, and after Cara got pregnant against Jack's will, Jack explained to her clearly that her new pregnancy did not change the facts; quite the contrary. Jack also told Cara several times that he would help raise the children and would support her in every way, but there would be nothing else between them because he had had enough of what they had already been through together. And I didn't understand, Cara, how she could expect a man she called crippled and shit, whom she humiliated and blackmailed every day, to go back to her. I just didn't understand it! I remained convinced that she was sick, that she was mentally unhealthy, that she was seriously damaged, because everything pointed to that. And I would rather believe that she was sick than that she would be consciously and deliberately evil. I felt sorry for Cara, but pity no longer dominated me when I thought of her; instead, I tried to think with her almost incomprehensible mind, what she was planning, what I could expect from her. And sometimes thoughts came to mind that frightened me. There were nights when I couldn't sleep because I was so afraid for Elsie. I thought Cara was capable of everything. Anything. Even hurting her.

In the first week of March, Cara's messages became more frequent. She wanted to know how she could finally get rid of her pregnancy and asked me about inducing labour. She was due to give birth at the end of March, and when she started writing to me, she had just reached 36 weeks of pregnancy. I replied that I couldn't help her with that. Babies are born when the time is right, when they need to be born, and it usually doesn't work out well when someone tries to force the birth. I offered Cara some folk wisdom, things that I knew couldn't do any harm: eat pineapple, curry dishes, go for walks, drink raspberry leaf tea, and look around maternity blogs to see what else she could do. She probably looked around too, because she started writing messages to Jack saying that sex was the only thing that would help her finally give birth to the baby... Jack rolled his eyes and made comments. Things like, he didn't know where Cara lost her mind, what she might be going through when she wrote things like that to him, and above all, why she wouldn't leave him alone. I bought Cara some pineapple and left it at her house, by the front door, one afternoon. I also ordered her raspberry leaf tea on Amazon and had it shipped directly to her address. On one hand, I understood Cara. I still remember how heavy and long a pregnancy could be; in the end, I could not wait for the labour to start with my children. But on the other hand, I couldn't get it, how somebody wants to induce her own labour before term, where there is an obvious risk for the newborn being born prematurely, having breathing difficulties.

At the end of February, Cara's mother made a surprise announcement that she was finally coming to visit her daughter after three years. She asked Jack and me to pick her up from the airport, a four-hour drive away. Even if it hadn't been so far away, we wouldn't have gone to pick her up, and we didn't understand why she was asking us to do so. Why us? How could she even think of such a thing? There could be only one reason for this: Cara had not been honest with her (either). We thought it most likely that Cara hadn't told her mother that she and Jack had been living apart for months and couldn't repair their relationship... Jack's mother-in-law probably knew nothing about the real situation. She was due to arrive a week before the scheduled birth date, as planned.

But in the second week of March, events accelerated. Cara had more and more intense contractions and became increasingly irritable and excitable. She went to the hospital every two or three days, but they sent her home every time.

> *"This baby is just messing with me*!" she wrote to Jack. *"Everything hurts, one day it wants to come, the next day it doesn't!"*

Cara asked Jack if labour started before her mother arrived, he should go to the hospital with her "if he wanted to". Jack had mixed feelings about this. Why should he be there when the baby might not even be his? But what if it were his baby? Maybe it would be better if he were there? What do I think about this? He asked me and asked all his close friends who knew about his life the same thing. Some said they definitely wouldn't go. "If this child is Jack's, it will be born against his will, so why should he be there?" Others said he should be there when the baby was born because they were sure that when Jack saw the baby, he would know and feel whether it was his or not! Most of those who held this view were Jack's female friends. Jack asked me too, and I thought about it for days, wondering how to answer. Finally, I told him that he had nothing to lose by going to the hospital with Cara and that, in my opinion, no one should be left alone when they are in such a vulnerable situation. I put it more bluntly than that. I told Jack that I don't even leave my dog and cat alone when they give birth... Jack finally weighed up the opinions and decided to accompany Cara.

I was waiting for this baby. And I felt very sorry for her, even if she was my grandchild, even if she wasn't. My aunt was also a midwife, and when I was expecting my own children, she often told me to be careful about what I thought and how I felt, because a foetus senses everything in its mother's womb and is affected by everything. I couldn't imagine what this little baby must have felt when Cara said things like she wished it would just die inside her... And when she tried for days to induce labour herself to finally get rid of it...

At the end of the second week of March, one early afternoon, Cara's waters broke, and her amniotic fluid leaked out. Jack immediately brought Elsie to me and took Cara to the hospital. Later, I went to work for the night shift, waiting for developments. Cara was sent home early in the evening again because she wasn't having any contractions, but she didn't want to keep Elsie with her because she didn't know what to expect during the night and when she would have to go back to the hospital. Jack stayed with Elsie, and I left home. I had barely arrived at work when Cara sent me a message, and from then on, she stayed in constant chat contact throughout my entire shift. I downloaded a contraction-monitoring app so I could get some work done. Cara sent me the measurements. At four in the morning, I texted her to go to the hospital, but I only did so because I felt she was very scared. By then, her contractions had become regular, and according to the measurements Cara sent me, they were already five minutes apart. Her amniotic fluid was leaking continuously, so I asked her to put in a pad so I could see what colour it was, and she sent me photos of that too. The amniotic fluid was clear, with pink smudges on the pad as her cervix dilated, but Cara thought the pink smudges were blood and was frightened by them. I thought it would be better for her to go to the hospital, where they could monitor her. At six o'clock in the morning, she texted me that she had been examined and her cervix was five centimetres dilated. They told her the baby would be born that morning, so I rushed home to wake up Jack. It was Cara's second delivery, so who knew how fast it would be?

Jack arrived at the hospital around 9 a.m. and found Cara still in the examination room; she hadn't even been taken to the labour ward yet. Cara's cervix was only three centimetres dilated, so she wasn't even in active labour yet. I didn't understand why she lied! Again. What was the point of that?

At noon, Cara was taken to the labour ward, where she was pretty much left alone and told to walk around as much as she could and not lie down. Jack walked with her in the corridors. At three o'clock in the afternoon, Cara was taken to the delivery room with a 9 cm dilation. Lilly was born a few minutes before six o'clock. She weighed exactly the same as Elsie. A little bit less than 3 kilograms.

Jack came home upset. I had to go back to work. I had been looking after Elsie all day; I hadn't slept, and another night shift lay ahead of me. Jack was upset and frustrated, saying that they, the midwives, had treated him very strangely, constantly watching him as if they thought he was suspicious, with the midwives keeping a close eye on him. It was also strange that, when Jack had to interpret the doctor's instructions, they kept asking Cara whether Jack had said exactly what he was supposed to say, and she was asked several times whether she had understood everything correctly. When Elsie was born, they didn't treat him like that, Jack said. But then he understood the whole thing. At one point, Cara asked him to open the window a little; beside it stood the midwife's desk. When Jack went over to it, he saw the notes on the desk saying that the child was born into an abusive relationship. The document sat atop the pregnancy record book, and its text was printed in capital letters. Then Jack understood why everybody was watching him and why they were looking at him so strangely. And he was completely shaken that, even though they didn't know him, everybody considered him to be an abuser... They let him cut the umbilical cord, but despite Cara's explicit request, they didn't let him hold the baby for very long. They took the baby from his arms, saying she needed her mother, and placed her on Cara's chest. With almost the same movement, Cara gave the baby back to Jack, saying she wanted to rest. I tried to imagine the scene. It must have been awful...

I will never be able to forget how they humiliated my son. Again, and again. Even if I forgive them, I will never be able to forget. This is what I thought about at work after talking to Jack, and even then, all I could think about was looking at the pictures of Lilly, whose identity no one knew, whether she belonged to us or not. She had a little round face and didn't look anything like the newborn Elsie.

Cara lost a lot of blood during and after the birth and had to undergo surgery because a piece of the placenta remained in her uterus. She also had an infection, just like during her first birth, so she had to be given antibiotics intravenously and was only allowed to go home after the third day. Even then, it was only because she wanted to go home at her own risk.

Cara insisted on being discharged at 8 p.m. on the third night after giving birth, against all medical advice. She was supposed to take three types of antibiotics, but she had no idea how to take them. She sent Jack photos of the medicine boxes so he could review them and explain how and when to take the tablets. The baby was healthy and received no medication.

Lilly, the newborn

The next afternoon, Jack had to go and pick up the baby. Cara said she had a terrible night and couldn't sleep at all. The baby cried, Elsie woke up and started crying too, and Cara sent Jack messages in the middle of the night saying:

> "*Man! I can't take this! I need to rest, I'm on medication. Elsie is terribly bad, but poor thing, I felt so sorry for her; she was just standing there on the bed, looking at us, and I couldn't even pay attention to her.*"

The next day, Thursday, I was working the afternoon shift. Jack brought the baby to my workplace. Lilly wore shorts, a top, and a thin cardigan, barefoot. She didn't even have socks on her feet. She was hungry, but she wasn't crying. She just whimpered. She looked so fragile, so vulnerable, and unhappy that I started to cry when I saw her. Our colleagues gathered around. They started to comfort me. Jack went away somewhere and came back with red eyes, so they tried to comfort him, too. That evening, he took Lilly back to her mother.

"Babies this small need their mother," Jack tried to convince Cara. And Lilly stayed with her mother that night, but she came back with Elsie the next morning, and her mother didn't want her back that evening.

> "*Let her sleep at your place, I told you, I couldn't handle her; I didn't want to take care of her. She doesn't want my breast. She doesn't eat. I want to sleep. I want to take care of myself at last. I've had enough!*"

I had to act quickly. I found a cot for free on the Facebook marketplace, so I went and got it right away. We bought some baby clothes, nappies, and formula at Tesco. Lilly ate well, 60-70 millilitres. The midwife came to see us that day and the next, weighed the baby, and did the screening tests. The midwife showed no sign of shock and was not overly surprised that the baby was with his father. She only wrote in the booklet, and only once, that "the mother is not present during the examination". The next day, she said nothing to suggest that anything was wrong. Why wasn't a five-day-old baby lying next to her mother in bed, feeding from her breast? The midwife was clearly not interested. No one else cared either. Jack wrote to the health visitor and informed her of the situation. The health visitor replied that she was on holiday and would return to work in two weeks. If Jack had any doubts or questions in the meantime, he should contact her colleague at this or that phone number... Jack had no questions or doubts; he just wanted others to have them. But no. On Saturday afternoon, Jack took Lilly back to Cara. Cara's mother arrived from abroad early that evening, and we hoped that with her help, Cara would find herself again. Her motherhood, that is. Sunday passed quietly. But on Monday, Cara again passed both girls along to Jack and wanted the newborn, Lilly, to sleep at our house, too. Jack asked several times in text messages if this was really okay. Didn't Cara's mother want to be with the baby? But Cara just said that this is what she wanted, and that was that. The baby should not be at her house; she should be with her father.

The paternity test was easy to do. Saliva samples from the father and baby were sent by post. If Jack had wanted a 100% accurate test, one that would be accepted by the court, he would have needed a sample from the mother as well. Then they would have had to go to a clinic in person, and the test would have cost three times as much as the simple "Peace of Mind" test. This would have yielded only a 99.00% result, which the authorities would not have accepted as valid, but Jack was not concerned with whether anyone accepted the test result, only that he himself could be sure whether Lilly was his daughter or not. And the test came back positive. Confirmed 99.9999% paternity of Jack.

Lilly was a dream baby. A very good little girl. It was as if she knew she had to behave well, that she had no other choice... It broke our hearts. We held her in our arms as long as we could; Jack and I were taking turns to cuddle her. Lilly woke up, ate, fell asleep, then woke up again two hours later, ate again, and slept. She never cried. She fed well from the bottle, hardly ever spit up, and burped very well and quickly after every feed. But at four days old, she no longer had an umbilical stump. Cara said it came off on its own when she was dressing her, but Lilly's navel was bleeding and oozing badly. She must have been dressed quite roughly if the stump, which hadn't even dried up yet, came off. The baby looked quite battered, en bloc, no matter how we tried to dress her, to wrap her tightly in the special newborn blanket, she looked terribly small, and all her baby clothes just hung off her. Her labia had not yet closed; they did not cover each other, and Lilly had tiny, thin chicken legs. She was premature, even if she was not officially considered so, as she was only born three weeks early, but her whole little body showed how underdeveloped and defenceless she still was. As long as Cara's mother was there with Cara, for two weeks, Lilly came over in clean clothes and spent a few nights with her mother, who didn't breastfeed her or take her into bed, but at least she was there, and Lilly could smell her. But after Cara was left alone, and her mother gone back to Europe, Lilly spent every blessed night at Jack's house. We took turns keeping vigil beside her, feeding and rocking her. And the baby began to gain weight nicely. We bought a baby weighing scale to monitor this, because Lilly was really tiny and Jack wanted to be sure she was eating enough. And she did. Within two or three weeks, we reached the point where Lilly had last eaten at 2 a.m., then often slept until six or seven in the morning. The tiny baby, who was perfectly fine except for needing to be fed and cuddled, had developed a secure routine for herself. That was her only need.

Jack tried from time to time to convince Cara to keep Lilly with her, saying that he would look after Elsie instead, which would be a greater help to Cara. But the children's mother proved adamant. Even if Jack took Lilly and Elsie home at noon the day after their visit, Cara would still call him that evening to ask him to come and get the baby because she couldn't cope. One day in early April, when Lilly was not even a month old, Jack and I were both working the night shift. Cara knew this. At half past one in the morning, she still sent Jack a message to go and pick up the child.

"But I'm working now, and there's no one at home!"

"You'll figure something out, you're her father. Take her away from here because she's keeping us awake. Neither Elsie can sleep! I don't want this baby!

So, Jack went to pick up Lilly in the middle of the night, brought her to our workplace, and she stayed with us until morning in her little baby carrier, sleeping soundly, breathing quietly... In the morning, we took her home and took turns resting. Not much, either of us. But we didn't mind the fatigue; we were just worried about Lilly. How she must be feeling. How could this tiny baby get through this period? Away from her mother, as my daughter Sophia said, "with her bare-naked nervous system". What kind of traumatic experience would remain with her? I often thought about what the poor thing must have gone through in her mother's womb. The constant rejection, the tension, and later the feeling that they wanted to get rid of her... Lilly had sad eyes and a deep, very sad gaze for many weeks.

THE EASTER INCIDENT

Back to court

It was Friday, Easter Friday to be precise, which they call Good Friday here. Early that afternoon, Cara sent Jack a message, for the umpteenth time, telling him to take care of Lilly because she didn't want the baby for even one more night. At most, Cara added, he could take her over for an hour or two during the day, but only if they had agreed in advance. And Cara asked that when Jack brought Elsie back from her visit that afternoon, he should keep Lilly with him and not take her back, because she, Cara, wanted to spend the next day and the weekend with Elsie, and she wanted to sleep at night! Early on Good Friday evening, Jack took Elsie back, then worked a few hours with Uber. I was left alone with Lilly. I wiped her little body with oil-soaked cotton wool, bathed her, put clean clothes on her, fed her, and made her comfortable. By 8 p.m., the baby was sleeping peacefully in her cot, and I was admiring her. It was already past 10 p.m. when Jack called to say Cara wanted Lilly back because Elsie had missed seeing her sister. Jack also said that he would be home soon and would take Lilly to Cara. But it was past 11 o'clock when Jack got home. We stood over the cot, looking at the baby, who was sleeping soundly. Outside, a stormy wind was raging, the kind of wind that brings spring floods, and it was blowing in from the sea, so it was cold. Jack looked at me, and I knew what he was thinking because I felt the same way.

“Call her then,” I said to Jack. “Call her and tell her that you’re not taking this baby out on the street at this time of night! She’s sleeping here, peacefully, warm, well-fed! This isn’t a toy; it’s a little child! This circus must end, like, right now! One of you must have some common sense! You can’t do this to a baby, dragging her around like this! A baby needs stability, warmth, and security! Lilly deserves that!”

Jack didn’t answer; he just went to the kitchen to get his phone. I followed him to see what was going on. Jack first sent Cara a message saying, which was what I had told him, only more politely. Then Cara started calling, which Jack didn’t want to answer at first, but after the sixth call, he could no longer ignore it and picked up. It was already past midnight. Cara demanded that Jack bring Lilly to her immediately. Jack quietly explained to her what he had written earlier.

- “Leave me alone with your mother’s shitty message. I know she wrote that message, not you! Tell her to suck it! I want my child! Right now!”
- “Cara, it’s almost half past midnight, the child is asleep, and I’m not taking her out into the cold. I’ll bring her to you in the morning.”
- “No! I want her now. Bring Lilly over right now!”
- “Cara, try to calm down. The child is fine, sleeping comfortably. You asked me to keep her with me today. It’s very late now, but I’ll bring her over tomorrow morning when you wake up.”
- “No! Bring her now! Bring my child! If you don’t bring her, I’ll wake Elsie up and come and get her, I’ll bomb and explode your house.”
- “Okay. Try to calm down. And don’t wake Elsie. It’s no use coming here; everyone will be asleep by the time you get here. Let me know in the morning when you wake up, and I’ll bring Lilly over.”

- "I don't believe it, motherfucker, I'm going over there right now, and I'm going to bomb your house, you bastards! Die already!"
- "Good night, Cara, see you in the morning!"

Jack leaned helplessly on the kitchen counter when he hung up the phone. Then a strange expression appeared on his face.

- "I think I recorded that call. The recorder on my phone was left on. Do you think she'll come here? Is she really capable of waking Elsie up and bringing her here? In the middle of the night?"
- "I have no idea. But I think you should call the police. After what she said. It wouldn't be good if she came here."
- "What's the point? What's the point of calling the police... They won't do anything anyway!"
- "Fine, if you won't call them, I will. For God's sake, only God knows what Cara meant by bombing and burning down the house. And that we should just die?! I've had enough of this, honestly! Someone needs to realise that what she's doing isn't normal! She leaves the child with you, then asks her back at 10 p.m., because Elsie misses seeing the baby before she goes to sleep. Then at midnight, when Elsie is fast asleep, she threatens you and wishes you dead if you don't bring the one- -month-old baby back to her immediately, but only in the morning... This is not normal, and it can't go on like this!

Jack nodded and called the police. We couldn't go to bed because the police said they would come out and make a report within an hour. They took down the details, wrote a report, and then left to talk to Cara. They wanted to arrest her, take her in, and question her at the police station, but because Elsie was asleep, they didn't want to wake her up, and there was no one to look after her. So, Cara got away with not being formally questioned again, just like she had a year and a half earlier. The police officer called Jack back and told him they had spoken to Cara and told her not to come to Jack's house but to stay home. If she did show up, the police officer said, Jack should call 999 immediately.

- "I'm sorry mate", added the policeman, "she really is a pain in the arse!"

Jack smiled for the first time in many months.

- "Well, I know", he said quietly.

"Finally, someone noticed," I thought to myself. And suddenly I felt a huge sense of relief. "Maybe someone will help us now. Maybe this nightmare will end, and someone will warn Cara that she can't force us to live like this."

We went to bed. Or rather, Jack went to bed, because that night I stayed up with the baby downstairs on the sofa in the living room. Jack looked terribly tired, and I wanted him to rest. We had no idea what awaited us tomorrow or even that night.

The next morning, we woke up to a loud bang at the door. I carefully pulled back the curtain to see who was at the door, even though I could have guessed. It was barely eight o'clock. Cara was knocking, banging, and muttering under her breath, I imagine all good wishes. Elsie was sitting on her arm. Jack called the police. They were there in less than five minutes. Four of them. Two came into the house, and two stayed outside with Cara, talking to her. They told her to go home. They repeated that after what she had said the night before, she was not allowed to come near the house anymore. Cara left, and the police officer at our house took a statement. It took quite a long time. When it turned out that Jack had recorded the threat, they asked him to voluntarily hand over his phone to the police so they could download the evidence. The police officers said Jack was not doing anything wrong by keeping the younger child with him, and that although they could not arrest Cara at this time, it would be good if he could take the older girl with him as well. The police officers said that they would report Cara for antisocial behaviour and threats once they had the evidence. Jack handed over his phone. It was Saturday, and nothing else happened with the police that day.

On Sunday, Cara and her mother kept sending us messages from abroad, telling us to take Lilly back to her mother immediately, because we couldn't keep doing what we were doing to Cara or the baby. Elsie was suffering too; she missed her little sister. I replied briefly to Cara's mother and urged her to be patient. I also asked her if she didn't know what was going on, it would be better not to interfere. She fell silent then. But I also learned from her that the police were still at Cara's house on Sunday, questioning her again...

We kept Lilly with us. Sophia commented, "At least the baby is where she is loved."

On the next visitation day, Monday, Cara didn't want to hand Elsie over, "because you're not giving my daughter back either," – but then she must have remembered the court order and decided to let Jack go and get the little girl after all.

We finally kept Elsie with us when we noticed red bruises on her back while bathing her on Monday. They were fingerprint-shaped bruises, and Elsie screamed when we put her in the bath; she didn't want to bathe, which she had loved before. At that point, we decided to keep her with us until the police investigation was over. On Wednesday, we didn't take her back to Cara because Jack's solicitor advised us to keep her with us. Cara, however, threatened us that we would be in big trouble for doing so. I was afraid she was right, because there was a court order regarding Elsie that specified exactly when and how her father could see her, and when he had to take her back, and her mother was named her primary carer. By not returning Elsie to her mother, we violated the court order, which could have serious consequences. But the solicitor reassured us that the judge would have no objection once he knew the reasons.

The only problem was that he didn't find out. In time. The judge didn't find out anything in time. Cara was quicker than us. She immediately got herself a free solicitor – she was entitled to one – who filed an urgent application with the court on her behalf for the immediate return of Elsie and the placement of Lilly.

PART IV – THE SYSTEM

The wheels of God and the police turn slowly. It took 20 days to download the data from Jack's phone. They said the code Jack gave them was wrong, then added that the officer handling the case had gone on holiday. And that's why the investigation was taking so long. On his solicitor's advice, Jack also filed a petition for the children's placement, but because he did not have free legal aid, he wrote it himself; it did not arrive at court on time. The hearing was urgently scheduled for 21 April, and only Cara's petition was included in the proceedings; Jack's was nowhere to be found, lost in the maze of bureaucracy.

If someone is despicable, they can be despicable without limits – it was time to learn that, too. Three days before the hearing, on 18 April, when both children were still with Jack, a police officer appeared at our door at 11 p.m. They wanted to search Jack's car because Cara had reported to the police that Jack was dealing drugs and making a living as a drug dealer. I was on shift that night, so I wasn't home. Jack fell asleep next to Elsie while putting her to bed, and he didn't even know if he was a boy or a girl when he opened the door to the police officer...

Three days later, at the hearing, it became clear that the judge had no idea what had happened. Nor did he know why it had happened. No one had told him that Jack had also filed a petition for custody of the children. All that the judge could see in the papers laid out before him was that Jack had violated the court order and unlawfully kept Elsie with him, and, as Cara put it, "took" the newborn Lilly away from her mother. Cara lied fluently and expressed concern for her children's welfare in her petition. She claimed she wasn't sure Jack was even taking care of the children. She described at length how the current situation could affect the emotional development of such young children, then went on to explain how she was breastfeeding and how terrible it was that the baby she was breastfeeding had been taken away from her. The judge needed no more, and he tore Jack down to the ground. Cara told the judge that after what had happened, she would not allow Elsie to go on holiday with her father this year. The judge agreed with Cara. Jack's lawyer referred to the elderly family members, the paternal grandfather, who had not yet seen the little girl and was ill, but the judge cynically remarked that, in that case, the little girl should not be taken on holiday, as a small child did not need to be among sick people! Our trip was already planned, everything was organised, and we had even bought the plane tickets. But it didn't matter. Neither did the fact that Elsie's grandfather had heart disease. He didn't have infectious hepatitis, but heart disease, and was awaiting an operation that he might not survive. But the judge wasn't interested in that or anything else; he was just constantly upset that Jack could have done such a thing, taking his children away from their mother, especially a newborn. Jack wanted to speak up several times, but the judge waved him off, saying that only his lawyer could speak for him, but now he wasn't even interested in what Jack's lawyer had to say...The lawyer did manage to say aloud that the father had been with the younger child, the newborn, since birth and had cared for her. Cara then laughed loudly, as if she had heard a joke, and looked at Jack with scorn and contempt. The judge, however, was surprised and later closed the hearing with this sentence: "Only the two of you know the truth here in this courtroom right now. But soon everything will come to light!" This sentence was enough to stop Cara from smiling. And this sentence whispered a faint hope into Jack's ear. Everything will come to light! The truth. Finally! How wonderful that would be! If only it were so! But unfortunately, this did not change the facts and the decision made at the time: Jack had to take the children back to Cara that very afternoon, with immediate effect.

We both cried. We tried to do it that way, so the children wouldn't notice.

During the 12 days they spent with us, they lived a beautiful routine, and so did we. The little girls were happy; they smiled, ate well, slept deeply, and woke up cheerfully. Elsie was talking constantly, forming two-word sentences and asking questions. She loved bathing again, was no longer afraid of the tub, learned to put on her trousers and socks, and ran out to play in the garden right after breakfast, weather permitting. Not once did Elsie head for the front door, not once did she look for her mother while she was with us! Not once did she mention "Mummy" and not once did she burst into tears! She didn't miss her mother, and that was terrible. Jack and I knew that. It was a telling fact that someone other than us might have found interesting. But no one was interested in the facts. People preferred to believe their own thoughts and feelings. Even those who, by virtue of their profession, should have remained objective.

During those 12 days, the health visitor came to see us twice, because she had to come every week to weigh Lilly, and on one occasion she brought a social worker with her. The social worker looked at Jack as if he were a mass murderer. She asked Jack how he could be so sure that the bruises on Elsie's back were bruises if he hadn't taken her to a doctor to have them examined. She explained that, based on the photos, she thought they were eczema... She explained to Jack that social services would only accept the abuse as abuse if it had been diagnosed and assessed by a doctor. Therefore, they did not believe that Elsie had been abused in any way. The health visitor was able to state that if a child is separated from its mother at such a young age, it will fall behind in its development and may not grow properly... At first, I thought I had misheard. And I actually regretted having more than 30 years of nursing experience, because it meant I was unable to feel ashamed like a normal person and go along with the shaming. But I felt even more sorry that I was able to simply freeze at the sight of such amateurism and such malice, instead of commenting and intervening in the conversation! Because I just sat there and tried to explain what had happened very quietly. To those who were completely indifferent to the truth... The health visitor was astounded by how much weight Lilly had gained. She weighed her twice to make sure she didn't write the wrong numbers in her red notebook. She was also amazed at how confident and open Elsie was, and how she greeted her in advance. "Wow, what a cheerful little girl, she must be having a good day!"

I think there are some people who really should be told to take a hike, or to get lost. Whatever. Of course, in a subtle, intelligent way, but in such a way that they understand. I was speechless. But at least we learned something. And got to know that abuse can only be verified by the GP. We didn't know this before. If we had known this, we would have taken Elsie to the GP surgery the moment we found the red bruises on her back!

After the court hearing, I took the children back to their mother. Because Jack said he didn't want to see Cara anymore, I had to take them back.

When Cara opened the door, she took the baby carrier from me, carried it into the living room in one swift movement, then took Elsie out of my arms. Cara didn't even look at Lilly. When she opened the door, there was a sly smile on Cara's face, but I pretended not to notice. I stood there for a few moments with the bag of Lilly's formula in my hand. I wanted to tell Cara what she had eaten, how we had fed her, how she had slept, and what her routine was like. But just as I was about to speak, as if Cara had suddenly remembered her role and what to do in such situations, she unexpectedly threw herself into Elsie's arms and pretended to sob loudly. It was so theatrical that it made me feel nauseous.

"Okay, enough of this circus! No one wants to see this!" I muttered under my breath, but in such a way that Cara couldn't hear the second half of the sentence. I put the plastic bag on the doorstep, turned my back, and started to go down the stairs. The sobbing stopped, and the door closed immediately behind me.

Well, well, well. If someone is sobbing with emotion, relief, or whatever, they're not going to immediately stop it, close the door, and lock it! Emotions don't change back and forth that quickly. What a circus. That's what it was. Artificial and disgusting. The baby was on the doorstep. All I could think about and see before my eyes, like a replay, was how Cara was taking Lilly, putting her over the threshold into the room, and not even looking at her! She didn't even glance at that tiny baby, her younger daughter!

God, it hurts so much... I burst into tears in the car. What will happen to these children?

I went to work in the afternoon, and so did Jack. He didn't come home until 3 a.m. then. The next day, he told me that he had walked 10 miles after work. He walked for three hours in the rain and wind, trying to calm down somehow.

THE EYE OF THE STORM

The story was not over. The judge ordered another investigation by child protective services, this time to assess the children's safety within six weeks and to prepare a safeguarding report. Perhaps they will come out now to do an environmental study, but it is also possible that they will just handle this with a telephone interview, - I thought. There will be another hearing (or hearings) after that, and the police will soon close the investigation. For now, they can't find the evidence on Jack's phone, which is among the audio recordings. The police officer said they had already had some of the messages translated, but found nothing threatening or abusive. No problem. When they returned the phone to Jack, he immediately sent the recording to a company that produces official translations. The transcript has already been completed and will be submitted to the court. Even if the police do not file a report because they deem the case not serious enough or cannot find sufficient evidence, the truth will come out. Because this is a serious enough case for Jack and me, it weighs heavily on our hearts every single day.

Jack hasn't been able to work for a month. He woke up every night to find his sheets soaked with sweat. He has lost 10 kilos in a few months; he was pale and exhausted. He forgot things, couldn't remember where he put his belongings, or what he had discussed with someone the day before. Sometimes he felt dizzy and had no appetite, and he ate only when the children were with him. He usually cooked then. He refused to see Cara for the time being, saying he couldn't go there and didn't want to talk to her a word, so I always had to bring and take the children on visiting days to collect and deliver them. Cara was furious about this, but there was nothing she could do: under the court order, I could also pick up and drop off Elsie and Lilly as a third party. Cara could only send Jack messages about this: Don't let your mother come for the children now! And, alternatively, she created all kinds of videos from the time she was still expecting Elsie, when they were still together, showing how happy they were. Cara tried to get in contact with Jack, but Jack wanted zero contact with her.

The nastiness didn't end there. After the hearing, and going back to the official child arrangement order, Cara couldn't cope. Cara had had enough of the children on the third day and gave Jack an ultimatum: if Jack didn't say anything bad about her to child services, they could work it out between themselves. Jack could have the children more often, he could even go on holiday with them, and they wouldn't have to go back to court...As long as Jack didn't say anything bad about Cara during the child welfare - safeguarding interview, everything would be fine, and they could agree on everything. This method, this kind of ultimatum, is still called blackmail, if I'm not mistaken! A big, fat blackmail.

Ten days after the court hearing, Lilly was already sleeping at Jack's again. Cara claimed she had found a job, so she asked Jack to change the visiting hours, saying she wanted to work and to let both children sleep at his place instead...

Two weeks after the hearing, Cara started begging Jack and me for money. The day after she received her benefits, she was already complaining that she had no money left. She gave me an ultimatum, too. She messaged me:

> *"You expect me to be nice to you, to let my child go on holiday with you, even though your son won't give me back the money I lent him."*

"Pardon?" I wanted to say. Jack had never borrowed any money from Cara. The truth was that Cara had sent Jack £300 after Lilly was born because Jack had given her a lot of money before the birth for taxis, food, and other things, and she said she wanted to pay him back. Now, this £300 that Jack received from Cara suddenly became a loan, money that Jack had asked for... Wow... Gaslighting, twisted truth – level X.

I couldn't imagine how this could get any worse! Cara's narrative was always different; it sounded unlike the truth, and, on top of that, it was completely malleable, changing however she wanted.

By early May, Cara was so desperate for money that she resorted to blackmail, threatening that if we didn't give her money, she really wouldn't let Elsie go on holiday. When Jack didn't respond, Cara bombarded me with messages. Until I sent her £40. But that didn't seem to be enough. Later that same day, she tried to trick Jack into giving her his Social Security number so she could claim a tax refund in his name. Cara wanted to claim the marriage allowance on behalf of Jack, a year after they broke up and had been separated. When Jack told her that he would not give her his social security number or any money, Jack became a "cold-hearted bastard" who was causing the children to starve, a "lying drug addict", a "soulless nobody" who "still lives with his mother, a Mummy's boy".

However, the "mummy's boy's mummy" was still good for one thing: if Jack couldn't be persuaded to give her money, Cara could try asking his mummy directly, over and over again. Two days later, Cara asked me for money again, this time for a taxi to take her to a job interview. I helped her. Again. Why did I do it? Because Cara was very clever in choosing her reasons for asking. If she asked for money for food, I simply couldn't bring myself to refuse her. And the job interview was something Cara knew I would support, as I had repeatedly stated that I would help her in any way I could if she wanted to work or study...

I helped her whenever she asked. But even that didn't stop Cara from deciding at the end of May not to hand the children over to me anymore, and she lied with a straight face in the child safeguarding report, saying that I was a very bad influence on my grandchildren, that they only learned hatred from me, and that since they had been spending more time at my house, Elsie had become downright mean...

Even if I had spent more time with the children, the quality of that time had not changed at all over the months. What had changed was that Elsie was slowly approaching the age of two. She could already talk; she knew how to express herself, and she increasingly wanted to assert her own will. She was trying to test her limits and set her own boundaries. She was no longer a baby. If she didn't like something, she was quick to express it. She was on the cusp of the terrible twos. Cara herself told Jack that after we brought the children back to her, Elsie would say "Daddy" and "Nana" for hours on end. Cara also wrote in a message that one morning, Elsie had packed her things, put her bunny and her dummy in a plastic bag, and gone straight to the front door, saying "Daddy, Nana," and trying to reach the doorknob. She wanted to come to us... That was the crux of Elsie's wickedness. That she loved us. Wanted to be with us…

INCIDENT

Cara couldn't stop me from officially collecting the children; she would have needed a Court Order for that. Jack continued to refuse to have any contact with Cara, so there was no other choice; I continued to do the handovers

One morning, Elsie was very fussy when I went to pick her up. Cara handed Lilly to me at the door and came down to the car with Elsie. I put Lilly in the child seat, then bent down to pick up Elsie and put her in the car, too. I picked her up, and she came into my arms without any resistance, but she was still whimpering. I started talking to her, telling her that Daddy, the doggy, and the kitty were waiting for her, but that didn't help. Elsie wanted something else, but she couldn't find the words and kept whimpering. Cara had already started back up the stairs towards her house, but suddenly she turned around and came towards us, shouting,

- "That's enough, give me back my child! Can't you see she doesn't want to go with you? Give her to me! Give me my child!" she babbled, reaching for Elsie.

I turned away to put the little girl in the car and didn't say a word, but it was too late. Cara took another step towards me and tried to take Elsie from my arms. I grabbed Cara's arm and held her back. I didn't hold her tightly, and I didn't hold her for long; I just wanted to stop her. I quietly told her not to make a scene, that today was the children's father's visitation day, and I was taking the children to their father. Then I let go of Cara's arm and put Elsie in the car in one swift movement. The moment she sat in the car, Elsie stopped crying, looked at the stickers on the glove compartment, and even smiled.

"See, everything's fine now, Elsie's all right," I said to Cara, who turned on her heel, gave me the middle finger, and stormed off. From the top of the stairs, she yelled back at me from the street, telling me to go to hell.

My legs were shaking as I got into the car, but I had to keep an eye on the children, so I didn't have time to be particularly upset by Cara's rudeness - again. I didn't care anymore. I was tired of it; my only goal now was to get as far away from her as possible and have as little contact with her as possible.

I told Jack what had happened, and he was genuinely sorry. We thought about calling the police about the incident, but we didn't see the point. We figured that the police probably wouldn't consider it an incident, since no blood had been shed and no one had been injured. And the police would probably not deal with the whole case beyond listening to the story and possibly interviewing both parties. Instead, we considered how to prevent similar incidents in the future and wondered how to protect ourselves. We wrote to our solicitor and ordered a miniature camera hidden in a pen to record all handovers and get evidence for Cara's behaviour if we ever need it. That was all we could do.

Cara, on the other hand, called the police. She claimed that when she handed the children over to me, I attacked her on the street, even beating her in broad daylight in the open street and shouting in front of her children that she was a stinking whore... The police called me two days later and asked what had happened. That's how I learned Cara had reported me. But I only found out what was in the report and what Cara's account of the events was a year later, from a document prepared by the child welfare services, which contained a detailed description of the incident.

This incident came in handy for Cara, and it is also possible that she fabricated the whole thing herself – we will never know. The following week, she told Jack she was going to ban me from seeing the children and wrote to her solicitor, who then wrote to Jack's solicitor, saying that from that day on, only Jack could pick up the girls and do the handovers. That was that. She would not hand them over to anyone else. What the previous court order said – and the fact that it had not yet been revoked by – was irrelevant. What the mother wanted and said would happen was what mattered. No one cared why Jack had not gone near Cara until then. If he wanted to see his daughters, he had to put up with emotional abuse and overt or covert verbal aggression. No one cared about anything. No one cared about the basis on which Cara wanted to ban me from seeing my grandchildren, whether she had any reason to do so, what Jack would have to face as a result, what he would go through, or the facts of the matter. Cara won the battle; she made sure she would meet only with Jack, and that he would be at her mercy, at her whim. And Jack sought protection in vain; he did not want any confrontation. Cara's wish has been included in the next court decision, so only Jack could take the girls. And from then on, he had to accept whatever came his way. Again. I thought it was a good thing we bought the little camera hidden in the pen. Jack and I decided to record everything we could. On video, on audio recordings. Wherever and whenever.

Court hearing and further incidents

For the next court hearing, the child welfare service prepared another report, again without a personal meeting, but at least proposed a further 12-week detailed investigation, including an environmental study, after which a final decision could be made on the children's placement.

By the time of the hearing, in early June, Cara had been so fed up with the children that she decided to let them go on holiday abroad with their father for two weeks. This included Elsie, who was not yet two years old, and three-month-old Lilly. Cara wanted to relax, have fun, and live her life, as she wrote in messages to Jack. She claimed that she was going to start working and get her driving licence. She wanted anything but to be locked up between four walls. Anything but looking after the children. We knew this well, but no one else was quite aware of it, as Cara had always presented a completely different image to the outside world. The judge was shocked and voiced her disapproval, but in the end, she upheld the mother's wishes and, with them, the father's desires. We were finally able to travel with the children. Our tickets were for the day after the hearing. We had also bought plane tickets for the children, because we were hopeful, and so we were, of course, very happy with the somewhat unexpected decision. The suitcases were already packed; if the girls couldn't come after all, I would just take out the two sets of clothes, and that would be that.

There were still a few hours left in the afternoon and the night until the flight the next morning. The children had been with me since the morning because I was looking after them during the court hearing, and because it was Friday, the day they usually spend with their father. Cara suggested she would like to see the girls before they left for two weeks, but she hesitated, unsure if she really wanted to. In the end, she decided that yes, she would like Jack to bring them over between four and eight in the evening so she could play with them a little longer. I had an incredibly bad feeling. All kinds of thoughts ran through my mind, but I tried to brush them aside one by one. My worst fear was that Cara would do something to the children that would only come to light once we were on our way, and then we would be blamed for whatever had happened. "I'm a complete psychopath now, I've become paranoid," I told myself and tried to focus on something else. Jack took the girls to Cara after 4 o'clock. I went to work at 2 p.m. for another afternoon shift, so I couldn't even say goodbye to them. My shift ended at 8 p.m., and a few minutes later, my phone rang.

- "Mum, Cara just called. Something happened to Elsie; she hit her head. Cara says she doesn't look good, she's bleeding a lot, I must go there, we have to take her to the hospital..." Jack said breathlessly.

The strength drained from my legs. I could hardly speak.

- "But how did it happen?"
- "I don't know, Mum, I'm going there now to see what's going on, I'll call you later."

I went home, waited for Jack's call, and tidied up the kitchen to keep myself busy. After 9 o'clock, a photo arrived on my phone, a photo of Elsie's head. It was taken from behind and from the right side, and there was a 3-4 cm long, deep cut, a crack in her scalp. It was in line with her ear, but almost at the top of her head.

How did it happen? How could this have happened?

When a small child falls, they fall forwards, backwards, or sideways... But certainly not onto the top of their head!

- "What happened? How did Elsie fall?" I asked Jack in a message because I didn't dare call him, knowing he was probably with Cara.
- "I don't know. I'll let you know. I'll be right there, I'll bring Lilly, please just put her to bed, we have to go to the hospital with Elsie," Jack replied.

A few minutes later, Jack arrived, looking distraught, rushing in. Lilly was breathing and sleeping peacefully in her baby carrier, and my son carried her through the door, but didn't come in.

- "I'll write to you later; I must hurry now. Elsie is fine, thank God; she doesn't seem seriously injured, but her wound is nasty, and you know what it's always like in A&E. I'll write to you from there. Or I'll call you."
- "OK," I replied and closed the door behind Jack.

I put Lilly in her cot, and she didn't even wake up from the multiple changes in position and environment. I restrained myself and sent Jack another message only half an hour later.

He didn't reply for a long time; they were on their way to the hospital. The next call came just under an hour later, after they had admitted Elsie.

- "How is Elsie? What happened?" I asked again before Jack could even speak.
- "We don't know..."

- “What do you mean, you don’t know? What do you mean?”
- “Just what I said. Cara can’t say what happened, how the child fell. She was there, not far from her, but she didn’t see what happened. She only noticed when she was lying on the ground, crying.”
- “What? Sorry. Pardon?”
- “I’m telling you. That’s what she said to the doctor. She doesn’t know how Elsie hit her head, or where. Supposedly on the edge of the door. Her foot probably got caught on something, and she fell against the door. Cara thinks that’s what happened.”
- “But how?”
- “Mum, how should I know?! I have to go back to the waiting room soon. I called you because I don’t know what’s going to happen! Listen, there are thousands of people here, I have no idea when we’ll be done... And will they even let Elsie out? I think they’ll have to stitch her head up.”
- “Oh my God...”
- “But I hope they let her out. Anyway, she’s fine, her head isn’t bleeding anymore, and she’s not in much pain. I don’t see anything strange about her, she’s just getting tired, I think... We’ll be sitting here for hours...”
- “Okay, she needs to see a doctor. That wound on his head looks pretty nasty. Really. Just keep an eye on her for now. So, what should we do? How are we going to travel? Can we even go? We should leave early in the morning...”
- “I have no idea. I’ll call you when the doctor has seen the child.”
- “OK. I’ll wait. Call me. Or text me, whatever!”

I put down the phone and looked at the clock. It was past 10 p.m. Jack, Elsie, and Cara had arrived at the hospital barely an hour ago. The average waiting time in the emergency room here is 6-7 hours. In England, it’s 4 hours. We would have to leave for the airport by 5 a.m. at the latest if we wanted to catch our flight...

Jack called again at midnight, and he said the doctor still hadn’t seen Elsie.

- "Go to bed, mum. And leave with Lilly in the morning," he said. "At least you'll be there at Granddad's birthday..."
- "No way am I leaving without you and Elsie! How could I leave alone with a three-month-old baby? Even if they let me cross the border, even though the baby and I have completely different names, I'm not going without you!" I was outraged by the idea.
- "That's true. But then I don't know what will happen. You can't imagine what it's like here..." said Jack
- "How is Elsie coping?"
- "She's very tired. She's terribly restless. I hope she falls asleep."

There was no Wi-Fi in the hospital, nor mobile phone reception, and we soon realised that Jack couldn't receive messages or make calls unless he went outside the entrance.

At two in the morning, he popped home to get Elsie's favourite teddy and some warm clothes, but I forgot to ask him for his flight booking reference, so I couldn't change his flight ticket. Elsie was seen by the doctor just before four o'clock in the morning, when they examined her and stitched up her wound, and they wanted to keep her in for observation until noon the next day because the little girl was very upset. We couldn't leave that day. The airplane's gone without us early in the morning. Jack came home at noon with the child, who was exhausted and fast asleep. We bought new tickets for the next day's flight. Jack told me that Cara had been provoking her throughout their hospital stay.

- "Are you very angry with me? You must be very angry now! What must your family think of me?! That you can't go on your trip after all..."

She then told Jack how sorry she was about everything that had happened and that she would buy new tickets for the next day, which of course never happened, but it didn't matter. We set off a day late. Thank God, Elsie was not seriously injured, so we were able to take her with us with the doctor's consent. The final report stated that the doctor had no reservations about the child's safety. Not because of the trip, but because of the circumstances of the fall. (No safeguarding issue – they wrote on the paper.) This was Elsie's fifth visit to the hospital emergency room in her short 21 months of life. But no one cared that the mother couldn't say exactly what had happened to the little girl, how she had fallen, where she had hit her head...If she had hit her head at all. I had bad thoughts. And when we were already on the plane, I knew we had made another mistake: Jack shouldn't have taken Cara and Elsie to the hospital; he should have called an ambulance! The injury, whose circumstances were unclear, should have been reported to the police. While waiting for Jack to take them to the hospital that evening, Cara sent Jack a message. Cara's message on Jack's phone said that she couldn't find any blood anywhere and had no idea how that was possible, since Elsie's head was bleeding profusely, and if she had hit her head somewhere, there should be blood, but there wasn't. This message also says that Cara is defending herself:

> *"But I didn't hurt her,"* she wrote, *"I couldn't have hurt her, you know that, because I was talking to you on the phone, you heard her start crying..."*

What mother would claim that she didn't hurt her child when they fell and hit their head? Would any mother claim that she didn't hurt her child when they fell and hit their head?

They should have called an ambulance and notified the police! I still can't get that thought out of my head. Because even now, no one knows exactly how Elsie was injured that night. The cut on the right side of her head, almost at the top above her right ear, had to be stitched up... It looked really bad. A three-centimetre-long, half-centimetre-wide straight line cut. What causes a wound like that? How does a small child hit the top of their head?

Cara probably noticed that her answer to the doctor's question was not right. So, she changed it. When the doctor on duty first saw Elsie, Cara claimed that she had no idea how the little girl had been injured. Cara said: She was in the kitchen and only noticed that Elsie was crying, and when she went into the room, she saw her lying on the floor with blood on her head. But by the morning, Cara's account to the other doctor, who wrote the final report, was as follows: She was in the other room changing Lilly's nappy when she heard Elsie crying, and when she went into the living room, she saw Elsie lying on the floor, crying and bleeding from her head.

The reality was that Cara was talking to Jack on the phone when Elsie screamed. Jack also heard it and claimed he heard Elsie crying from close by, not from a distance, and certainly not from another room. Jack also claimed that, immediately, the moment Elsie started crying, she told him that Elsie had hit herself, was bleeding from her head,

– "Oh, she's bleeding badly, come here, come here right now!...

So, she was right there next to her! How is it possible that she didn't see what happened? How is all this possible?

At the hospital, no one had any safeguarding concerns, doubts, or questions. I find this astonishing. Even though I know and understand that two different doctors examined the child, and the second doctor may not have been aware of what the mother had said about what happened when she arrived. It is still astonishing that no one had any questions, even if the mother's explanation of the injury the next morning is acceptable: she was busy with her other child in the other room when Elsie was injured in the living room... I ask again, and I know I am repeating myself, but it really bothers me: how does a two-year-old child injure herself in the living room in such a way that the skin on the top of her head is cut in a straight line over an area of three centimetres? How?

And no one notified the police... The final report only states that the social worker must be notified of what happened.

During the first few days of the holiday, Cara called Jack several times. Not to ask how Elsie was doing, but to ask Jack to send her pictures of the children, because she wanted to know what they were doing and where they were going. After the thirtieth call and message, Jack began to tire of the constant supervision. He told Cara he would send her pictures every day, but asked her politely not to call him, as he wanted to spend time with the children. Cara got angry and didn't write or call for a few days.

It was a wonderful holiday. Elsie was relaxed and behaved like a happy little girl, chattering nonstop, laughing loudly, and making friends with the little Viking, my grandson, who was her age and with whom she became very close by the end of the holiday. Elsie finally got to see her great-grandparents, her paternal grandfather; she swam in lakes and streams, went to the beach and a farm, petted little goats, saw the musical fountain on Margaret Island in Budapest, and ate a lot of delicious food! And Lilly? Lilly was a dream baby who smiled at everyone and could hardly be heard except when she cooed. We travelled back happily and relaxed.

However, upon our return, the nightmares began again. Cara asked for Lilly as soon as we got home that evening. Jack had to take her to Cara immediately. The next day, Cara wrote messages saying, "*Look at the poor little child's body.*" She claimed that Jack had handed over the baby in a dirty nappy and hungry. Luckily, we had filmed ourselves changing Lilly's clothes and cleaning her up, and we had also taken photos of her body before we handed her over. Cara wanted Elsie back the next day, too, because she'd somehow forgotten that Elsie still had three days left of her two-week holiday, and we didn't have to take her back yet.

Then came the begging for money again. We had to send money, but as soon as possible, immediately, because Cara couldn't buy formula for Lilly. She didn't have a penny left. She hadn't had to take care of the children for two weeks. She had received her benefits for that month a week earlier, but she had no money left... Jack simply replied that he would send the maintenance money as usual, every week, and that Cara would have to manage with it, because he could not give her any more than that. Neither before the maintenance money was transferred, nor after. The response came immediately. Cara replied, "OK. If Jack isn't going to send her the money, he should return the children's passports, since there's no reason for him to keep them any longer.

– "What do you need the passports for if you're not going anywhere? Or are you going somewhere?" Jack asked, but this only led to

> another argument. The passports belong to her, the mother, and she must have them because she currently has custody of the children, and the court has ruled so! Cara hissed and promised that if she did not receive the documents, she would go to court again over the matter.

The drug test was repeated, and both tested negative. Jack drank an average amount of alcohol, occasionally. The fact that she had falsely accused Jack again, and that it was now becoming clear to everyone, made Cara increasingly frustrated and nervous. She wanted to exercise control and power increasingly aggressively, and she wanted to get the children's passports back more and more. Finally, she had her solicitor summon Jack to return the documents on the next day of contact. Jack had no choice but to consult his own solicitor again. According to the judge's decision, the documents should indeed be in the mother's possession. However, in recent weeks, Cara had repeatedly made it clear she intended to leave the country. Again. Jack had countless messages about this, saved on his phone, and he was rightly afraid to hand over the children's passports to Cara. Jack was afraid that Cara would suddenly disappear and that one day he would go to pick up the children and find them nowhere to be found.

Cara's intentions and plans for the future were unclear and unpredictable. She began harassing Jack again, asking him to sleep with her one more time, just one last time. Perhaps she was lonely, hungry for affection, which seems natural at the age of 22, or perhaps she wanted to accuse Jack of rape afterwards, only God knows what Cara's motive was for these messages; we couldn't know that at the time. Jack had no desire to see her, let alone sleep with her...

Cara's whole lifestyle seemed quite chaotic that year. She had accumulated high debts from utility bills, and in early spring, the heating and electricity in her house were cut off twice because Cara had not paid any bills until her social worker had the meters replaced with prepaid cards. Even though her benefits amounted to a full salary, Cara could not budget her monthly income. In addition to her benefits and child support, and the fact that Jack bought all the children's nappies and formula, Cara was constantly begging for and borrowing money from both of us, and never had any. At the time, we didn't understand why. Cara didn't make any friends; she was lonely, and perhaps she felt in danger of losing her children. Jack saw a strong possibility that Cara wanted to escape and leave the country. But not by asking anyone's permission anymore. Just like those who have no other choice. She would suddenly disappear from one day to the next. Just as she had arrived. With a small suitcase. Jack thought Cara was so insistent on obtaining the children's passports so she could keep this option open for herself if all else failed. And Jack was afraid of this, afraid that it might happen. Anytime.

As for Elsie, the court ruling included a prohibited steps order, barring her removal from the country without permission. But Lilly's custody proceedings were not even over yet. Cara's sister-in-law Elenor, who lived in London, could easily have helped Cara get the children out of the country. Every fibre of my being protested against the idea of Jack handing over the passports to Cara. Jack translated Cara's messages to the lawyers. We tried to delay the passport issue for as long as possible. We knew that if Cara fled without permission, she would be at a disadvantage and Jack would have every chance of getting sole custody when the police brought the children back from Europe... if they could find them. But all this could take months. Or years. And we had no desire to go to court in The Hague. Jack didn't want to take any chances either. The world isn't that big, just a small village, really, but it's easy to disappear in it, everyone knows that you can disappear for years, decades, you can make people disappear. Legal system here, police there; there were plenty of examples of these kinds of child abductions.

After seeing the translated messages, no one mentioned for weeks that Jack should return the passports to Cara. The lawyers remained silent.

Later, when the matter could no longer be postponed, it was agreed that Jack would hand over the passports to Cara's solicitor at her office, where they would be kept in safe custody until the court granted one parent permission to travel abroad with the children. This seemed to be a safe solution.

Father's Day followed shortly after the two-week holiday. According to the court order, the children could spend an extra day with the relevant parent on Mother's Day and Father's Day. But Cara didn't miss the opportunity to play a little game.

- "I'll give you the children for a few hours," she promised Jack, but in the end, she didn't do so, because Elsie started crying in the car.
- "See, she doesn't want to go anywhere with you; she doesn't want to be with you! „Cara said to Jack and took the little girl out of the car before her father could calm her down. Lilly stayed in the car.
- "You can take her! Take Lilly," Cara said, smiling triumphantly at Jack, then pressed a bag of sweets from her pocket into Elsie's hand as if it were a reward.

Jack came home feeling terribly frustrated. He had all kinds of plans to take the children to the city centre, buy balloons, go to the amusement park, and, for the first time in their lives, really celebrate together that he, Jack, was the father and that Elsie and Lilly were his little girls. For some reason, this was very important to Jack, who had been planning and talking about this day for weeks. Instead, he slumped down on the kitchen chair, drank another cup of coffee, and decided to mow the lawn. Lilly was asleep in her baby carrier, just as he had brought her in from the car, and didn't even wake up to what was happening around her.

An hour and a half later, Cara called Jack to ask him to come pick up Elsie if he wanted to, because she couldn't cope with her. "Now, she said, she's sure that Elsie will go with Jack too; she'll be happy to stay with him." But Jack didn't go to pick up Elsie that day. He took Lilly back to Cara in the early afternoon and was silent all evening.

There had been no news about the police investigation since Jack got his phone back in May and sent in the evidence he had officially translated. We had not been notified whether the case had been closed or what had become of it. One afternoon in June, Jack called the police for information.

This time, he asked to speak to the officer's superior. The superior, familiar with the case, told Jack that, due to insufficient evidence, no proceedings had been initiated against Cara. The Metropolitan Police website provides a detailed description of how the police should proceed if threats occur more than twice or show an increasing trend in severity. Jack had been suffering from repeated threats, false accusations of different things, and assaults, including physical abuse, for a year and a half. The police knew about all of this, almost everything. But they did nothing to Cara. Why? Because they did not see it as justified and did not find the evidence sufficient. Jack looked at me incredulously, phone in hand, and put the call on speaker. "I see," he said to the police officer. The officer then said something very strange to Jack:

- "What exactly do you want to achieve?" he asked. "What would you like us to do with your wife? Would you like her to go to prison? Do you really want us to put the mother of your children in prison?"

Jack suddenly couldn't answer that question. Even after a few moments, he could only manage a few fragmented sentences.

- "Not necessarily... I just want this to be over. Because I can't go on living like this. I want someone to at least warn her that she can't do this... someone to tell her she can't treat people like this... She keeps threatening me with everything. She blackmails me with my children, she accuses me...
- "All right," replied the police officer. I'll send a colleague to see you next week, and you can discuss this with him. He'll take another statement, and we'll take it from there.

Jack hung up the phone and looked at me, unsure of what to do.

- "What kind of question was that from the police officer?" he asked. Do I want to put the mother of my children in prison? Isn't that some kind of emotional thing? How can a police officer ask something like that? And what should I have answered?"

I didn't know what the right answer was either. The most appropriate answer came from my son Joe, to whom we later recounted the conversation.

- "All you had to say, Jack," Joe explained, "was that you just want the principle that the law applies equally to everyone to prevail. All you had to do was ask the policeman how the police would have treated you if you had done to Cara what she did to you! If you had punched her so hard that her lip split, if you had threatened to take her child away, if you had taken her money, if you had repeatedly humiliated her, and if you had threatened to set fire to her house... What would they have done to you, as a man? The same thing they did to her. I don't think so! You'd be in prison by now and would have a lifelong criminal record... Just because you're a man, the law treats you differently. Accept that. In this country, what would immediately lead to prosecution for a man is overlooked and ignored when it comes to a woman. That's the truth." Joe added in a resigned tone, and I had to admit he was right. On the "Accused. Me" website, which I had unfortunately come across by then, there are thousands of examples of how this happens every day in practice to innocent men.

There was nothing we could do but wait.

The police officer did come, not at the appointed time, but a day later, and unexpectedly, but he did show up. He took another statement, took the evidence, and said he would be in touch after discussing the case with his superior. We heard nothing from him for weeks.

We've been waiting ever since. We're waiting for the police to call, for their decision, for the case to be closed, for anything, we don't know yet. Meanwhile, life went on and continues to go on.

After one of the long weekends, Cara handed over Lilly to Jack again, as she usually did. In a dirty, sour-smelling shirt, in an awful representation.

Jack began bathing the baby in the morning. But as Lilly tilted her head back in the warm water, the folds of her neck became visible. And in them sat clumps of curdled formula. The lactic acid had burned the baby's delicate skin bright red. As Jack wiped Lilly's neck with oily cotton wool, the little girl cried bitterly under his hand. After the bath, we rubbed her skin with Sudocrem, which is the only thing that works for this. The next day, Jack asked Cara to pay a little more attention to the child. Cara smiled. She hadn't noticed what had happened, she said with a shrug, but she would put some breast milk on it, and everything would be fine, and it would heal anyway. And then she blamed us:

> *"Why do you have to make such a big deal out of everything? Why are you so mean? Why do you always have to talk about everything so negatively?"*

During her next visit, the health visitor simply told Cara that this often happens in hot weather, that babies' necks and skin folds turn red, and that she shouldn't worry too much about it...

"It's a common problem in this hot weather." The health visitor said.

Cara relayed the health visitor's message to Jack and shrugged her shoulders again, smiling.

I couldn't believe my ears. Pardon? What is the common problem? Sour milk residue in the baby's neck, which is causing a moisture lesion? Or a baby without a bath and clean clothes? "This is quite a common problem, said the health visitor. It was echoing in my mind. I was starting to lose my patience, and I was so tempted to ask:

"Really? On which continent? And in what culture? Where exactly?"

But I realised that it would be pointless to ask these questions. In the same place where people don't wash their hands before touching a baby… Even after Covid-19, a pandemic that lasted three years, the health visitor was unwilling to ask where she could wash her hands upon arrival, whether she could have a towel, or whether we could provide her with hand sanitiser...The health visitor never once washed her hands when she came to visit my newborn, infant, and toddler grandchildren. For me, born in the homeland of Semmelweis, this was a shock.

But life went on.

At the end of June, rats moved into Cara's house. They had already been there in the winter; we know that because Cara complained about them, but now they were back, in full force. Cara couldn't catch them, but she saw and heard the rodents, and she said that the food left out on the kitchen counter kept disappearing. Cara bought poison, laid it out, and it disappeared too. She was hopeful. But the rats came back; they did not die, and they seemed to have increased in number. Cara called Jack to come look at her house and go inside to help her get rid of them. She went to the council and demanded another flat. She couldn't live like this! She said to anyone who would listen. And Jack was a useless bastard again, who wouldn't help her at all, who couldn't be counted on for anything! The neighbours were to blame for putting out the rubbish; the council was to blame for not collecting it on time; everyone was responsible and to blame for the fact that she, Cara, and her children had to live with the rats...

"Jack should take the children and look after them until the rats are gone or until I get a new flat. The children should sleep at Jack's place every night until then. During the day, they should go over to Jack, or they could just stay there." That's what Cara said and wanted, and so for three consecutive weeks, from Sunday evening to Thursday noon, the children stayed with Jack. And all day Friday too. Five days a week.

Elsie settled in completely and was visibly very happy with the situation. We went on lots of trips, played in playgrounds, went to the swimming pool, and her cousins came to visit. Elsie was already bilingual by then, repeating a few English words to me in German and mixing up words, saying "wasser" instead of "water", for example, which is how I realised that she also speaks German. She was an incredibly intelligent little girl. However, it was still impossible to teach her not to mention the word „Nana" too often in front of her mother.

In the fourth week, Cara withdrew her previous requests for childcare and told Jack that she wanted everything to be as it was in the court order, with only three days and three nights with the children, and that it would be good if only Jack was with them now, because Jack would see that she would make sure that no one else could be with them...That „no one else" was me. Cara was terribly jealous. She couldn't stand Elsie calling me Nana in front of her; she couldn't stand that my granddaughter loved me, that she was attached to me, she simply couldn't stand that the little girl enjoyed being with me...

By mid-July, Cara had arranged for herself to get a new council flat. She was told she could move in within two weeks. Jack was completely devastated. Before the guardianship investigation, Cara could move into a freshly painted, clean new home, away from her totally dilapidated house, which had been just as beautiful and clean when Jack took it over and renovated it, but which had since been overrun by rats. Where the stove no longer works, where Cara sold the brand-new furniture she bought on hire purchase, where the walls are dirty, and the wallpaper is torn. Cara is moving into a new property where nothing will show how she has lived with her children for the past two years. Where the circumstances that reflect her real life will not be visible, but rather those that the guardianship authority expects in a child custody case. The health visitor and social workers helped Cara with this trick. A fair and correct procedure. Certainly.

However, she would have to pay a fee to move, a few hundred pounds. And she would need boxes and someone to help her. – said Cara. Of course, she expected Jack to do all this. To lend her money, bring boxes, and help her move. But no one else could know her new address, where she would be living with her children. – Cara also said. And that „no one else," of course, was me. Again.

Cara hates instinctively. She hates everyone she can't manipulate. She hates Jack, too, when she can't manipulate him. When Jack is setting up borders, he cannot be manipulated, not obeying her, then he is a drug dealer, a junkie, a bastard, and a shitty father. But when she needed him with the children for extra time, childcare, etc., then he's not a junkie, he's not a cripple, and he's not a shitty father.

"Be amicable!" The judge instructed Jack - and Cara too, both parents, I suppose - at the end of the hearing.

Shared parental custody presupposes that the parents treat each other kindly and respectfully for the safety and emotional well-being of the child(ren).

I would now like to know whether the judge considers all the behaviour, spoken and written words that Cara has constantly directed at Jack – and not only at Jack – to fall within the category of "amicable". Or does only the man, the father, have to be amicable?

Because a 21-year-old woman is not subject to the law or instructions? Can a 21-year-old woman, by giving birth to a child, override all rules and do whatever she wants with anyone?

Will the truth ever come out to the judge? And to the health visitor? To the social worker? Will the eyes of those in society who are currently blinded by indifference or ignorance ever be opened, those who have sworn to serve the truth and should be making responsible decisions and thinking about the welfare of children? Or is everyone Lillith's daughter, Nox's child? And do women, just because they are women, stick together? Do they protect each other with their heads buried in the sand, even at the cost of lies, even if it means harming the innocent and causing pain?

A young woman came to this country and deceived everyone. She had never worked anywhere in her life, but she immediately received all kinds of support. Through her husband, she acquired real estate, but after repeated abuse, her husband moved out rather than stay with her. And the charade continued: after the break-up, Cara became the abandoned young mother who had to be supported with all possible means. With monthly benefits above the minimum subsistence level and donations, and if she doesn't feel like cleaning and her home is infested with rats and bedbugs, she can even get a new house. Indeed, families with several children have also been waiting for council housing for months, including two of my colleagues, both born here. But that doesn't matter. Cara has priority. She has given an Oscar-worthy performance, and anyone could learn from her. And it's a huge system failure! Or the fault of the officials working in the system... But honestly, when I think about the whole story, I always come to the conclusion that I can't blame anyone. Cara deceived me, and I missed it, too. How could anyone else not, someone who doesn't live with her, who doesn't know her, who can't recognise her behaviour?!

No one knew, and no one knows today, whether Cara has any kind of diagnosable mental illness, or whether she is just inherently cunning, a liar, crude, and rude. But this was the moment Jack first wondered whether his marriage was nothing but a scam.

However, we didn't have to worry about Cara's flat swap for long. She didn't have the money to pay the few hundred pounds she owed for the house move, and Jack wouldn't support her financially any more than he did for the children. When the traps Cara had bought were filled with fat rats, Cara asked Jack to come over to dispose of the dead animals. I wouldn't have done that either, but I didn't tell Jack that. I understood his motivations, I think. He didn't want to be blamed again for not helping, and he tried to avoid any conflict.

Late summer merry-go-round

We still had a long summer month ahead of us. Until then, Elsie and Lilly were with their father three, four, five times a week, sleeping there, and overall spending much more time with him than with their mother. Lilly was already smiling, cooing at Jack's face, and often asking to be picked up. Elsie was always very sad when she had to go back to her mother, saying a long goodbye to the dog and cat and waving her little hand at the house as she and her father walked out the garden gate. She never smiled in the car on the way to her mother's house, she never said "Mummy", she showed no joy, only concern. When her mother opened the door, however, Elsie smiled, but it was a very different smile from the one Jack and I knew. Her father always waved and called out a loud goodbye as he walked down the stairs, but Elsie didn't respond right away or wave back. She always looked at her mother first, like a radar, trying to gauge Cara's mood, and only then did she start waving and shouting "Bye, Daddy!" if her mother's face showed no sign of anger or agitation. Elsie is not yet two years old...

I was also worried about what would happen. My little granddaughter is not even two years old, and she clearly knows and senses what is going on around her. She is a cautious, thoughtful, and very intelligent little child. She has also become tactical, without anyone suspecting it. This filled me with despair and fear.

There was still no baby gate at the top of the stairs. Lilly had recurring thrush all summer, and Elsie no longer slept in the afternoon because, according to her mother, if she put Elsie down then, she would have trouble falling asleep at night, and she believed a two-year-old should not be sleeping in the afternoon anyway. The little girl was constantly tired and very fussy when she came to our house, almost always falling asleep in my lap or in Jack's arms as soon as they entered the house. Elsie always had lots of blue-green bruises on her body, on her legs, arms, and little elbows, probably from falling when she was tired.

I often wondered what else would happen. Does something very serious have to happen before someone finally takes the trouble to look behind the scenes and see what is going on, and then realise where and what really needs to be done to help?

Do we really have to wait for a tragedy to happen?

TURBULENT AUTUMN - FALSE ALLEGATIONS RELOADED

No tragedy occurred. But everything close to it did. Autumn rushed by with full force into the rainy winter here; events swept us along like the wind sweeps leaves, so that we fell, dry and weary, into the beginning of the new year, like into a muddy puddle, where loudly squelching rubber boots and shoes will trample on us until we disappear, are destroyed, or become invisible.

It's good not to know what lies ahead, which is why I never liked asking fortune-tellers for help. In most cases, it's better not to know what's coming, because if you did, you might give up, be horrified, lose your strength, or lose all motivation.

So, Cara's move to the new flat didn't happen. We considered this good news. The Early Help Hub, part of the child and family protection service, had been dealing with Cara, Jack, and the children's situation since June, but it did not support Cara moving out of her two-bedroom council flat into a one-bedroom flat in a housing estate.

During the monthly meetings that were arranged for Cara and Jack to help them become parents, some rather strange things happened. At one of these meetings, Cara was unable to control herself and had a heated argument with Jack in front of the social workers, who then recommended her therapy. They concluded that Cara had anger issues. Finally, someone noted something, we might think, but nothing really happened. Cara went to the therapy group recommended for her once and then never showed up again.

Social workers tried many times to visit Cara to offer help, and during one of their visits in August, they discovered that Cara was using marijuana daily. The cigarette butts were scattered in front of the front door. When asked, Cara herself admitted that yes, she does smoke weed. Of course, the narrative was that she was terribly stressed and couldn't manage her life any other way. The interpretation was perfectly characteristic of her: immediately after her confession, she asked for help, saying that she wanted to get rid of this terrible habit, but needed help to do so...

The hearing scheduled for September was postponed because, at the end of July, Cara submitted another request to leave the country, which had to be investigated separately by the child welfare service (Cafcass). By the time the application had been investigated, and it had been determined that leaving the country was still not in the children's best interests and could not be supported by child welfare services, Cara had changed her mind and withdrawn her application. She stated that her situation had changed (improved) a lot since then; she had received help, made friends, was starting to fit in, and had even started a new relationship. The new partner appeared at the end of June, and since then their relationship has become serious, Cara said. Well, at least we understood why the children were spending more and more time with Jack, 4-5 days and nights a week by the end of the summer... Only the stress that Cara might take them away, or that they (the Court and the officers) might let her take the children abroad, was something that no one could erase or make us forget...

The court scheduled another hearing for October, but the guardian requested a postponement because, at the very end of the investigation, literally on the last day! Cara called the child welfare officer and asked for help... The essence of her request for help was that Cara expressed her fear that Elsie might have been sexually abused by her own father, Jack, or, if not by him, then by his friends. Cara was certain that something had happened, as Elsie's behaviour had changed, she said. Elsie would occasionally refuse to have her nappy changed, complain of pain down below, and sometimes did not want to go to her father during visiting hours. The guardian did his job: a report of this gravity had to be investigated, so he asked the court to postpone the scheduled hearing and to allow social services to intervene, assess the situation, and make a final decision on the children's placement only then.

Just when you think things can't get any worse, the pit really opens beneath you...

Jack couldn't sleep or eat for days, weeks on end. Neither could I. The court did not revoke Jack's visitation rights, but the new hearing was set for December, and social workers from the Children's Services were knocking on Jack and Cara's door daily. A meeting was called to renegotiate visitation rights and the schedule, and Jack drafted statements and attempted to defend himself against the false accusations.

Elsie turned two. The terrible twos arrived in her life right on schedule, a milestone that affects every child who is developing normally. The period after age two is called the "terrible twos" here. At this age, young children discover they can undertake tasks, become independent, assert their will, and increasingly demand autonomy over their lives. They won't get dressed or eat if they don't want to, they won't wear the teddy bear T-shirt, they want the pink ballerina one, they won't let you wash their hair if they don't feel like it, and they won't ask for cocoa if they want a banana milkshake instead.

Cara has always had problems with nappy changing, but at this time, the problem became permanent. Elsie had sensitive skin, which quickly turned red from infrequent nappy changes, and the nappy rash became permanent, so, of course, the little girl signalled pain down there, down below.

Elsie started nursery school at the beginning of September. At Cara's request, Jack enrolled Elsie in the nursery they had chosen together, but, as with everything else, Cara did not actively participate in this decision as a parent, and it was left to Jack to take Elsie to the nursery school every morning. I don't know if it was a conscious, manipulative decision on Cara's part to never once take the little girl to nursery school. However, there is no doubt that Elsie lost considerable trust in her father in just a few weeks.

"Daddy comes to pick me up, but he doesn't take me to his house; he takes me to strangers. They say I'm a big girl, and yes, I want to be one, but I don't want to lose my sense of security! My little sister can stay at home, but they're taking me to nursery, where I don't know anyone or anything, where there are new customs, and I have to learn new things. Yes, I want to learn lots of new things, but not when there's no one I love with me..." Elsie must have been thinking to herself.

And so began the morning, crying and begging. Anyone who has had a small child at home or has one now knows what this is like. A few weeks, 1-2 months of torture. For the parent and most small children. After all, what two- or three-year-old likes to find themselves suddenly in a new, unfamiliar environment, leaving the warmth of home behind and integrating into a community of children? Almost none. Not even those who grow up in a complete, loving family. And Elsie, an introverted, withdrawn little girl, certainly didn't. The nursery teachers unanimously stated that Elsie would cry for a few minutes upon arrival, then happily play with the others, and was a very sociable, intelligent, and kind little girl. They swore that the morning tears would disappear within a few weeks and everything would go smoothly, that Elsie would love the community and being there. As is usually the case with children. But in September and the first weeks of October, Elsie was still at the very beginning of this new adventure that was nursery, and her little mind linked this whole pleasant-unpleasant experience to her father's presence... Their relationship had weakened. The terrible twos and this fact came in handy for Cara to fabricate another false accusation...

Thankfully, the social workers did not doubt that Jack had not committed any violence against his own daughter. They wrote their report to the child welfare services and the court, in which they expressed this. But no one reprimanded the mother, Cara, for her false accusations. They did not even ask her why, if she had such serious concerns, she did not take Elsie for a medical examination to obtain certainty. And no one warned her that allegations of sexual assault and molestation are not a game.

Final Court Hearing

The trial was in December, which was (supposed to be) the last one for a long time, and the court granted joint custody to both parents, with equal visitation rights. Holidays and vacations would have been shared equally. And peace. But Cara was not happy. A few weeks before the trial, she said to Jack:

> *"I know you're a good father and you love being with the kids, but I don't want them to spend as much time with you as they do with me, because then I won't get as much support and benefits. If the kids are with us equally, I'll get a lot less money. I need to stay the primary carer, I must keep the" live with" order for myself..."*

This conversation took place between the two of them, of course, and there were no witnesses...At that time, unfortunately, Jack did not make any audio recordings.

Before the hearing ended, Cara became so angry that she got up from the table without saying goodbye and left the courtroom. She slammed the door behind her so hard that it rattled. The judge was surprised, as were Jack and the lawyers. The next two days were Cara's time with the children, and when Jack got them back, he found a large purple bruise on Elsie's shoulder. He notified the social worker, who further investigated the matter. On 15 December, Cara was visited by the social worker and two police officers. According to the report, Cara became extremely nervous and angry when she saw the social worker and wanted to slam the door on her, but she couldn't because of the police officers.

On 17 December, Jack's court-approved 10-day Christmas break with the girls began. On the morning of 18 December, Cara refused to hand over the children. When Jack's solicitor asked her to comply with the court order, she did hand over the children, but she called the hospital and the police too, to report that Jack had probably sexually abused Elsie. The police dismissed the report – I think – because no one came to Jack's house; only a social worker called him to inform him that he had been accused again. Jack calmly said that this was nonsense and offered to take Elsie for a medical examination if anyone thought it was necessary. The social services staff did not consider this necessary. But they still did nothing about the false accusations. And the Police neither. They both remained passive.

After handing over the children, Cara tried to be friendly with Jack again for a few days. She sent him messages saying she had broken up with her boyfriend, that their relationship, which had begun in June, was now over, and that she was deeply upset by everything that had happened and wanted peace. She also sent a screenshot of an email she claimed to have received from the local health service, stating that she had been examined and they were happy to inform that they had found no malignant abnormalities in her brain, no tumours, but that she needed further tests to determine the cause of her complaints and symptoms... The screenshot of the email was suspiciously strange, and we couldn't be sure if it was real or if Cara had edited it, just like she had done a year earlier with the ultrasound images and video of her alleged pregnancy.

I understood the situation less and less: accusing the father of my children of sexual assault, then initiating reconciliation a few days later, and trying to elicit sympathy, emotionally manipulating him with a hospital incident?!... Wtf? – to quote the British expression again – What is going on here? What is wrong with this young woman? Is Cara bipolar? – I had so many questions. But there was no one to turn to. The social services and the child welfare services were all hostile towards us; they were clearly biased against Cara, and I was afraid that if we said or reported anything about Cara, they would turn it against us and try to prove that we were malicious and/or wanted to alienate the children from their mother...I didn't know what to do, what could be done, or how to do it. So, I turned my attention to the children instead.

The winter holiday started well, and every day was filled with joy. We took the children to the music-sensory group, where they met Santa Claus. We took them to a nearby farm, where they got to pet reindeer and llamas and dance with the elves. They got presents and enjoyed every moment, Elsie and Lilly.

But two days before Christmas, the girls came down with scarlet fever. They were listless and feverish. We took them to the doctor, who prescribed antibiotics, and from then on, we nursed them. They slept a lot, but thankfully, they still had their appetite, so Jack cooked them all kinds of delicacies, and after three days, the children started to feel better.

However, two days after Christmas, we had to return them to Cara, who was taking them to Austria for her ten-day holiday. She informed Jack via the court-ordered Parenting app that she didn't care how sick the girls were, she was leaving with them, and she wasn't going to miss her flight, so Jack had to hand over the children on the evening of 27 December. Jack cried as he dressed the girls. They no longer had a fever, but they were very lethargic, pale, and weak. Personally, I had to beg Elsie for 20 minutes to come downstairs from her father's room, where she was playing with her stuffed animals, pretending that they were all scared and wanted to stay and sleep in the cot bed…

- "Come on, Elsie, go to Mummy, then you can come back later and continue playing, but now you must go! Come on, hurry up, Mummy is waiting!"
- "No, no! Elsie sleeps here. The elephant is scared, Nana, see? Tiger is scared; Cookie Monster is scared. Elsie sleeps here,

Nana", - the little girl pointed to her sister's cot, and I tried to stay calm and not to show what I was feeling, not to say what I was thinking...Very slowly, I tried to convince her, give her the jacket and hat, and soon after, Jack took her to Cara together with Lilly.

PART V – THE INVESTIGATION

Falling into the deepest pit in hell

The children were left with Cara for 10 days as per the Court Order. Cara was supposed to show Jack their return tickets and travel details, where she would be staying with the children while abroad, and which flight they would be taking back. Cara provided no information other than her parents' address. Jack stated on the Parenting app and wrote to the social worker that he did not consent to the children being taken abroad because 1. they were ill, and 2. he had not received the information necessary to give his consent. This did not achieve much. It was the end of the year, between the holidays, and no one was interested in a case involving a mother taking her children abroad without the father's consent. Cara told Jack, somewhat sarcastically, not to worry; she wasn't stupid enough not to come back; she would be back on time, after 10 days; and she would send him a photo of the ticket for the return journey as soon as she had the money to buy it on 4 January. I tried to reassure Jack that everything would be fine, not to worry, really! Cara had complied with the court's orders to date. She had tried to resist, but the court's decision had always been sacred to her, and surely it would be no different now...

Jack wasn't very reassured, but he kept himself busy with work and talked a lot with his friends, so he wouldn't think about his fears.

He received photos of the girls every two or three days, mostly of Elsie, with almost nothing of Lilly, but Cara assured him that both children were well, had recovered, and no longer required antibiotics.

Cara promised every day that she would send the ticket and flight number and asked Jack to pick her up at the airport because she wouldn't be able to get home with the children on her own. She broke up with her boyfriend in early December and can no longer count on him, she explained to Jack again, and she won't be able to get home with the children on her own. Jack didn't reply, and later he didn't have an opportunity to do so.

On 4 January, Cara failed to purchase her return tickets as she had promised before her departure, and she went silent online, disappearing from the Parenting App for four days. She did not respond to Jack's questions and refused to state when she would return to the country. She was supposed to return on 7 January and hand the children over to Jack for visitation on 8 January. On 8 January, on the advice of his solicitor, Jack went to the police to report that his children were abroad and that the court order had been violated, as their mother had not handed them over for visitation. Cara was unreachable until 11 January.

On 11 January, a long message landed on the Parenting app, in which Cara said that she was unlikely to ever return and that Jack would probably never see the children again because she had taken Elsie to an Austrian hospital for a medical examination, where it was determined that Elsie had been sexually abused by someone...

"Elsie, Cara wrote, *"she has a very wide vagina, her hymen is not visible, and she is afraid of all men and cries when a stranger is near her. The sexual abuse is a fact, DNA samples are now being taken from her family, and Jack will also have to give a sample, either in Austria or England, but if the truth comes out that it was Jack who abused Elsie, then Cara assures him that Jack will rot in prison...*

I felt nauseous, which had become a constant feeling of mine by now. I didn't even know what was making me feel worse: the fact that my grandchildren's father, my son, was being falsely accused time and time again, or the fact that no one was stopping this from happening again and again? But what horrified me most was that I couldn't be sure if anything bad had actually happened to my granddaughter. Had someone hurt her, someone who had an interest in proving that the little girl had been molested? I was literally physically ill at the thought that someone had done something to Elsie, my granddaughter! That they had hurt her, just to get my son sent to prison and to stop Cara from having to come back to the UK? I was paralysed with terror, unable to cry or scream. My stomach just turned over and over. Jack handled those hours much better than I did, apparently, although I have no idea what was going on inside him; he remained calm. He called the social worker, who came to our flat and read Cara's messages. He promised to take action. He didn't tell us how or what he was going to do, but we trusted him. We later learned that he had contacted Cara by email because he didn't have her phone number, and that he had also contacted the Austrian police and social services.

Cara arrived with the children the next day, on 12 January. She informed Jack of this and said he would not be allowed to see the children until after the official medical examination.

The duty social worker on the social services helpline was in contact with Jack throughout the weekend. Jack knew that Cara had an appointment for a medical examination at the hospital on the 13th. They also told him that there was nothing to prevent him from getting the girls and that he could go to the examination. But Cara did not take Elsie. Cara asked Jack to take Elsie and her to the hospital, but Jack declined. Jack offered to pay for a taxi, but Cara declined and ultimately did not attend the examination with Elsie on the 13th; she went only the next day, on the 14th, when her boyfriend, whom she had broken up with in December, arrived and took them. The examination found that Elsie had not suffered sexual abuse. On the morning of the 15th, Jack was finally able to pick up the children and was happy to see them again, but he couldn't do so without a cloud over his head. Immediately, he had to go to the hospital with Lilly, who, according to her mother, had eaten cigarettes that morning. Cara refused to take Lilly to the doctor, and she could not say how many cigarettes the 10-month-old baby had eaten...Jack did not want to risk Lilly's health and decided to have her checked in the hospital. Thank God Lilly was sent home because she had no symptoms of nicotine poisoning. After a few hours, Jack was finally able to be with his daughters, whom he had been waiting to see for 19 days.

A few days later, the social worker informed Jack that Cara had been unable to show him the Austrian medical documents that would have proven that Elsie had been molested or even examined regarding the molestation. The social worker suggested that visitation rights should continue as per the court order and that Jack should try to forget what had happened. In the meantime, the authorities would investigate the case and, if necessary, recommend a review of the children's placement.

A week passed peacefully. But on the second week, after the visitation, when Jack handed the children back to Cara in the morning, Cara called the social worker in the afternoon and reported that Elsie had returned from her father, Jack, with bruises and contusions. The social worker called Jack and asked him what he knew about Elsie's injuries. Jack replied with what he knew: Elsie had no injuries whatsoever. The social worker sent Jack the photos she had received from Cara. Jack sent them to me. At that moment, my patience ran out. I called the social worker from my own phone, and I have no idea what I said to him, but the gist of it was that I'd had enough! I also asked him to go out and see my granddaughter for himself, to check if Elsie was okay, what injuries she had, and when they had occurred. I had my suspicions that the injuries couldn't be real, because before Jack handed over the girls to their mother, I didn't see any marks on them, so if they were there, they couldn't have happened at our house, and it would be good to know what happened to the children in such a short time. I still hadn't forgotten Elsie's head injury from last June, and I was seriously concerned that Cara might have done something to the children. I still had enough presence of mind and common sense to end the phone call by saying: I find it strange that Jack handed the girls over to their mother in the morning, and Cara only called the social worker in the afternoon, early evening, to say she had found injuries on them... The social worker remained silent for a minute, then said only that he considered my request justified and would arrange for someone to go to Cara's to check on the children.

I am a grandmother. It is the fate of grandmothers to dote on their grandchildren. Grandchildren are a reward, the reward for raising our children, they say. Grandchildren are a source of joy, unconditional love, the joy of being able to love, give, adore, and relive the miracle of teaching and guiding tiny little human beings, now with all our experience and wisdom. Grandmothers take photographs. They have a good habit of wanting to capture every moment they can spend with their beloved little creatures, their grandchildren. I have thousands and thousands of photos and videos on my phone. As it happens, I took a few that morning too, including some while I was getting the girls dressed. I sent these pictures to the social worker. There were no marks or injuries anywhere on Elsie's body that morning. The social worker thanked me for my cooperation. He called Jack later to tell him that he had spoken to Cara and warned her that social workers would be coming to see Elsie the next day. He also informed Jack that Cara had called her back half an hour later after hearing the warning and told him that the marks on Elsie's body seemed to be fading and that they might just be dirt marks, not injuries... I knew exactly what had happened, and I wasn't the only one! Cara wanted evidence against Jack. If the sexual assault charge didn't work, she was in trouble and had to come up with something new. But she didn't expect the photos she had taken wouldn't be enough! She didn't know that the social workers would go out and look at the injuries on Elsie's body themselves...

The next day, Cara couldn't get Elsie to undress in front of the social workers. Elsie cried bitterly and begged her to stop undressing her. The social workers then ordered Cara to take the children to the hospital and called Jack to attend if he wished. Jack went to the hospital to determine what had happened. They sat him down next to Cara in the corridor. In the presence of the police and social workers, Cara whispered to Jack, asking him if he really didn't want her anymore. She said she had reconciled with her boyfriend and was starting a relationship with him again, but that if Jack wanted to, he could contact her anytime, because he would always be a priority for Cara. Jack, as they say, was speechless. The offer was so obscene and so inappropriate, so completely out of place in the situation, that Jack couldn't speak, couldn't react at all, he told me. Luckily, the door opened just then, and the doctor called them in, so he didn't have to answer.

After six hours of waiting and examination, the doctor determined that the children had no visible injuries that could have been caused by abuse, and in fact had no injuries at all. However, the entire story and sequence of events raised very disturbing questions, so social services decided they had to investigate the circumstances. The police were also present during the investigation. The children were removed from Cara's custody and placed in Jack's care. The social workers decided that my grandchildren would be placed in a child protection programme and that their mother would only be allowed to see them under supervision until the first hearing. Jack was also instructed to file a petition in court to review the children's custody rights.

From then on, events accelerated. Cara also picked up the pace. She hysterically demanded her children back, wrote God knows how many letters and emails, made countless phone calls, and told all sorts of lies, and the gaslighting went into overdrive. By the time of the child protection conference, Cara had come up with a new story, claiming that Jack (and I) had painted make-up marks on Elsie's body to get her into trouble, because we knew she would report them to the social worker, and we also knew that they weren't real injuries and so we could get her into trouble... Seriously, if it hadn't happened to us, I would have been interested to find out what the hell was going on! What the human mind is capable of. How the truth can be twisted and what kind of charade has to be played to deceive even educated adults, so that in the end, it all works out for the benefit of those who are least innocent... If it hadn't happened to Jack and me, if it weren't about my grandchildren. But it did happen to us.

The social services network was unable to provide childcare for the child protection conference, the first child protection meeting, as promised, so I stayed with the children and was unable to attend the meeting. All family members who play any role in the children's lives should attend this conference. The parents, relatives, police, health visitor, and appointed social workers are also present. But I couldn't attend. By accident. Due to organisational difficulties. It's regrettable that, a few days earlier, the social worker informed Jack that Cara had said she would not attend the meeting if I were also present...Cara could refuse my presence because she has parental custody, which only a court can take away from her. As a grandmother, I have no rights, but I should have been present at the conference. According to the law. However, the law also gives Cara the right to exclude me. Why did Cara do this? Why did she want to exclude me from attending the conference? It's not difficult for anyone to determine. I am the one who knows everything and remembers everything. The fake pregnancy tests, the ultrasound images, all the false accusations, and all the truths she distorted. The abuse that my son, the children, and I suffered. In my presence, she cannot, and could not, manipulate those who know little about her, or do not know her. In my presence, she cannot lie because I have answers to everything, and not only answers but proof as well. Jack also knew everything, but perhaps he did not remember everything so clearly. He was in shock, numbed by what had happened to him, and Cara was fully aware of Jack's innocent nature and spirit. Jack was gentle, a pure empath, who avoided conflict and never wanted to hurt anyone.

Interestingly, I, the grandmother in whose house my grandchildren were born and with whom I have spent the most time since they were born, after Jack, was not permitted to attend the child protection conference. But Cara's partner, with whom she broke up in December and has since reconciled, was permitted to attend the conference and speak as her steady partner, who is like a stepfather to the children. This man, whom Cara has known for barely eight months, whom the children barely know, whom Cara broke up with after six months of dating, and who is the third man, male partner in Cara's life in the last three years. Andrew sat there and supported Cara in every lie; he probably didn't know they were lies. However, this does not excuse him in any way.

The first child protection conference found out that my grandchildren had suffered emotional and psychological abuse from their mother. However, it also found that the parents were unable to communicate and were blaming each other. Perhaps I could have said that Jack's accusations against Cara (the injuries, the infections, the tone below criticism) are well-founded, but Cara's accusations against Jack are false, lacking any evidence, so perhaps they should not be judged equally... But I did not have the opportunity to say this. All I could and can trust today is that those who currently have control over my grandchildren's fate will realise this for themselves, sooner or later.

The conference concluded that the mother's mental state needs to be investigated. It was also concluded that the mother has used or is using illegal drugs and that the current situation also needs to be investigated.

A new social worker was appointed to supervise the children and maintain contact with the parents until the court hearing concluded. The conference took place on the last day of January. The emergency court hearing was scheduled for a week later. However, the judge did not receive the social services reports and therefore was unable to make a decision. Instead, he requested a new safeguarding report and ordered the parents to comply with social services' instructions until the next hearing, which was scheduled for early April.

The conference concluded that it was in the children's best interests to remain with their father, while ensuring that their mother retained visitation rights. However, it was no longer deemed necessary to order that the mother could only see the children under supervision. Good old gaslighting works well, doesn't it?

"Really, who painted the marks on the children? Really, are you sure they weren't raped? Yeah, the medical examination was completely negative, so it's not possible, but, you know, I am just a concerned mother who is overly protective of her children. I didn't say or think that their father or one of their father's friends molested my daughters, I didn't say that - I was just very worried..." Cara kept saying this new narrative to the social workers, as later revealed in the guardianship authority's documents.

Classic gaslighting: „*What has happened wasn't like that, it was something else, it happened differently*", „*I didn't think, and I didn't say that*", "*I don't understand why you think this or that, you must have misunderstood something*" ... Everybody knew very little about gaslighting that time. Including me. Gaslighting is awkward. And when it happens, it happens so fast! Barely recognisable. And if it happens in a talented interpretation, it seems to be the absolute, honest, undeniable truth.

1ST OF FEBRUARY - THE CHILD'S CONFESSION

This day remained etched in my memory forever. It was the first time Elsie spoke openly, half asleep and therefore presumably completely honestly, about how her mother, Cara, had hurt her. My little granddaughter was two and a half years old, and I thoroughly enjoyed seeing her mind blossom. She talked more and more each day, and she was incredibly cute. It was different experiencing all this as a grandmother than when I was a mother. Back then, technology was less advanced; there were no mobile phones with cameras or audio recorders, and I thoroughly enjoyed being able to capture nearly every phase and moment of my grandchildren's development. I also recorded the bedtime stories.

Our routine is that when Elsie gets into bed, we briefly discuss the day in a way that even a little toddler can understand: what was the best thing that happened that day, what happened, and what are we planning for tomorrow, where would she like to go, what would she like to do the next day? All this has become part of our daily routine, processing the day's experiences after the bedtime story. That's how it was this evening too. Elsie drank her milk from her bottle with relish; we talked a little – for about fifteen- twenty minutes – then she curled up against my chest and breathed peacefully. I thought she had fallen asleep when she suddenly spoke up:

- "Nana, Nana!" - she said very quietly, almost whispering.
- "Yes, sweetie?"
- "Nana, you know, Mummy is not good!"- I didn't answer because I couldn't think of anything to say. And Elsie continued:
- "Mummy hurts me, Mummy hits me. She hit me. Here," said the two-and-a-half-year-old girl, pointing to her head where she had been injured last year.
- "Mummy hits me and kicks me. Mummy is not nice."

Oh, my God. I wouldn't wish this feeling on anyone! My thoughts raced: what could I say to this? I searched for words, searching for an answer, suddenly shocked, terrified, wondering what to do now. Finally, this is all I could come up with:

- "But why? Why did Mummy hurt you? I don't understand... Elsie, my darling, no one will hurt you here! No one will hit you here. Daddy is here. Nana is here. No one will ever hurt you here, ok.? We won't let anybody hurt you! Sleep well, sleep peacefully!"

Elsie didn't answer, but I could feel her little body relax and, all of a sudden, fall into a deep sleep. I was completely distraught. I showed the recording to Jack, who was shocked and decided to mention what had happened to the social worker and the health visitor at the next meeting.

However, only the health visitor attended the next meeting. So, Jack did not show the recording; he just recounted what had happened, what Elsie had said, and how she had confessed to being abused before falling asleep. The health visitor's response was: „Children of this age say all sorts of things, you know, they say this and that, you shouldn't read too much into it."

When Jack told me what happened at the meeting and repeated the health visitor's response, I thought I had misheard. I didn't understand. How could anyone say such a thing?!

In the next few days, I searched the internet for the opinions of child psychologists. I was primarily interested in whether a two-and-a-half-year-old child can lie and exaggerate things. In theory, they are not capable of this before the age of three. I also asked two child psychologists online for their specific, personal opinions, but they did not provide them. They said they couldn't examine or interview Elsie because it's very difficult to assess children at this age. They advised me to inform the health visitor and social worker of what had happened, as they would know how to address the situation. "We've already done that," I thought to myself, "thank you very much." And there was nothing else to be done. I retained the memory of that evening.

There were two months until the next hearing. The new social worker assigned to the case was also a woman. The mother cried and sobbed on the phone about how much she missed her children. *She didn't do anything wrong, she didn't mean it that way, her words were twisted, it was an unfortunate accident that the baby ate cigarettes (three times), but it won't happen again, the mother promises. Besides, she now has support, a stable relationship, and Andrew is always by her side. He loves the children very much, and he will help! The mother cries, yes, she admits she made mistakes, yes, she used drugs and smoked weed in the summer, but she doesn't use them anymore, she did quit! Her two children are everything to her; she will do anything for them, she has always taken care of them, and now they have been taken away from her! This is terrible. Help her, someone, please help her!*

And everything started all over again.

The new social worker visited the mother and the father. After the third week, she told the father the following:

- "Well, OK, the mother may be very agitated and use bad language, - I can see this on the parenting app, - but the mother is very upset because her children have been taken away from her, I think, if the mother uses bad language and makes threats, it's just a reaction to the situation"...

She also asked Jack:

- "Why do you think the mother has violated the court order? What do you mean? How has she violated it? Why do you object to giving the children unsupervised contact with their mother? Why don't you want the children to spend more time with their mother?"

And in the fourth week, the social worker informed the father that, as a social worker, she had conducted an environmental study and found that the children are safe with their mother and that she can spend as much time with them as she wants, so the father should hand them over at this time and on this date. A summons is issued. The judge instructs the parents to cooperate with social services. Jack had no choice but to follow the social worker's instructions and to comply.

They say the flying monkeys can be more dangerous than the ones they serve. They believe everything and act in the name of a holy cause, and they have the power to act, give orders, and do the bidding of those they represent.

My favourite quote from social workers is:

> "Most of the accusations are historical."

And the accompanying explanation:

> "Most false accusations are historical; they happened in the past. And the only way to put things right is to leave the past in the past. Let's do that, shall we? OK. So now we draw a line under it, here's a new chance, now everything can be put right, we'll give everyone this chance, now everything will be different!"

How would everything be different? How could everything be different?

It made my hair stand on end.

Past behaviour predicts future behaviour. That's a psychological fact. If there is no change and no intention to change, nothing will change, and all past behaviour will be repeated. Past behaviour patterns predict future behaviour. The past points to the future.

Most of the social workers' intention by „ let's give a chance and forget the past" might be very humanistic and merciful if there is a single incident, one sole mistake, but might be an absolute failure if there is a repeated pattern of behaviour, and the social workers refuse to see the whole picture, to get to know the whole family history. With all the details. Because the devil is always hiding in the details.

Cara has been trying to separate Elsie from her father for three years, and Lilly from her father for a year. Cara intends to leave this country with the children permanently. Cara constantly threatens Jack that she will send him to prison, and he will "rot there", and the girls will never know who their father was. Cara wants money from the children because she receives benefits for them, but she doesn't really care about them. Every week, I cut Elsie's nails, and Jack washes her hair, ever since this little girl was born. And Lilly? She has lived with us and continues to live with us. Two days after she was born, she was transferred to her father for custody, but when it came time to submit the benefits paperwork, Jack was required to take her to Cara several times, and Cara insisted on being able to state that the baby was living in her household. Cara didn't even try to breastfeed Lilly, sent multiple messages about it to Jack, but she lied to the Court and to social workers that she did, and she still breastfeeds Elsie to this day to comfort her or express her love for her. Elsie gets everything, while Lilly doesn't even have new clothes. She only gets cheap formula and used toys. On Lilly's first birthday, Elsie wears the "Birthday Girl" badge in the photos. If Cara is narcissistic, then Elsie is the golden child, and Lilly is the scapegoat who did not live up to expectations and whose birth did not bring Jack back to Cara. And sooner or later, Lilly will be blamed for everything. It's already started. She is already the reason Cara can't spend enough quality time with Elsie. *"Because Lilly is always here,"* says Cara. *"She's still small, it's difficult with her, we can't go to nice places with Elsie, because of her."*

It's sad. It's cruel. For all of us. Especially for the children.

No one will readily believe me, because even my oldest son, Joe, found it inconceivable that Cara would forget Lilly's first birthday!

- "Come on, Mum, no woman could forget the day she gave birth to her child! Cara's not good, but let's be fair, she is not that bad!" said Joe, and I could see in his eyes that he was trying to figure out how serious I was about what I had said. That Cara would probably forget Lilly's very first birthday.

However, I noticed that in the week leading up to Lilly's first birthday, there were no messages from Cara on Jack's Parenting App requesting additional time off to celebrate her daughter's birthday. Every day I asked Jack:

- "Didn't Cara write to you? Didn't she write to tell you which day she wanted to celebrate Lilly's birthday?" Jack just shook his head.

After that, I just asked Jack not to tell Cara anything, not to warn her.

A mother should know when her child's birthday is – that's the bare minimum, I think, even if she doesn't love the child that much... - and I was curious to find out if Cara was really capable of forgetting the birthday of the child, she had given birth to a year ago! Jack agreed and promised to keep quiet about it.

As it happened, the next Core Group Meeting, a small-group meeting attended only by parents, social workers, health visitors, teachers, and those directly involved in the children's lives and care, was scheduled for the day before Lilly's birthday. Somehow, I managed to get to this meeting because Elsie was at nursery and we were able to take Lilly with us. At one point during the meeting, Jack asked the health visitor when she would next visit us to see the children. The health visitor stated that she would return when Lilly turned one. She would come a few days or a week after that date. And she asked a question right away.

- "When is Lilly's first birthday exactly?" – She opened her notebook and held her ballpoint pen to write down the date.

Silence fell in the small room. No one answered. I glanced at Cara, who was sitting across from me. She wasn't looking at me or anyone else; she was watching her own knees, her legs moving as if she were listening to music. Jack didn't answer either; he was also looking at Cara, watching her, waiting for her to speak. But nothing happened. The health visitor repeated the question:

- "Hm? When exactly will Lilly be one year old?" - I waited a moment, but then I felt I had to answer if no one else did:
- "Tomorrow. Lilly will be one year old tomorrow," I said quietly.

The social worker sitting next to me suddenly glanced to my side and looked at me. Her gaze met mine, but her expression betrayed no emotion. There were a few seconds of silence. Then the social worker suddenly turned to Cara:

- "Cara, you know, I hadn't even thought of that, so it's good that it came up! Would you like to spend some time alone with Lilly tomorrow to celebrate her birthday?"

Cara, who seemed very happy about this, replied:

- "Of course! Thank you very much! That would be really great!"

But her gaze remained cold as ice. I will never forget it. Not the moment, not the tone of voice, not the silence. Nor the pain that I felt when we got home from that meeting, and I hugged Lilly tightly in the kitchen. The little girl whose own mother had forgotten her first birthday. My innocent little lamb. Lilly knew nothing, felt nothing, suspected nothing; she only knew our love and happily wriggled in my arms. She held my face in her little hands, held it between her palms, and smiled at me.

"We'll have to make up for it for the rest of our lives," I thought, and it didn't hurt me, because I'll be happy to do it and Jack will be happy to do it too, I'm sure of that, but it touched me, in fact, I would rather say that it crushed me spiritually when I understood, when I sensed the extent of the kind of lovelessness that could lead a mother to forget her child's very first birthday! Bottomless...

I didn't cry until Lilly's father had taken her away. I went to the bathroom and cried there. I don't usually cry, not easily, but now I had to. I felt that if I didn't, my heart would break into pieces. The pain was so enormous. I cried badly. For a long time.

I knew, I could feel, that this incident had not escaped the social worker's attention. But I also knew that she was still biased towards the mother, Cara. There were many small signs of this. For example, she hardly ever communicated with Jack about anything. She only called Jack when she had instructions for him: when and where to take the children. She never asked Jack if he needed anything, how he was doing, or if everything was all right. She simply reduced contact to a minimum. It wasn't that Jack missed a social worker calling him; he would have liked Annie to tell him her plans a few days in advance rather than giving him ad hoc instructions. Jack would also have been happy if Annie had answered her phone calls sometimes, on those rare occasions when Jack wanted to ask her something. But that rarely happened. Annie was a flying monkey and remained so for a very long time.

However, she wasn't the biggest one. The staff at Action for Children were. They were supposed to help the children, but they gave the mother everything imaginable: money, a telephone, free furniture, carpets, dishes, food parcels, and they accepted the mother's lies without any question. Help, help the poor, vulnerable young woman. The social workers were exactly the same until certain things came to light, the mask slipped, and Cara became entangled in her lies. But the support workers at The Action for Children did not wake up. I would have loved to tell them all that I understood they wanted to help. But if you want to help, then get Cara a diagnosis, "get a diagnosis for her"! Find out why Cara behaves the way she does! The greatest and only help for Cara would be to get her affairs in order. And for her to live a happy life, she needs to be diagnosed! What is wrong with this young woman? Is she bipolar? Borderline? Paranoid? She is afraid of everything! She is afraid of everyone and avoids all unfamiliar situations! Is she antisocial? Sociopath? Has she ADHD? Autism? Or is she just "simply" antisocial with narcissistic traits? It needs to be found out, and there needs to be a cure, a solution, a treatment! If Cara can be treated and agrees to treatment, then she and everyone else can finally live happily. That would be the most important thing for my two grandchildren. But even though several people at the conference stated that the mother's mental state needed further investigation, no one did anything, and the suggestion disappeared into thin air. This information was lost. Or it was made to be lost, disappear...

At the court hearing in February, after adjourning the case, the judge simply said to Cara and Jack again:

"The truth will come out. Those who lie will regret it very much."

I didn't want anything else either.

With all my heart, I wished for nothing more than for this to be true!

And then, for the story to finally come to an end. That's what I wished for, that's what I hoped for.

But that's not how it turned out. We still had to wait for the truth to come out. We had no idea how long or how.

What else would prevent the truth from coming to light? Even in our worst nightmares, we could never have imagined what would happen next...

"It's going to get worse" – Rapülők

There was a band 30 years ago, back in my home country, that composed a song titled "Don't worry, everything is just going to get worse." I never liked Péter Geszti for this hit song. I always thought it was a terribly negative attitude. How could anyone sing something like that? Into the airwaves, onto the World Wide Web? If I had known thirty years ago that he was right and that it was realism rather than negativity, I would have forgiven him long ago. In the summer of 2024, I could have hummed this song endlessly.

No decision was made at the April hearing regarding the children's placement or custody.

The judge instructed the local authority to continue monitoring the family and ordered another Section 7 investigation, which had already been conducted twice by the independent guardianship authority (Cafcass). It was now up to the social services to do so.

All this happened because the local authorities continued to fail to provide the requested data and their reports to the court, and the judge knew virtually nothing about Cara's desire to stay abroad with the children, nor about what happened in January: the false accusations against Jack, the marks painted on the children's bodies, and nothing else. All the judge could see in the papers was that the joint custody decision made in December 2023 was failing, as the parents were back in court... The children were placed on the Child Protection Register, and social services took over most of the control over the children's welfare. The Judge had no choice but to assign additional tasks to the child welfare services to obtain detailed information and, if necessary, make a new decision. The judge then postponed the hearing until June. By then, he was supposed to receive a detailed report from the child welfare services, including an environmental study and assessments.

The ground slipped away from under Jack's feet. I was stunned to hear that we would have to wait another three months. Neither of us could understand how an authority could fail to fulfil its court-ordered duty. How was it possible that this had no consequences? But we didn't have time to dwell on it too much. We cared for the children, welcomed the social workers who regularly visited us, ensured that the mother had her visitation rights, and, all the while, we worked to pay our bills.

By then, Cara could spend three days and three nights a week with Elsie and Lilly – she had the children from Monday morning to Thursday morning. We spent Fridays helping the girls relax and return to their peaceful and familiar routine. They usually arrived hungry and thirsty, eagerly throwing themselves into their games, loud and unrestrained. I bought half a kilo of Sudocrem for Lilly's bottom because she had to be treated for nappy rash every week. Jack also had to take both girls to the doctor because they had thrush again. We exchanged messages regularly with the child protection officer.

We intended to go on holiday in the summer. We had already paid for the holiday last year and purchased the plane tickets for June. We had to contact child protection services and request permission for the holiday. We had planned to raise this issue at the next Child Protection conference, but I proposed inviting Annie, the social worker, to our home and asking her for advice in person. Annie came; I thanked her for taking the time to see me. We sat down on the living room sofa and began discussing the children. I showed her the photos from last year's holiday and told her that the children's grandfather and great-grandfather were elderly and ill, and we would like to visit them again this year. This is also because this may be the last time. I told her everything honestly. I didn't expect to cry while doing so. I didn't plan it, I didn't want to. The British don't like it when someone shows their emotions. They don't consider it appropriate or acceptable. I was afraid of how Annie would react, so I apologised. But surprisingly, she placed her hand on my arm and said she was very sorry and understood how I felt. She advised me to take the albums with me, to speak with Cara in person before or after the conference, and to ask her to permit the children to go on holiday with Jack.

The next conference. It was on the last day of April.

This time, I was invited as a direct participant who plays a role in the children's lives. Taking Annie's advice, I took the photo albums from the previous year's holiday with me, with the intention of showing Cara how much fun the girls had had and to formally ask her to hand over the children's passports and agree to the 10-day holiday, which was due to take place at the beginning of June.

But the atmosphere was so awful that none of this plan came to fruition. When Cara saw me there, the hatred that emanated from her descended on the room like a fog and hung in the air. She sat up stiffly. I tried to ignore it. We sat in a semicircle: the two social workers/guardians, Cara and her partner, the health visitors, and the flexi social worker who was supposed to teach the mother, Jack, and me. I could see Cara from the side, but I didn't have to look her in the eye, nor would I have done so.

The conference began, and ten minutes later, Cara stood up and rushed out of the room, gasping for air. Her partner, Andrew, followed her. It took a few minutes for them to return. Some people were concerned, while Annie and the social worker beside her were simply surprised. But everyone asked Cara if she was okay when she returned. "Panic attack, I just couldn't breathe," she replied.

Conferences like this can be terribly slow and boring for those who are not involved in the case. Each participant read their official statement regarding the past three months, and then they had to decide together whether there had been any progress, any positive developments, or any developments regarding the children's concerns. The executive read my short statement aloud, and at that moment, Cara's psyche snapped. Without anyone asking her, she started talking loudly and rapidly, which, after a while, escalated into shouting:

"Why is she even here?" - she pointed at me. - "The grandmother? She has no right, no parental responsibility! Everyone knows that the children are fine; they love being with me and want to live with me. I want my four nights back! Just like it always was! I want four nights, and they can stay with their father for three! That's why I'm here. I want my four nights back. If I don't get them back, I will exercise my parental rights and keep the children with me the next time they come.

The conference leader and Annie jointly reprimanded Cara. Annie noted that this request required investigation and that she was about to recommend reducing the mother's contact time because she had doubts that, although the mother loved her children very much, the mother's primary motivation for requesting four nights was financial. The children's health and educational needs were not being taken into account: when problems arose, the mother did not take them to the doctor or to nursery, and the girls regularly missed nursery. Cara's voice cut through the sudden silence:

- "I am a good mother; I take care of my children! The children want to be with me, not with their father! I want back the four nights I can spend with them!"

I suddenly had to cough. I couldn't help it; I couldn't hold it back. Cara turned to me and, even without any mental or spiritual gifts, I could see exactly who I was dealing with. I immediately bowed my head. But by then, Cara was already shouting:

- "There! That's what I'm talking about! What kind of disrespect is this! She's laughing at me out loud! She never respected me, and now she's laughing at me out loud; it's intolerable, it's unacceptable!" Cara was incredibly aggressive; she was overflowing with hatred. Her partner finally spoke up.
- "He was just coughing, didn't you hear? Calm down! Try to calm down, Cara!"

After the incident, it was clear that the meeting chair and Annie no longer wanted to discuss anything and were trying to end the conference as quickly as possible. All that remained was the vote; everyone had to score on a scale of 0 to 10 how much the children were still at risk of emotional harm. Where 0 was the worst, and 10 was the best. Each participant had to justify their score in 2-3 sentences. Everyone scored 0 or 1. So the children remained on the register. I was surprised by the flexi social worker's score and explanation. She said:

- "The mother's behaviour raises doubts. Also, in the sense that the mother regards the grandmother as a third party, not entitled to have an opinion. That's why I gave her a score of 0..."

The Conference ended. Nothing has changed, neither in the contact arrangement nor in any other respect.

To relieve our tension, Jack, the children, and I went shopping after the conference. Annie's words, which I overheard when she was talking to the other social worker, were running through my head. Cara had 30 days to prove that the children lived with her and that she had custody. If she can't prove it, she won't receive any further benefits from the state; at best, she'll receive the minimum, about £300. She can't pay the council flat rent, the bills, or even live on that. That is why she seeks to regain full custody, which will occur only if the children spend four nights per week in her household. The other guardian ad litem shook his head, but listened attentively and did not respond while I was within earshot. On my way out of the courtroom, I asked the presiding judge, the chair of the Conference:

- "What should we do? How can we consolidate the situation?"
- "Someone has to step back. For the sake of the children." She responded.

One thing I knew for sure: Jack wasn't going to step back or back down. And I suspected Cara wouldn't either. She needed custody of the children to make a living and secure her status.

MAY INCIDENT – FORGING EVIDENCE FOR FALSE ACCUSATIONS

Was this the last and lowest point?

I wasn't so sure anymore.

I planned to visit my father in mid-May. He wasn't well, and his partner had serious doubts about his mental state the previous year, which were confirmed at the beginning of the year: my father was diagnosed with Alzheimer's disease in January. We had a lot to discuss in this regard. My stepmother, who had actually been playing the role of my mother for 15 years, had had Parkinson's for a few years and was finding it increasingly difficult to manage her daily tasks. They were unwilling to go to a nursing home, which they had both made clear years before their health problems arose. My stepmother believed there was little time left for either her or my father. She wanted to put things in order in a reassuring way. She requested my assistance with this. I arranged the trip to coincide with the children, Elsie and Lilly, being with their mother. I left at noon on Monday and was due to return at dawn on Thursday.

It was a beautiful spring day. The plane took off from rainy Albion and landed in the middle of the sunny Carpathian Basin, where the air was filled with the balmy scent of flowers. The cherry trees were in full bloom in my father's garden, and the cat was napping at the foot of the fence, purring. They cooked and baked, even though I asked them not to, as I was bringing food with me. But they insisted on setting the table with their finest tableware and serving meat soup, meatloaf, and the inevitable homemade sour cherry brandy. "Let's toast!" said Erika, and Dad raised his small glass with a smile. Dad was in good shape; the only symptom that suggested something was wrong was that he wasn't talking. Almost nothing. He uttered only one-word sentences. It was clear he was trying to follow the conversation and contribute to the dialogue, but whenever he tried to say more, his speech faltered after a single word. It was heartbreaking to see, but we knew, we suspected, that he understood almost everything, because he laughed appropriately at the jokes and his face clouded over when worries were mentioned. That's how we avoided discussing important matters and concerns about him in his presence. We chatted easily while waiting for Dad to retire for his afternoon nap. I showed him photos of his great-grandchildren on my phone. We sat outside on the terrace, drinking coffee. That's when the phone call came. It was Jack. I put the call on speaker because I wasn't expecting what he was going to say.

- "Mum, there's a problem! Something has happened to Lilly, and Cara won't tell me what! All I know is that they've taken her to the hospital, Annie took her, and another social worker is there with them. But Cara won't tell me exactly what happened; she just wrote that she can't talk to me for now. The police are there too!"

- "What happened? Did she fall from somewhere? Is she hurt? Is she alive?" All the strength drained from my legs. My God, Lilly, my little star! She's barely 15 months old. She walks well but falls often because she does everything hastily, imitating Elsie in every way. She must have fallen from somewhere! That's the only explanation!
- "Please call me as soon as you find out anything! - I begged Jack. I'll try to call Annie from here; I'll text you when I reach her!"
- "All right! Keep trying," Jack said. "I've already tried calling everyone, but no one is answering their phones!"

I started calling everyone I knew, left messages, emailed Annie, and asked her to return my call. However, no one answered the phone or responded. Time passed slowly. Dad finally went to his room to rest, and for the first time, I was glad that he might not really understand what was happening. Erika and I discussed a few things, including the fact that she felt she could die at any moment... "There's never a better time for such serious conversations!" I tried to offer some comfort. I laughed awkwardly: "Dying isn't that easy, don't worry!" But Erika also wanted to know what to expect, and she wanted to know exactly how Parkinson's patients usually die... I told her briefly, omitting certain details, what I had experienced. She seemed to calm down. Regarding my father's placement, she asked me to visit the nursing home they had already chosen, talk to the director, and submit an application form for my father. Erika looked at me seriously and quietly. I knew, I felt, that what none of us wanted to happen was about to happen, but we had to accept it. I felt very sad. When Erika leaves, another era will come to an end, an era with memories and feelings that can never be fully recaptured. There would be no more Eri, no more hesitant, trembling movements, no more tight hugs, no more silences between conversations, no more smiles, and there would be no more little house with a porch and a cherry orchard, no more fruit soup, the laid table, the lemonade – everything connected to her will disappear from our lives, as if it had never been. And that will hurt a lot.

Jack's call startled me out of my sad moment.

- "Mum, I found out that Lilly is in Cardiff Hospital because she started bleeding during the night and apparently bled heavily. Cara notified the flexi social worker this morning and also called the ambulance emergency line."
- "Bleeding? But where was she bleeding from?"
- "Well, ... from her vagina."
- "What???"
- "Yes, that's what Cara wrote."
- "Lilly is 15 months old! She can't bleed from her vagina; she can't bleed vaginally! What did Cara do to her?"
- "I have no idea, Mum, I don't know if she did anything to her, but I think she's accusing me of something again..."
- "But Jack, this is no child's play. These are serious allegations, and Lilly was fine yesterday morning when you transferred her to Cara. If the little girl was really bleeding, then Cara must have done something to her during the night... Oh my God! I can't believe it! My God, poor child!"
- "Cara wrote that she's being examined now and can't talk to me, but she'll write to me about the results of the examination."
- "She can't talk to you... Who said that?"
- "The police and Annie."
- "Then they suspect you of doing something to Lilly! Do you know what that means?"
- "I know exactly what it means, Mum..."
- "Please call me as soon as you have the results!"
- "I will."

I put down the phone, sweat running down my back in a thin stream. It was very hot, almost like a summer heatwave, but I was shivering. My God, what if Cara had hurt Lilly! What had she done to her? Was the little girl really bleeding? Or was this just another case, like the one in January, with purple and green marks painted on the children's bodies? I hoped so, I hoped so with all my heart, although the fact that it could be true did not reassure me, as she had accused Jack again, this time of sexually abusing his 15-month-old daughter... This is a nightmare! Someone, please, wake me up! My thoughts raced ahead, far ahead in time. What if, what if it's not true, what if this is just another false accusation with fabricated evidence, then this is the second time! What will be the third? If Cara sees that this fabricated evidence has not led to results, will she really abuse the children and cause them real harm?

- "Don't think the worst, don't jump to conclusions! Don't see ghosts!" Erika put her hand on my arm. I hadn't said a word since I hung up the phone, but she knew exactly what was on my mind...
- "This is terrible, Eri!"

She nodded.

- "I hope it will be over soon, my dear."

Jack called again half an hour later. He said Cara had texted him to say, "Thank God, Lilly is fine, she just has nappy rash"...

I amended my ticket to return to Jack on Wednesday instead of Thursday. I was glad I did, because Annie and another social worker announced that they would be visiting. "After all", they said, "We need to talk things over."

Annie and Tony, whose real name is Antonia, arrived together. Later, Becky, their supervisor, joined them. They brought a letter with them stating that they were initiating a PLO investigation, which could result in the children being removed from the family and placed with foster parents or put up for adoption. My world turned upside down several times during the conversation. On what grounds do they want to take the children away from us? Jack hasn't done anything wrong, and we haven't endangered the children in any way! We were completely paralysed, like rabbits caught in a corner, unable to respond properly, and it took us a while to gather our thoughts. Annie tried to reassure us. "This is mostly just a formality. We have to take this step to be eligible for a full investigation. I don't think there's any danger of anyone taking your children away from you! But we need to see clearly. Everything!" All this talk did not reassure me. How could it not be clear what was happening?

Who was causing the problem? Who is endangering the children? What can anyone bring against Jack? Why isn't Jack above suspicion from the outset? Why does he have to be thoroughly investigated? Just because the false accusations against him are so serious, and because he is a man? He is a father, and a father accused of any wrongdoing is always compelled to defend himself. Is everything a woman says gospel truth, impossible to be a lie, not needing to be investigated? Must it be accepted without question? Does the presumption of innocence not apply to men and fathers? I would have loved to ask all these questions right there and then, during that meeting. But I couldn't. I had to keep quiet. And there was nothing we could do. After extensive internet research and discussions with our solicitor, we realised that there was nothing we could do. We had to obey and go with the flow. We had to cooperate with the authorities and be available. And trust, believe, hope, pray that the truth will come out and that justice will follow. The 12-week assessment began. Nothing was more characteristic of my paralysis than the fact that I did not even notice that the document ordering the PLO investigation did not cite the incident as the reason – namely, that Lilly was hospitalised because her mother had falsely accused Jack of sexual assault – but rather as "emotional harm" and held both parents responsible for the children's emotional harm due to their lack of contact and communication. I only noticed this obfuscation, this incorrect procedure, months later, and only then did I realise it. By then, the investigation was long over, and we were facing even more serious problems...

PLO

First, we had to provide a list of 3-5 people who could be considered as potential foster parents. I was on the list, along with Sophia and my two older sons. Tony took over the case, replacing Annie. She said she would come to our house every week for six weeks and compile a complete profile of Jack. She would ask about his past, his childhood, his education, his family background, his work, his financial situation, his relationships, his relationship with children, everything. We didn't mind, let everything come out!

However, I was terrified by the fact that, despite everything that had happened, the social services would continue to allow Cara to have contact with the children in the same way as before! Three days a week, three nights, from Monday to Thursday. It was time to take out the audio recording I had made in February of Elsie's evening routine, right up until bedtime, in which Elsie said, "Mommy is not good, mommy hit me and kick me, mommy did hurt me." – I sent this audio recording to Annie, who was still in the office, after their visit. After receiving the email, she immediately responded that they would return the next day to discuss further. Although I had to explain why I was making audio recordings of my granddaughter, they understood that the confession itself raised doubts. Not insignificant doubts, in light of the past few months. They decided to restrict Cara's visitation rights and allow her to see the children only under supervision for a while. We were relieved because it meant the children were safe. At least for a while...

Supervised contact meant that Cara could see the children for four hours per day, from 9 am to 1 pm, on three days per week, with a social worker being present. We had to take the children there and pick them up. This went on for six weeks. Until then, we breathed a sigh of relief. Although little Lilly fought her own battle every single day, crying desperately and refusing to go to Cara. She turned away from her father's embrace and sobbed, "no-no-no." No one cared. The social worker sometimes carried Lilly up the stairs to her mother, who was still sobbing in her arms, but none of this was mentioned in the later reports...

Our hearts broke every morning, but at least we were reassured that nothing would happen to the children as long as they were with Cara. Because a social worker was present to observe her and assess how she treated the children. The investigation began, and Tony was a pleasant surprise, listening attentively at every meeting, trying to slip jokes into the conversation to ease the tension. She also gave us details about Lilly's "bleeding" and informed us that the forensic doctor had found no evidence of injury or bleeding, even though the little girl had allegedly bled at 1 a.m. and Cara had only arrived at the hospital at noon the next day, so it was questionable whether the bleeding could have occurred earlier, since "small children recover very quickly from their injuries" ... WTF ... - sometimes I regret being a nurse ... I wanted to scream, and

I could have: "if a child is bleeding vaginally, and heavily at that, as her mother claims, it is impossible for the bleeding to stop within 12 hours and for there to be no visible injury, as if it had never happened! No one can bleed heavily and then, within a few hours, leave no trace of it!" I simply did not understand, and still do not understand, why it was not possible to write down clearly and unambiguously that the child had no injuries, no bleeding, and could not have had any! The doctor suggested that Lilly might have had a nappy rash, which could cause some bleeding. The social workers noted this in their reports. The only problem was that, in the photo Cara sent, Lilly clearly had no nappy rash. On that photo, there was only the blood-looking substance on her tiny labia, but no nappy rash at all; her skin was nice, clean, and intact.

Tony also told us that they took a swab from Lilly and that there was a nappy confiscated by the police with bloodstains on it. Tony also said that although Cara said she suspected Jack had abused the little girl, she later withdrew this statement and did not mention it again when questioned by the police. On 10 June, Tony told us that social services would request the nappy from the police and that the police would not be investigating the matter further because no crime had been committed. We were still in shock and trusted the authorities, which we shouldn't have done! We didn't know what we could or should do. We thought it was clear to everyone what had really happened here and that someone would take action, investigate the case, if not the police, then children's services, and that there would be some kind of consequence! We were very naive. We were busy taking care of the children, our work, and trying to survive all this. And then what happened next? We had no idea...

MID-SUMMER MISERY – THE ARREST

Jack decided that since he had not received any detailed information from anyone, had not seen the report, and found it suspicious that children's services would just "ask" the police for the nappy, he would take matters into his own hands and go down to the police station to talk to an investigator about what had happened on that night in May, what was in the reports, and he was planning to possibly request an investigation. He left home at 10 a.m., so I looked after the children. Jack called me after 3 p.m.

- "Hi, so what did you do? Did you get to talk to anyone?" I asked before he could speak
- "Yeah, not really, they arrested me, Mum."
- "What?"
- "I was arrested. I called you to tell you that I don't know how long I'll be here."
- "That's a great joke, Jack. When are you coming home?"
- "I'm not joking. Who would joke about something like this? They really arrested me. They took my phone, so I couldn't call you. I just got my phone back, and only long enough to call you!"
- "But why? What happened? I don't believe it! Why did they arrest you?"
- "I don't know yet. I'm about to be interrogated; they're arranging for a court-appointed solicitor to come here, and they won't tell me anything until then. They handcuffed me and arrested me... I'm now locked in a room. I have my phone back, but they said I must hand it over so they can search it for evidence. A police officer is sitting opposite me now, watching to make sure I don't delete anything. They only allowed me to call you and told me that, if I wanted my own solicitor, I would have to arrange it myself. But I don't have a solicitor...for this."
- "And when will they question you? When will you find out what you are being charged with and why you were arrested?"
- "I have no idea. I'll try to check in."

I went to the park with the children to pass the time, as I couldn't stay in the house with all these thoughts in my head. But I don't have many memories of that afternoon. I waited anxiously for Jack to call again and couldn't imagine why the police had arrested my son when he had only gone there to ask for information!

There was no further communication from Jack thereafter. I went home with Elsie and Lilly, gave them dinner, and put them to bed. I wrote to my eldest son. I didn't want to disturb the others. Sophia was working that day, and it was late; they were probably already asleep. I tried to call the police station where Jack had gone and was being held, but I couldn't reach him; you can't speak with an adult defendant after they've been arrested. I didn't know that. How could I have known? I could have remembered that this was also the case in 2021, when Cara hit Jack, and Jack slept in a cell for 10 hours before being questioned and released. They didn't let me talk to him that time either. But I didn't remember that. It seems I had buried that night deep inside me. Now I had been told that Jack's interrogation was still ongoing – it was 9 p.m. – and that they would pass on my message: I had been looking for him, and he would call me when the interrogation was over, if he was able to make a phone call.

I wouldn't wish these hours and these feelings on anyone! I went into Jack's room, desperately searching for something that might explain why he had been arrested. Of course, I hoped I wouldn't find anything, and that's how it turned out. I turned the whole room upside down, then put everything back in its place. It was almost midnight when the door opened.

Jack stood in the middle of the kitchen in grey overalls, his eyes red, and immediately lit a cigarette.

- "What about the kids? Are they okay? Are they asleep? Is everything all right with them?"
- "Of course! But tell me, what happened? Don't you want to eat?"
- "No." Jack stopped by the kitchen table and pushed an A4 sheet of paper towards me. The paper stated that he had been released on bail, was under investigation, had had his phone confiscated, and was not permitted to approach, contact, or speak to Cara. If the children had to be handed over or picked up, it had to be done by a third party.
- "What did that little bitch say about you? What did she come up with this time?" I asked. I couldn't control myself anymore.
- "She claims I raped and sexually assaulted her three times," Jack replied, and with a strange grimace on his face, he finally sat down at the table. "You didn't tell me you like my new uniform. This is what people get at the police station when they're arrested.

So I decided to keep it as a keepsake and bring it home. – he tried to make jokes.

- "It's not funny, for God's sake! Jack. But you weren't even in a relationship! There's been nothing between you since 2022! You avoided Cara as much as you could!"
- "Come on, Mum, don't worry! That's just it! The whole thing is nonsense! I was glad not to see her, let alone rape her!"
- "Son, you've been arrested, you're under investigation, and we're in the middle of a child welfare investigation. How can you expect me not to be worried? You can't hand over the children, you can't arrange contact, you can't even talk to Cara, either verbally or in writing!"
- "That's good news, at least I don't have to answer her, or talk to her, - that's at least good news." Jack smiled.
- "OK. I understand that, but what will the child welfare services say about this?"

Jack's face clouded over.

- "I don't know. I must tell them tomorrow. I'll call Tony."
- "That's good, yes. They need to know about this. Did the police tell you in detail what Cara is accusing you of? Where, when, and how did you rape and sexually assault her? Just so we can defend ourselves and seek evidence. What did the court-appointed solicitor say?"
- "Nothing. Just that I should make a statement, which I did, and that everything will proceed as course; they will determine whether what Cara said is true and will let me know. Until then, I should do what is on the paper."
- "When will you get your phone back?"
- "They didn't say. They just said they would download the data from it and let me know when I could pick it up."
- "Great."
- "Apparently, Cara reported me to the police in April. The one morning you didn't come with me to drop off the kids, remember? Cara claimed that I raped her last summer and sexually harassed her this year in April, on that morning."

- "Then how come they haven't arrested you yet? How come they haven't come for you?"
- "Apparently, this case was not a priority for the police; it was not a top priority, because the story was largely about events that happened last year. The solicitor will send us the detailed report later, he said."
- "There were messages from Cara on your phone... from last year, too. I remember some of them. I saved them with screenshots. I'll take a look! Have something to eat, then let's go to bed."

I looked at Jack, who nodded. His face was pale and worn, and there was a broken light in his eyes, as if he were an old man who had worked hard all his life or had lived through and survived a war. He didn't look thirty, more like twice that age. I waited for him to shower, eat, and go up to the children. I stayed up all night looking for evidence of his innocence so that I could send it to the solicitor the next day. I found a few messages in screenshots that I had saved when we were preparing for last year's trial. Not only did Jack not rape Cara, but he also constantly rejected Cara's sexual advances. He even went so far as to write: "I can't do it anymore; I think I've become impotent." The next day, we drafted a statement for the court-appointed lawyer, attached the screenshots, and we asked him to send it to the police along with Jack's testimony.

The supervised visits with the mother were changed to unsupervised contact the following week. But even with the supervisor present, an accident occurred. Elsie injured herself on the playground, with a large purple bruise and a bump on her forehead under her hair, but we only noticed this when we got home. Jack called the social worker, who replied, "Oh, yes, Elsie fell off the climbing frame." Jack did not question why no one had mentioned this when the children were handed over, nor did he ask why no one had followed the usual protocol for head injuries... We took Elsie to the emergency room ourselves. Because all head injuries must be examined by a doctor, even according to the rules here. Fortunately, Elsie was not seriously injured.

The child welfare services were not concerned about Jack's arrest. Tony said they already knew about it in May, as the police had informed them that Cara had filed a complaint against Jack. Tony said not to worry too much about it, as almost everyone was certain that Jack had not committed any crime, which was why the police had not arrested him earlier, in April or May or June, and if Jack had not gone to the police station on 7 July, he would still not have been arrested as yet either... I was surprised by this information. Jack authorised me to submit the additional screenshots I had found of Cara's messages and to prepare another statement on his behalf, supplementing his previous testimony and statement. Thank God I found all of Cara's messages from two years ago on Jack's computer. We also received a letter from the appointed solicitor containing the charges. Cara's report contained serious inaccuracies. At the time of the alleged rape, Jack was not even in the country; he was on holiday with the children, and the day before, Elsie had injured her head and had to be taken to hospital to have her wound stitched up. But Cara told the police that Elsie had been injured when Jack raped her in the middle of the living room... The only problem with this was that Cara had sent Jack a message that day saying: "I don't know what happened, you know I didn't hurt her, because I was on the phone with you, you know that," which was also included in the hospital's final report, "the mother cannot give a precise explanation of how the injury occurred," and then the final report included another explanation: The mother was changing the younger child's nappy in the other room when Elsie was injured. But Cara was now able to report to the police that Elsie was injured when Jack raped her in the middle of the living room, and Elsie fell onto the threshold. My hair stood on end. How could someone be so twisted, so evil?

We were able to refute all allegations because Jack had all the evidence he needed in the official documents. Thank God I also found the report of the independent guardian ad litem from the same year that Cara reported the assault. In October 2023, the guardian ad litem's report stated the following from Cara's testimony:

> *"Jack and I tried to repair our relationship in June 2022, but we soon realised that it wasn't working, so we didn't continue. Lilly was conceived from that one encounter that happened at that time. After that, we were no longer in contact."*

In addition to all this, I found a dozen messages in which Jack was not harassing Cara, but rather the opposite. Many messages received from Cara said things like:

> *"Don't you miss me? Won't you come over for a bit? We can be friends with benefits, no strings attached. If you were here, you don't know what I would do to you. Please come over and sleep with me, just one more time, for the last time!"*

I sent all the documents as they were, re-sent them to the solicitor, and also sent them to the police. I also wrote to the police officer, on Jack's behalf, directing him to the original messages in the reports and on the confiscated phone. However, I did not receive a reply to my emails.

The following week, unsupervised visits began, and with them, the problems began, too. Nappy rash, scratches on Lilly's face, bruises on the children's knees and elbows, dirty clothes, and hungry children every afternoon when we came home. Elsie was already attending nursery school, but the summer holidays had begun. In August, the children's services increased the four hours of unsupervised contact per day to six hours, so the children stayed with their mother from 9 a.m. to 3 p.m. Since Jack couldn't drop off or collect the children, it all fell on me. Tony said she didn't understand how I could do it, looking Cara in the eye every day, knowing exactly what she had done to my son... I replied that I didn't know how I could do it either, and that it wasn't easy, but I was doing it for the sake of the children. I didn't add that I know exactly what we must do to satisfy social services so that they don't take the children away from us... We must comply with everything. Even if the mother has access to the children pursuant to a social services order. Even if we don't agree with this. So, I went with the children. I tried to reassure Lilly every morning, and she cried less. But I could see on her little face that she didn't understand why I was doing this, too. Why was anybody forcing her to be where she didn't want to be, where there were problems, where no one looked after her... And her questioning look broke my heart every morning. Again, and again.

Cara behaved terribly most of the time. She didn't say a word to me, but her face said it all. Cara didn't even say hello; she just took the children from my arms, turned her back on me, and went into the house. After a while, I developed a strategy and technique. I greeted her loudly and visibly, wishing her good morning on behalf of the children: "Hello Mummy, Good Morning!" Turning to the little girls, I said, "Have a good time, I'll be back soon, have a nice day." I didn't look at Cara's face, let alone her eyes. This worked: I didn't get so upset; the children understood that they had to go now but that I would return for them, and they behaved much more calmly. Until that afternoon, when I wasn't strong enough, and an incident occurred.

One afternoon, when I went to collect the children up the stairs to the front door, I noticed that Cara had left her key in the door. I took it out of there kindly, thinking I would give it to her when she opened the door. But then I noticed the key ring, which was nothing more than a gift I had bought for Elsie a long time ago in Devon when we visited Uncle Joe. I could hardly believe my eyes. Had Cara taken Elsie's toy and put it on her key ring? Even though I thought Elsie might have offered it to Mommy herself, it was a gift, a memento from me! I couldn't control myself... The door opened just as I realised this, and of course, Cara immediately attacked me when her gaze fell on the empty keyhole:

- "Where's the key?"

I shrugged my shoulders because I couldn't speak. I took Lilly, who was smiling and reaching out her arms to come to me

- "Give me back the key, I know you have it, only you could have taken it!"

Cara's eyes flashed with hatred and anger.

- "I don't know what you're talking about," I muttered to myself, then took Elsie's hand, who didn't quite understand what had happened, and started walking down the stairs.
- "There's a camera above the door; everyone will see that you stole my key from the door!" Cara hissed.

I didn't answer. I threw the key onto the street beside the neighbour's bin. I was ashamed of myself for behaving like this, like a child, but I was completely paralysed by the hatred that was directed at me. Later, I regretted not at least removing the little keyring charm from the key ring... From home, I called Tony and the social worker who had assessed me and told them everything honestly, what had happened and how. Of course, Cara also reported the incident and exploited every opportunity it offered. She wrote to the social workers and told the police that she didn't feel safe in my presence anymore, not even in her own home, because who knows if I had copied the key and would break in one night to assault her or, even worse, kill her?!... I could only hope that no one would take what she said seriously. But I knew I had made a huge mistake.

The investigation, which was intended to determine whether I was fit to raise the children if neither parent was capable of doing so, was progressing well. In parallel with Jack's PLO investigation, which Tony was conducting, I was assigned a separate social worker. She visited me five or six times and asked me pretty much the same questions that Tony had asked Jack. Amanda was a nice young woman, and she told me candidly that, after reviewing the reports, she couldn't understand how Cara could have been granted unsupervised access to the children in light of recent events. Neither did I, nor did Jack, and I think Tony did either. I suspected that someone at the managerial level had decided, and was deciding, what should happen, and that thought was not reassuring to me. The following week, Tony announced that, as planned, the mother's visitation rights would be extended to include Sundays, so that instead of three times a week, Cara would see the children four times. Jack asked about the next steps, and I could see he was genuinely upset. Now it's four times a week! Eight meetings with Cara, eight car trips there and back, four mornings of waking the children, who liked to sleep late, four times of getting them dressed and mentally preparing them to go, and then coming home... I was also shocked and was very curious to know who developed all this and what the plans were. However, we haven't received the document, even though we asked Tony to provide it. Tony said we would talk about it later, in due course, because nothing was certain yet; nothing had been decided; the investigations were not complete; and even they did not know what would happen. For the time being, they were just monitoring the mother and seeing how the visits were going. We had to be content with that. What else could we have done? At that time, we didn't know, we weren't aware of our rights, and we were terrified that those in power would suddenly decide to take the children away and place them with foster parents or in state care. We were afraid. And fear is a terrible advisor.

In early August, Cara filed a petition with the court, seeking to initiate another child custody case and requesting full custody of both children. In her petition, she tore Jack down to the ground. Cara wrote again that Jack had abused her and neglected the children, and she also wrote that Jack stored drugs in his car and dealt them. But Jack was not Cara's only target in this petition; Cara also complained about Tony, accusing her of bias and indifference, and condemned her own lawyer for not helping her in the proceedings to date. After this, her own lawyer resigned from representing Cara. The court did not accept the statement of claim, stating that a child custody case was pending, the PLO investigation was underway, and the Court's Legal Advisor said that Cara's complaints and allegations would be addressed at the next hearing. We urgently called Jack's lawyer to ask whether we should respond to the allegations or issue any statement, but the lawyer said we did not need to respond at all.

After six weeks, in mid-August, the police finally returned Jack's phone. But they extended Jack's bail - conditional release - because, as they wrote, they had not yet completed their investigation. I didn't understand. The evidence was on Jack's phone, which I had submitted on his behalf, and Jack's statement was there as well. Jack hadn't been in contact with Cara for two years, avoiding her whenever he could, only meeting and talking to her for the sake of the children. How could this not be obvious to everyone? The solicitor said he was sorry, but we had to accept the police's decision and let them investigate. So, we waited. There was nothing else we could do.

The PLO closed at the end of September, and the court hearing followed in early October. Three days before the hearing, Tony brought us the PLO minutes and showed us the first page, which contained the decision of the children's services, but she did not allow us to read the sixty-page document. Instead, she just said that he would send the entire document to the solicitor before the hearing, who would then forward it to us. Tony came in with a bright look on his face, just popped in, she said, because she wanted us to know the good news: the guardianship authority was recommending that the court place the children with Jack and that the mother have limited visiting rights, only during the daytime. Cara did not cooperate with Tony or the other social workers. She refused to attend any courses, did not provide her family's contact details, and did not permit child welfare services to contact her family members residing abroad to obtain information regarding Cara's past and personality. Accordingly, this decision was made. We were very happy about everything. Finally, we could see the light at the end of the tunnel. This nightmare would finally be over, and perhaps we would no longer have to fear for the children! However, the first page of the PLO document also stated that the child welfare services would request a further 12 months of so-called assistance orders from the court to monitor contact between the parents and children. Reading this sentence, it is difficult to describe how I felt. I knew that this sentence negated all the previous sentences. I felt that even if the court decided to grant Jack custody, we would still have to remain under the close supervision of social services for another whole year. During which time anything could happen. During which time anything could change. They could take the entire case back to court and overturn all prior court decisions. Knowing that it was unclear who was in control and what exactly the children's services wanted to achieve for Cara and the children, this sentence about the assistance order seemed dangerous, very dangerous. Alarm bells were ringing in my head: nothing is certain yet; we can't relax; something is wrong; something is not clear here! I hoped that my sixth, seventh, and whatever sense would not be right this time. I knew instinctively that something was wrong, that there could be trouble... I didn't tell Jack what I was thinking. I wanted him to feel relieved and calm down a little.

The hearing took place, and the outcome was as recommended by child welfare services. Jack was granted custody, the mother was granted visiting rights, and the child welfare services were granted an assistance order. They immediately announced that the mother's visitation rights were flexible: if she cooperated and completed the assigned courses, her visitation time could be varied and increased. I asked Tony whether this meant the children might be able to stay with their mother overnight. But Tony replied that I shouldn't worry: a lot would have to change for that to happen...

Jack and I only received the 60-page summary of the PLO Assessment after the hearing, and that's when we read it. The report contained shocking lies. Cara made false statements about her childhood and family background. For example, she stated that her mother and father had been married for thirty years, had a very good marriage, and that she, Cara, and her three brothers were all from the same parents and loved each other very much. Cara also claimed that her grandparents lived in Austria, just one street away from her parents' home, and that they always went to their grandparents' house after school. According to the report, Cara was a good student and graduated from school with a high school diploma. These were blatant lies! When Jack pointed out to Tony that Cara had given false testimony in the investigation report, Tony said she suspected something was wrong, but Cara refused to give him her parents' contact details, so she couldn't verify whether what Cara had told her was true. And so, she could only write down what she heard from her. I could raise my eyebrows, but it didn't matter. The PLO Assessment was over, and we were past the court hearing. Jack decided not to pursue the matter further or file an official report. It was a shame. It was a mistake.

A few days after the trial, a post appeared on Cara's social media page. Cara wrote: "I'm very tired, but I will finish what I started." – a real indirect harassment toward us that we couldn't prove because of its nature, it was indirect, not naming anybody. I didn't feel any calmer; in fact, I didn't feel calm about anything, not at all!

The future didn't look very promising, but we were safe in the present.

The children were fine, and that was the most important thing for us.

Elsie left the small group and became a big preschooler. She is a beautiful, smart little girl! She posed proudly at the nursery graduation, and we received a beautiful photo album. She moved to another building, and we were concerned about how she would fit into the new community, because Elsie is an introverted little girl, very precise and organised, and she likes things to stay the same, so everything happens the way she is used to. But she took the obstacles in her stride. There are thirty children in the nursery group, but the room is much more spacious, with many new toys and many new things to discover. Elsie was willing to attend school. Lilly began to speak, forming sentences with more and more words. Two girls, two little stars, each increasingly intelligible. They were both very active and happy children. They loved nature and wanted to be outside whenever possible. Elsie was no longer afraid of bugs; in fact, except for earthworms and spiders, she happily placed all bugs on her palm to examine them. We took them swimming, to parks, for walks, to bouncy castles, and to play centres.

During the autumn break, we were finally able to travel abroad with the children and visit their grandfather, great-grandfather, aunt, and cousins. The present was cloudless, the future looked foggy, but we tried to enjoy every moment. Cara, of course, made our lives difficult wherever she could. She didn't assist with anything, never once picked up the children or returned them, and I continued to take the girls to see her eight times a week. When I raised this, Cara told me to consider it a privilege that I could do this and care for my grandchildren in this way, and not to complain. Tony remained our social worker, and we exchanged messages in the group chat she had created. Cara's style remained unchanged, and it seemed impossible to change it. If I were five minutes late for the handover and didn't bring the children on time, she would flood me with complaints. If she was late bringing them back in the afternoon, she didn't understand why I asked her in a message where she was or why I told her I was waiting for her at the agreed-upon place. She said I was aggressive. I could have been more patient. Tony didn't interfere in the conversations, but she could observe everything; she knew everything.

When we finally went away for a week, Cara wrote every day, asking what the girls were doing and demanding that I send her photos. When I sent the photos, she accused us of lying to her because we weren't where we said we would be. She wrote at length about how worried she was because she didn't know where her children (MY children – she wrote, the girls always been apostrophed as HER children) were and expressed her fear that we wouldn't come back from abroad and would steal her children...She exercised terrible control until I sent him another dozen photos of the children and ended the chat. Jack got away with it because of the police investigation; he still couldn't contact Cara. He was calmer and more balanced, and he looked to the future with confidence. I was the only one who suffered from this massive coercive control.

Autumn passed slowly, in relative calmness.

My assessment was also completed, and I would have been suitable as a foster parent for the children, but this was not necessary, as Jack was granted custody and the mother retained her parental rights, so my file was closed, and I did not appear before the committee (panel) that would have stamped the minutes. That appointment has been cancelled.

Toward the middle to end of November, Elsie's new educational institution reported certain problems to the social services. Tony informed us about this. The nursery teachers noticed that Elsie was particularly fond of one of the nannies and gave her special attention. What could be the problem with that? I thought to myself that most young children have a favourite nursery teacher. However, Tony said the nursery teachers were concerned because Elsie had expressed her affection for her in physical terms. She asks to be held, rocks herself, strokes her, puts her hands on the nannie's chest, strokes her there, and pulls their hands down to her tummy so that the nannie strokes her too... Tony asked, almost apologetically, whether Elsie behaved similarly towards us, or whether we had noticed anything unusual about her that might bother us. According to Tony, Elsie is just overly "sensory," and since she does not yet speak fluently, she expresses her emotions through touch, which, in her opinion, is not a problem but rather completely natural. Her children behaved similarly, - Tony said, - but based on the nursery teachers' report, she now has to conduct an investigation... Tony was embarrassed and apologetic. My hair stood on end. Again. What is this all about? I didn't fully understand, but I felt it was something Jack would have to defend himself against again. And that, after all the past suspicions and false accusations, the fact that the nursery teachers found Elsie's behaviour suspicious and overly sensory did not bode well for Jack.

My cortisol levels must have been sky-high; we had to play for survival, and fortunately, I remembered things. That Elsie's love language is physical touch, hugs. To this day, her mother picks her up and puts her onto her breast when Elsie is sad or tired. I explained this to Tony, and as I was talking about it, I suddenly remembered Cara's message and advice to Jack a year and a half ago: *"If you want her to fall asleep quickly, stroke and caress her down there. She always asks me to take off his nappy and stroke her down there..."* I told Tony this. I told her that Jack had received a message from Cara with this advice. I still remember the look on Tony's face. Her eyes widened; she was completely surprised. "Could you send me that message, please?" she asked. I sent it to her that same evening. I translated it because at that time, Cara hadn't written it in English yet. Tony thanked me. She returned the next day and said it was a very unusual, harsh message. Her supervisor at social services agreed that it was very concerning, but because the message was written a year ago, they could no longer investigate the matter. But Tony reassured us that she would attach it to the investigation she was conducting, which, so far, had only shown that Elsie was highly "sensory". As she was leaving, Tony turned back from the door, shook his head, and asked me if I thought this „thing" could be something cultural? Some kind of tradition? That the mother takes off the child's nappy and puts her to sleep by stroking his genitals? It was my turn to be shocked. What kind of question is that? I replied emphatically that I knew of no culture or cultural tradition in which it was customary to put small children to sleep by stroking their naked genitals... Tony nodded, apologized, and said goodbye. She probably closed the investigation because I never again received any questions about why my grandchild likes to sit on her favourite nursery teacher's lap, why she likes to touch her, or why she waits to be hugged and caressed... Jack was outraged, completely baffled, asking why the nursery teachers hadn't come to him with their doubts and questions, and what the hell was all this about?! I didn't understand "what the hell it was all about" either, but I had my own opinion, which I didn't share with Jack, thinking it was better if he didn't know.

In November, another incident occurred. Elsie's necklace disappeared. The necklace I had given her for her birthday. It wasn't hugely valuable, but it was made of precious metal and was a memento. Elsie had chosen it herself from a catalogue and wore it happily. One day it was there, the next day it was gone. It was about two or three days later that I noticed it was no longer around her neck.

- "Where's your necklace, Elsie?"
- "Mummy took it off."
- "And you didn't bring it back? Is it not in your pocket?"
- "No. Mummy took it off."

I asked Cara about it in a message the next day. She stated that Elsie had asked her to remove the necklace because it was causing her neck pain. But she would look for it and send it over next time, Cara said, when the children go to visit her. I didn't reply, I just said thank you.

The necklace never turned up again. Cara „couldn't find it". She also claimed that she had put it in the nylon bag with the clothes that she had sent back once. Of course, it wasn't in any of the bags with the clothes, not even once. But I didn't argue, I was too tired of the whole thing. The necklace was tuition money, and I never let Elsie take anything more valuable or memorable to her mother when she went to visit. I didn't let her take her toys either, which sometimes caused a little resentment, but when her favourite stuffed cat disappeared and never came home, I think Elsie understood why I was so strict about this issue.

Cara didn't change at all. She continued to hate me, and that hatred flowed towards me from somewhere deep inside her, from her very guts. When she looked me in the eye, her gaze was so cold and bright black that it drained the strength from my legs, a cold rock settled in my stomach, and fear ran down my spine like an electric shock. After a while, I made it a habit not to look at Cara, or at least not to look into her eyes. It was relatively easy. I turned to Elsie and little Lilly, talked to them, and kept them occupied while I handed them over. Because I still had to arrange for the children to be handed over. The police extended Jack's three-month conditional release by another three months because the investigation was continuing and the case against him had not yet been closed. Eight meetings with Cara, four days a week. I had to go to her place, take the children there, and bring them back. Cara was unwilling to come pick them up, let alone bring them back. She did not take part in the handover duties. She lived an 8–10-minute walk from us. A 3-minute drive. But Cara didn't have a driving licence or a car, and she would have had to walk up a hill...

"The hill is too steep, it's difficult for her to push the pram up it. Anyway, Jack gets all the child benefits. Jack took away the benefits she was entitled to because Jack was awarded custody of the children. She, Cara, can barely make ends meet, she is struggling not to become homeless, she has no money for anything, she can't pay for a taxi to pick up or bring back the children, and her boyfriend is not a taxi driver to help her, petrol costs him money too." Cara said these words to the social workers at the child welfare office when Jack suggested they share joint parental responsibilities to facilitate the handovers.

I suppose I would have been the evil mother-in-law if I had ever mentioned that she could look for a job and go to work so that she wouldn't have to be homeless because of the lost benefits... Countless beautiful thoughts ran through my head. This was Cara's way of taking revenge on us at that moment; in those times, it was her only option. And she did it. This did not bode well for the future. We could expect that anything that did not go her way would continue to be punished at any time. Cara had not changed at all. She wasn't even willing to pretend to change. When Tony suggested that she could perhaps help with transporting the children, since I was, after all, an old woman who might get tired, Cara simply repeated that she messaged me earlier and replied:

"Grandma should be happy to help! Consider it a privilege to take the children back and forth! The Grandmother should be grateful instead of

making complaints all the time." – Nothing was more characteristic of Cara's character than this sentence...

CONCERNS - STRANGE THINGS

More oddities about Cara. One late afternoon, Cara sent a message asking Jack to bring one of the toys Andrew had bought for Elsie to the viewing the next day. She also informed Jack that she, Cara, had marked the toys to indicate which belonged to her and which to Jack's household, and that she had severed the limbs of the figures she had purchased. That was how she marked them. This is what the message said:

> *"I did cut off the legs and the arms of the toys I bought, so that I would know which ones belonged to me..."*

The mutilated toys stayed on my mind for days. Jack sent Cara's message about this to Tony. Tony found it strange that Cara would mark her children's belongings this way, but she honestly said there wasn't much she could do about it. Tony promised to forward this story to the family support worker who will be starting parenting classes with Cara, and that worker will then take appropriate action. She will discuss with Cara that there are better alternatives for marking toys, such as felt-tip pens...

Windy Winter - new incidents, big changes, and losses

At the November Core Group meeting, Cara lost her temper again. We don't know why, as Tony didn't tell us. Tony stated only that the meeting, which was now held separately because Jack was not permitted to contact Cara, even online, was scandalous. Tony wrote that she had to end the conversation because Cara was literally shouting, and that she had to report Cara's behaviour to the social services' legal representative because it raised doubts.

Tony was good to the children and to Jack. Because of her, we learned what a real social worker is like: what it's like when a social worker supports the family and the children, when she does her job and does it well. Tony purchased theatre tickets for Elsie, Lilly, and us, so the girls could attend the theatre for the first time in their lives and see the fairy-tale play Jack and the Beanstalk. Every time Tony came, she asked Jack if he needed anything. He never needed anything, but it made Jack feel good. Tony always answered the phone when Jack or I had any questions and replied to every email. In June, when she was assigned to Jack's case, along with the PLO Assessment, Tony promised to remain with us until Jack's and the children's cases were closed, until the very end. She was our fifth social worker since Children's Services became involved in the family's life, and she stated that even that was too many; a case should have one social worker from start to finish, permanently, because families need consistent support. We were happy about this; it was reassuring because we felt the same way. Tony's presence alone was reassuring because she remained impartial throughout, and somehow, she didn't turn into a flying monkey. She saw through Cara from the very beginning. I think.

But after the meeting at the end of November, on 2 December, Tony unexpectedly called Jack to say she would stop by before she finished work and pop in to visit us because she had something to say. And when Tony arrived after 6 p.m., she said she had to hand over Jack's case because she suddenly had too much work, and Jack and the children's case was already on track; she had done what she had to do. We were speechless. But Tony tried to reassure us.

– "Believe me, everything will be fine. This case doesn't need a social worker anyway anymore; it's more than enough to have a family support assistant to handle it further."

We were very disappointed; I remember the feeling exactly. And the first thought ran through my mind: "An unqualified family support worker... and Cara..." - alarm bells were ringing in my head. Again. "Oh my God! Oh no!"

A blessing or a curse? The seventh sense, the capability of predicting the future?! Which I have sometimes. God knows. I needed to let the worries go. The holiday season was fast approaching. Tony still came at Christmas and brought two huge boxes of presents for the children. Elsie prepared a small gift for Tony, and we presented it to her as a thank-you for her assistance and good work.

After Christmas, we travelled with the children to celebrate the New Year with Great Grandpa and Grandma. We visited Erika and Dad, celebrated a belated Christmas, and Erika gave Elsie and Lilly musical storybooks as gifts. The larger storybook played classical music, while the smaller one played children's songs and nursery rhymes. We had a wonderful evening together. Erika and Grandpa happily watched the children playing in front of the fireplace. Erika seemed very tired, but I never imagined that at noon the next day I would receive a phone call telling me that she had passed away...

I drove down to the little country house in tears. Erika's children and grandchildren were already present. And Erika was still there, too. After an unexpected death, we all had to wait for the coroner, the district medical officer. It was New Year's Eve. We were supposed to come the next day to welcome the new year together. Lentils were soaking in a porcelain bowl on the kitchen counter, leftovers from lunch were on the table, and Eri was lying on the floor between the kitchen and the dining room. It looked as if she had just fallen. "She'll get up in a minute," my Dad thought. And he wanted to help Eri up. His Alzheimer's disease prevented him to realise what had happened.

- "Why are we leaving her on the floor? She'll catch a cold!" my dad said, pacing back and forth between the living room and the kitchen. He bent down several times to look at Erika and took her hand. Then he burst into tears. "Is she dead?" he asked over and over again.

My heart broke into pieces that evening. Seeing my elderly father mourning, after losing my mother, now losing the woman he had known since childhood, with whom he had both been widowed, found each other late in life, and with whom he had been companions for almost two decades. They grew old and fell ill together with Erika. But thank God they had many wonderful years together before that happened. Theatres, short trips, city breaks, concerts, gatherings with friends and family... Now it's all over. And Dad, like a lost, abandoned little child, now stood there in the middle of the lovely little house, where just the day before the Christmas candles had been burning, which barely more than 24 hours earlier had been filled with laughter and hugs. It's impossible not to feel heartbroken... I tried to calm Dad down and sat him down in the room where Eri's relatives were talking quietly. I gave him some water and sat down next to him for a while. We had to wait a long time for the coroner. Later, I went into the small room to collect Dad's clothes and documents. I knew he couldn't stay there alone in the house. When Erika was taken away, everyone would go home. But this was Dad's home. Even though he had a small flat in the capital city, they had lived here with Erika for years. Now that it was over, I had to pack his things and take them with me. I didn't even know what to do. Jack and my two grandchildren were sleeping in that flat, in Dad's property. We used to sleep over there whilst on holiday. The little flat will be overcrowded if I transfer my confused Dad there, I knew. But there was nothing else I could do; nowhere else I could take him.

We waited for the doctor and then set off with Dad towards the city. A terrible night awaited us. It wasn't difficult to assess Dad's condition, and I honestly didn't understand how Erika could take care of him on her own. Dad was completely demented, confused, and even more confused by what had happened. I think he was in shock. His short-term memory was completely gone. So, as his long-term memory. He didn't recognise his own flat and kept asking where we were and why we weren't going home. He didn't mention Erika's name, but he was looking for my mother and for his own mother. He was worried about them, wondering if they were okay, if they were still alive...

In three days, thanks to divine luck and the help of friends, I managed to place Dad in the hospital where I used to work. I took him there for an assessment so that, before he could be admitted to the care home that Erika and I had chosen, his medication could be adjusted, and we could get an accurate picture of the care he would need. Jack, the children, and I were required to return to the UK within three days. My workplace was waiting for me, and Cara needed to see the children. She was supposed to have contact time with them. But because of this tragedy, we were unable to return to the UK until five days later. Cara was furious.

"I don't care about your family, I don't want to hear about them, they have nothing to do with my children! I don't want to hear about your family anymore. Please don't write to me about them anymore, because I don't

care! I want my children at the agreed time, or if you don't bring them, I'll go to court. I'm calling my solicitor right now!" - She wrote to Jack.

Zero empathy. We knew that already. But now Jack was grieving too, and this sentence did hit him hard. He loved Erika as if she were his own grandmother. He had known her since he was a teenager, and Cara's words hit him like a whip. Jack exploded on the way home when we got off the plane:

- "How can anyone be so cruel? How can she say that she and the children had nothing to do with what happened? Erika was our children's great-grandmother!"

We were sad and bitter, and the children could sense it. We had to explain it to them in their own language so they could understand what had happened. It was the first time Elsie had encountered death, and I thought she understood perfectly well that Eri Mama was gone, that we would never see her again, because Eri Mama had gone to be with the angels. Her eyes filled with tears. We tried to comfort her. Just how intelligent Elsie was at three and a half years old was evident from the question she asked after she had calmed down a little:

- "What will happen to Great Grandpa now? Where will he live? Who will take care of him?"

I stroked her clever little head and explained it to her as best I could.

It was difficult to return home, but upon arrival, everything gradually returned to normal. Cara calmed down and, of course, she did not go to a solicitor or back to the Court.

In the first week of January, after six months of investigation, the police finally dropped the charges against Jack for lack of evidence and closed the case with an NFA (No further action). Jack was now allowed to meet Cara during the children's handovers. Jack was unhappy about this, but he had to get back on the treadmill because I had to travel home every other week to take care of my Father's affairs. I continued to accompany him and the children to most handovers, and I recorded them from the back seat of the car. Just so that what happened last April wouldn't happen again. Cara couldn't come up with anything to accuse Jack of.

PART VI – PARALYSIS

SPIRITUAL WARFARE IN FULL FORCE

Tony was still on duty with us in January, but we haven't seen her. On the 1st of February, she introduced the family support worker who would be taking over her job and said her final goodbyes.

That's when our real ordeal began, and we didn't yet know it. There were two social workers, who were not qualified social workers but support workers. One of whom began "working" with Cara to develop her parenting skills, while the other, who replaced Tony, was responsible for supervising the parents' relationship and the contact arrangements. Cara prevailed over them both in less than a month. The children came home every week with blue and green bruises, hungry and dirty, again. However, when Jack raised this, Laura, the support worker on duty to supervise the parents' relationship, did not respond, or only said that Jack was too critical and that he should stop, as it wasn't good for the children if he was constantly criticising their mother. Laura didn't understand why Jack expected Cara to pick up the children or bring them back. Why did Jack want to share this task? According to Laura, Jack should realise that, without a car, it would be difficult for Cara to walk up the hill for eight minutes and that pushing the pram would be far too difficult. Laura believed that a man should support a woman and that a father should serve the mother, especially if he has custody. Then the father could at least do that much to arrange things so that it would be good for the mother...Laura did not care about what had happened in the past; she did not care about the family history.

To demonstrate her good intentions and enthusiasm, Laura bought the mother a new pram, a sporty one that would be easy to push up the hill if the father required her to come and pick up the children, or if the mother was required to take the children to school. She purchased the pram either from her own funds or from taxpayer funds; we don't know. Cara did not use that pram, not even once.

INCIDENT

It happened in mid-February 2025, when it was still dark at the afternoon handover. Elsie rushed to Jack, but Lilly was asleep, wearing a thick winter coat with the hood up. Cara handed her over to Jack from her arm, and it was only when Jack got home that he noticed something was wrong with Lilly. The little girl didn't want to get out of his lap; she was difficult to wake up and was whimpering. Jack undressed her, and then he saw the bruises on Lilly's face. Jack immediately wrote Cara a message, asking what had happened to Lilly. But Cara didn't reply. Lilly came round with great difficulty, while Elsie sat quietly on the floor playing with her doll's house in the corner. As Cara didn't reply, Jack asked Elsie too:

- "What happened to Lilly, sweetheart? Did she fall? How did she fall?"
- "It was Mummy," said Elsie. "Mummy hit Lilly, she pushed her." Jack looked at me.
- "Write to Cara, please, maybe she'll answer you," he asked. "Ask her what happened to Lilly."

I wrote a short message that said:

"Hi, please reply to Jack or write to me here and tell us what happened to Lilly, because she's not well, she has a nasty bruise on her face, and we may have to take her to the doctor. It's okay if she had a fall, just write and tell us what happened so we know exactly what to do."

Cara did not respond for a while, so Jack asked me to call the on-duty doctor to determine whether we needed to take Lilly to the hospital for evaluation. I started making phone calls, then noticed Cara had replied and left a message in the chat. I quickly checked it whilst I was waiting for the doctor's advice. Cara posted a crying-laughing – meaning laughing loud – emoji as a comment under my message, and then wrote:

> *"Oh, come on, don't be so dramatic! Send us a photograph of the bruise so we can see it. Lilly was fine when I handed her over to you. She fell off her bike in the room and struck her face slightly, but there was no injury; it won't even be visible tomorrow! You don't always have to make such a fuss!"*

I was completely stunned by this message, but the doctor picked up the phone, so I didn't have much time to think about it. The doctor said he definitely wanted to see Lilly, so we started packing and getting dressed. We had a long night ahead of us at the hospital emergency room.

They examined Lilly, but fortunately, they didn't have to keep her in the hospital because, apart from some really nasty bruises, Lilly was fine. By the time the doctor saw her, she was completely herself, playing, chatting, coming and going. The doctor tried to call her mother to find out the exact circumstances of the accident, but her mother did not answer the phone. Elsie refused to repeat what she had seen of the accident, and when the doctor asked her what had happened to her sister, she just lowered her head. The doctor also called the on-duty social worker, who advised us not to hand the children over to Cara until the police arrived the next day and the social worker assigned to us took action. Jack came home with the children at midnight. I had to go to work, as I was on shift that night. Elsie and Lilly slept well.

The next morning, however, we waited in vain for the police. However, only Laura arrived, accompanied by a young social worker in her twenties whom we had not previously seen. Laura asked with concern how Elsie had interpreted the events of the previous day. She shook her head and said the same thing as the health visitor said to Jack one year ago:

"Children of this age say all sorts of things; they say this and that, their statements cannot be taken as gospel."

Laura said that before coming to us, she had gone to Cara and asked her what had happened to Lilly. Cara gave her roughly the same answer she had given us. That Lilly had fallen off her bike and hit the door. Laura, the social care support worker, examined Lilly's face and concluded that the mother's account was consistent with the appearance of the injury. So, Laura agreed that this was what must have happened. Lilly had fallen off her bike.

"It was an accident, nothing else," said Laura. "It could happen to anyone."

I could see from Jack's face that he was in a state of mild shock again. He didn't say anything, just hugged Lilly tightly. I was upset. Elsie was already three and a half years old at this time, spoke fluently, and expressed herself without difficulty. When her father asked her what had happened to Lilly, she would have simply replied that she had fallen off her bike, if that had been the truth, if that had been what had happened! She would not have said that Mummy had hit her and pushed her! I pointed this out and dared to ask Laura the question:

- "All right. But if that's how it was, okay. Then I only have one question left: Why was Lilly riding her bike in the room, inside the flat? And if she was riding her bike there, why wasn't she wearing a helmet or protective gear?" Laura looked at me coldly.
- "I think Cara was about to leave to take the children to their father. "It's a very small bicycle," Laura replied, and then, somewhat incoherently, repeated, "It's a small bicycle. And I think Lilly just sat on it for a minute before they left, and unfortunately, she tipped over, fell off, and hit the door... Nothing else happened." Then she added, "Don't wait for the police, because no one is coming. We've already spoken with the police, informed them that we're investigating, and reported it as an accident. This kind of accident can happen at any time with such an active little child. So, the police aren't going to investigate anything."

The door slammed loudly behind them. It wasn't the first time I felt I'd had enough. It wasn't the first time I considered how different the situation would have been if all this had occurred under Jack's supervision. The woman who arrived with Laura attempted to engage in direct work with Elsie before they left. She tried to coax Elsie into confessing indirectly. They played with little figures on the floor. The Peppa pigs went on a trip. Mummy pig took them on a trip, but Daddy pig stayed at home because he was too fat and couldn't fit in the car. Daddy pig, while his children were on a trip with Mummy pig, climbed onto the roof because he was very silly and fell off.

"Silly, silly Daddy Pig," Emma, the social worker, repeated. Her voice and intonation echoed in my head for months. – "Silly, silly Daddy Pig! How can you be so silly? Silly, silly Daddy, how can you be so silly..."

"We've already spoken to the police" - this sentence also echoed in my head for weeks. So, in this country, social services are in direct contact with the police and, behind the back of the parent with custody, the children's legal representative, they discuss the children's condition with the police without the parents' knowledge. This is what happened last year, in 2024, when social services staff requested and obtained evidence of a crime from the police, the bloody nappy, and asked the police not to investigate the case, saying that they, the social services, would investigate the case instead, because the children were already on the Child Protection Register, anyway.

I was not, and still am not, sure that the social services acted in accordance with the law. "Fabricating evidence for false accusations" is a criminal offence in the United Kingdom. By concealing Jack's identity and destroying the evidence, social services prevented the police from investigating a criminal offence and thereby obstructed the course of justice in 2024. Social services swept what happened on 15 May last year under the carpet, and they are doing the same this year. That's what I thought, and I also thought that we couldn't let this go, either last year or this year! But I had no idea who to turn to. Where can I find a solicitor willing to take on the social services and the guardianship authority and bring a lawsuit against them? And where would I get the money for all this? After all, it could cost an astronomical sum! We were in a hopeless situation; I had to admit it and accept it. As immigrants in a foreign country, with low incomes, but actively working, which means not entitled to free Legal Aid, we had no chance of fighting for our rights and justice, even in a civil democracy, and this was the sad reality.

Should have been, but no investigation was conducted; no investigation was required. For Jack and me, it was not necessary to conduct an investigation to understand what had happened. A few days later, Elsie pretended that one of the dolls had fallen off her bike and hit her head badly on the door because the other doll (the mommy) had pushed her. The picture came together, making the story completely clear. But we didn't tell anyone about Elsie's game. It wouldn't have made sense. They wouldn't have believed us, or even if they had, no one would have pursued the matter further. "It was an accident," they would have said, "and as we know, children say things like that, so we shouldn't read too much into it."

The days passed quickly, and every day something happened. Small scratches and purple marks appeared on Lilly's arms and face. Elsie always told us what had happened, but she only told us once and never repeated it, as if she always realised while she was talking that she mustn't say anything, anything bad.

"Mummy grabbed Lilly's face, Mummy pinched Lilly, Mummy was angry because Lilly didn't want to eat. Mummy grabbed Lilly's arm tightly because Lilly ran away and didn't want to walk nicely on the street."

Elsie, while she was being honest with us, was always scared; at least I saw fear on her face. I asked Jack not to ask the little girl any questions because it was obviously making her uncomfortable. My son agreed with me, and we agreed on this.

One afternoon, after the children came home from Cara's, Elsie was very sad for some reason, but she didn't want to talk about it. She sat quietly, nibbling on her snack while watching cartoons on TV. I sat down next to her on the sofa. We didn't talk; I just sat there quietly next to her, watching the cartoon together. One episode had just ended when Elsie suddenly said:

- "Nana, why don't you take Mami out to the sea, far away, and throw her into the water with her clothes on? Then she wouldn't be able to return. Then Mami would never come back..." I was shocked, suddenly not knowing how to respond wisely.
- "You can't do that, sweetheart, you must never do that. Then Mami would go to the angels, and we can't send her there," I replied quietly to Elsie after a moment's thought.

Elsie bowed her head, sighed, and continued watching the next episode of the cartoon. Jack looked at me in shock; he had heard Elsie's question, too. Later, in the kitchen, he said to me in despair:

- "Poor little girl. But there's nothing we can do about it. If we disclosed to anyone what Elsie said about her mother, they would conclude that we were teaching Elsie to say such things. They would turn against us, too."

I had to agree. They would twist our words and the story. We couldn't allow that to happen, since nearly all the officials were already against us. Jack and I agreed that at some point in the near future, Elsie would definitely need to see a child psychologist. Somehow, we have to help her through these things, the traumas, the processing of her own feelings. We can't do this alone. Our love is not enough. This requires professional assistance.

It was March, early spring. On Sundays, the children always stayed at Cara's for a long time, only coming home in the early evening. One Sunday evening at the beginning of the month, Elsie and Lilly entered Jack's car, looking upset, and began speaking at the same time. Lilly had large bruises on both knees, her trousers pulled up above her knees, and pen-drawn patterns on her shins: houses, flowers, and butterflies. This wasn't the first time Cara had drawn all sorts of things on the children's bodies with a pen. hearts, suns, little houses. She regularly used the children's skin as canvas, drawing on them. Jack was always angry about this because the drawings were difficult to wash off the children's skin during bath time. I was also somewhat angry and confused by this, because I couldn't understand why anyone would want to do this. But that wasn't what we were paying attention to most. It was Elsie's excitement. We asked Lilly to be quiet so we could better understand what Elsie wanted to say. And Elsie began to tell us with a frightened look on her face:

- "Lilly fell because we were running fast on the street. And there was a man, an evil man, with a knife in his hand. And Mummy was crying..." Jack was driving. He didn't stop the car, but he glanced back and repeated Elsie's words in a question:
- "An evil man with a knife in his hand?"
- "Yes, Dad, the bad man with a knife in his hand."
- "Where was the bad man, Elsie? On the street?"
- "No, Dad, we were just running down the street to Mummy's house. The bad man was there, and Mummy was crying."

Elsie was very upset. Lilly was quiet, stroking her knees and looking at them, crying silently. It was difficult to put Elsie to bed that night; she kept coming back to the man with the knife, and we didn't understand what it could be. Jack told Laura this story the next day. A few days later, Laura replied in an email and wrote the following:

- "Don't worry, I went to see Cara and asked her what she knew about the man with the knife, but Cara said she didn't know anything and that Elsie had never talked to her about men with knives."

I read Laura's sentences 3 times. Then I thought again, not for the first time, that we were in a hopeless situation...

Strange things Concerns:

More strange things about Cara. In addition to drawing butterflies, hearts, and houses on the children's bodies, Cara also liked to stick fake nails on Elsie. She didn't do this to Lilly because her nails were still too small, or maybe, as usual, she wasn't that interested in Lilly. Cara didn't like her and didn't want to spend so much time with her. She just painted her nails purple, red, and pink. But for Elsie, Cara liked to stick fake nails. Cara played with the children like a girl playing with her dolls, which is fine, as this is usually a passion of girly mums. Dressing them up, playing beauty salon with them, preparing the little girls for their grown-up life. She bought artificial nails for little girls in every colour, and Elsie regularly came home to her father wearing them after every visit to her mother. At home, she would soon ask her father or me to take the nails off because she couldn't play or draw with them on. Elsie was not yet four years old. I found the sight of a toddler's hands with artificial nails repulsive, as did the sight of makeup, blusher, and eyeshadow on her face, but perhaps I was just getting old, I thought... Different parenting styles, said Becky, the practice lead social worker, there's nothing wrong with that. And Laura, the support worker, was absolutely thrilled with Elsie's make-up and artificial nails. – "She looks so cute!" – She stated a couple of times...

Later, towards the end of March, Lilly and Elsie also fell ill, catching an early-spring virus and developing a fever a week apart. Lilly started it. When Jack picked her up from Cara one afternoon, Lilly seemed very lethargic. We took her temperature. It was 39.2. Jack sent Cara a message asking whether she had given the little girl any medication, such as a fever reducer. He only asked so that he wouldn't overdose her on medication. Cara replied indignantly:

> *"Lilly was fine. Leave me alone, don't always make up all sorts of things. What are we trying to achieve with this? Why don't you leave me alone?*

Jack didn't respond; he didn't address this at all. Lilly is a fortunate, resilient little girl; whenever she caught a viral infection, she always recovered easily. Jack gave her Calpol. Lilly was seen by the physician, did not require antibiotics, slept a lot this time as well, and recovered within two days.

After the bicycle accident, Laura removed me from the online chat group where parents, family support workers, and I were together and where we discussed matters related to the children, such as when and where to hand them over, and whether there were any problems we should be aware of. Laura removed me from the group at Cara's request because Cara claimed that I was harassing her and writing her „hostile" and unnecessary messages. Laura decided that my communication was not helping to restore the relationship between the parents and maintain peace... Because I dared to ask how Lilly fell and why she wasn't wearing protective equipment while riding her bike... Cara didn't give up; she was "tired but wanted to finish what she started," and over time, she achieved what she always wanted. She worked seriously and systematically to ruin Jack's life and also to eliminate me. She provoked me to react badly, lied about me, and reported me to the authorities. Cara told me back in 2022 that she was going to remove me from the children's lives, and she kept telling everyone that I had no rights and no business being involved in „her" children's lives. This was in accordance with local law and practice: a grandparent has no say in the lives of their grandchildren unless the parents authorise them or the court grants them parental rights. In early spring, Cara also wrote several times to the family support workers so that I would finally know my place. I think the family support worker, Laura, came to the same conclusion – that I, the grandmother, should not interfere in anything. And she removed me from the group. Jack then showed me all the messages. From the messages that came in, I could see that Cara began to play along. Suddenly, she did a complete 180-degree turn and became the kind, caring mother whose sole focus was on the children's well-being. Cara sent the group photos of the little girls playing beautifully, doing well, and eating delicious food. She photographed the children's plates, the playground, and the storybooks.

At the end of March, Laura wrote to Jack, noting that social services had observed that the mother had changed significantly and had completed all the parenting skills courses, and therefore believed that the children were ready to spend nights with Cara again. First, one in mid-April; then, if all goes well, two; then three. Jack was a little shocked. "This wasn't discussed," he whispered. Cara hasn't changed at all. She may have completed the courses, she may post pictures of flowers, bees, the children's snacks, and playgrounds, but she hasn't changed in her communication with Jack at all, and the children are more hurt than ever! I also found the idea of the children staying with Cara overnight astonishing. The accidents, the knife-wielding man, the unexplained and untreated fevers, illnesses... I didn't understand any of it. I couldn't find any logic in it. The crying-laughing smiley came to mind when we received the answer to our desperate message and question about what had happened to Lilly's face... Jack wrote a counterargument and opposition statement to Laura explaining why he couldn't agree to the overnight stays at this time. Jack asked the social workers to proceed slowly with this change and to wait until the children were older and it was safe for them to sleep at Cara's. But this email, like many others, went unanswered.

Under the court order, if social services workers propose any changes, they must report them to the court, and all parties who retain parental rights must agree to them. To Jack's knowledge, the social network had not notified the court, so he appeared in person to inform the judge and request that his objection be filed. However, the court informed him that no one remained to handle the case because it had been closed. We had no idea what to do next. Jack's former solicitor had been transferred elsewhere, and the new solicitor at the same firm was unfamiliar with Jack's matter and had nothing substantive to add. What's more, he demanded an exorbitant advance payment before he would even consider taking Jack's case. Our sense of hopelessness only grew; we had no one to turn to for advice or help.

- "There's nothing we can do, Jack!" I said to my son. „We have to agree to what they want. They are the authorities, and they are obviously biased towards Cara. I feel like there's nothing we can do."
- "Well, I'm not going to agree to that!" - Jack shouted angrily. - "I'm the children's father. There was a good reason the court granted me custody. It's no accident that the children live with me, not with Cara! Am I supposed to expose them to whatever might happen to them again? What's going on here? Has everyone forgotten what happened last year? Barely a year ago? It hasn't even been a year.
- "No, I don't think anyone who knows what happened would have forgotten. I think Laura doesn't know because she hasn't read the notes and the minutes. And her boss doesn't want to

remember. But I don't know what they're playing at. We need to find out what they want to achieve and how far they're willing to go. How much contact do they want to give the mother?

Jack tried to speak with Laura's supervisor, Becky, but it was difficult to reach her. Becky didn't answer the phone; she messaged Jack, saying she would rather come out to see us and then discuss what to do. This never happened.

However, under Becky's leadership, the social services team scheduled another meeting for the following week to address the issues that had recently arisen. In this case, the problems stemmed from Jack, and one of them was his refusal to consent to sleepovers. The head of the nursery, the health visitor, Laura, Becky, and Jack were present at the online meeting. Cara was not present. They held a separate meeting with her. Many matters were discussed, and I listened to the entire proceeding from the kitchen. The primary agenda item was Cara's change, her transformation, and how well everything had turned out according to the social services. Jack stated that he could not agree with this because Cara's communication with him had not changed; she was just as arrogant as before, unfriendly during handovers, did not say hello, and often did not say a word. The bicycle accident and the children's injuries were discussed, and Laura stated that she had investigated all cases and that the children's injuries resulted from accidents. The social workers went so far as to say that, in their opinion, it would be abnormal if the children had not been injured... The mutilated toys were also discussed. To my great shock, Laura commented on the toys with severed limbs with the following words:

– *"But those toys weren't mutilated, their legs weren't cut off, they just broke, - those are just damaged toys..."*

At that point, I went into the room because I couldn't listen to this any longer without saying anything: I asked to speak and apologised, and all I said was that I wanted everyone to know that Cara herself had said in a message that she had marked her own toys by cutting off their limbs, mutilating them. The toys were not damaged; Cara mutilated them.

There was a frozen silence; no one said a word. Then Becky cleared her throat and suddenly said:

- "The word 'mutilated' is actually a very exaggerated term, and it should not be used in this case in relation to the toys."

Laura immediately agreed. After that, Becky didn't let me say another word; she did not let me talk any further; she had to ask the nursery manager something very quickly. I went back to the kitchen, feeling confused. Laura, the family support worker, had lied openly and blatantly in front of the health visitor and all the other child protection professionals. She lied right to our faces, in front of our eyes and ears. Becky, her supervisor, allowed this misrepresentation to occur and silenced me. What was going on? What was happening and why? I didn't understand anymore. And I began to feel afraid. If they could do this, they could do anything! All of Cara's mistakes, carelessness, transgressions, and even her crimes are swept under the carpet – are they really acting in the best interests of the children? The child protection, the children's service staff? – In addition to my shocked amazement, I also became angry and began to feel resentment. It was a small flame flickering under the pile of twigs and brushwood that had been brought there. That afternoon, I began to feel anger towards everyone who endangered my grandchildren in any way. Until then, I had hoped for help. I trusted and believed. But my hope was lost, and anger took its place.

Elsie loved going to nursery, but she didn't really feel comfortable there. I think she was just a good girl who wanted to please her father and her mother and live up to expectations. My eldest grandchild is the type who likes things to run smoothly and for everyone to be happy. This included her acting in a way that kept things running smoothly and kept everyone happy. But Elsie had no friends at the nursery. She didn't take part in the carnival; she didn't want to dress up in a costume; she wouldn't let the school photographer take her picture in her little uniform; and not a single photo the teachers took showed Elsie smiling. At the Easter parade, she just sat on her mother's lap, not even thinking of going up on stage or joining the other children to play. The parents went to the Easter parade together, and I was there too, in a distant corner. Lilly ran up and down, but Elsie just sat there quietly. When we took her home, we took her temperature because she felt very hot. It was 39.5. I remember feeling terribly angry at that moment, too.

- "I can't believe Cara didn't notice that she didn't feel it! This child is burning up, she's like a stove, and she sat there in Cara's lap the whole time during the ceremony!" I whispered to Jack in the kitchen because I didn't want Elsie to see how angry I was. She would have understood every word! Jack just grimaced and gave Elsie Calpol the fever reducer before he called the doctor.
- "What can I say to that, Mum? It's a nightmare that the kids will be sleeping at Cara's next week..."

We took Elsie to the GP surgery, and the doctor prescribed her antibiotics.

And the following week, they were already sleeping there, in their mother's house on Sunday night. Jack was literally threatened by social worker Becky that if he didn't agree to this, there would be consequences, and proceedings were initiated against Jack because his unfriendly behaviour towards the mother endangered the children's emotional well-being and could cause them long-term damage. I thought we had fallen into a bad dream again. I didn't understand how they could do this, how they could turn the story against us like this. I was also accused of bad faith; they claimed that I was rude and that I was making unnecessary video recordings of the handovers of the children, because this was also emotionally damaging to them. And anyway, "the mother feels uncomfortable with me making videos and being present at the handovers... It frustrates her greatly," as they wrote in the Child Protection Conference minutes, which they initiated because of the „risk of emotional harm". Has everyone forgotten why I am there? Does no one care or find it disturbing that I was absent just once, and the next day, Cara reported Jack to the police for sexual assault? Do social workers think that I wouldn't rather drink coffee in my own kitchen after working the night shift than sit in the car with my grandchildren, looking at their sad little faces and trying to comfort them, telling them that everything will be fine with Mummy? I didn't understand any of it. Another child protection conference was initiated, and the children were put back on the child protection register, this time for alleged emotional abuse caused by Jack noticing the children's injuries, reporting them, and being reluctant to agree to Cara having more contact with them. Also, because I am present at the handover of the children and behave unfriendly towards their mother...

The safety plan agreed upon at the child protection conference also stipulated that no recordings of the handovers were permitted. Jack felt he was expected to handle the handover and the children's collection on his own. I noticed this. And I decided that I would no longer be present. If this helps to prevent further false accusations, then so be it. I will pray for him and hope that Cara does not provoke Jack and does not come up with anything that could land my son in prison... Jack sighed.

- "I don't know how it will turn out, Mum, but I'll be careful. Even if I can't make a video, no one can say anything if I keep my phone in my pocket and record the handovers on audio, just so I can refute it if Cara claims that I harassed her in any way, made advances towards her, or was rude to her."- I nodded in agreement.

The social workers still did not disclose their further plans. Jack asked them several times, but to no avail. "We'll discuss it," they always said. But this discussion never took place. They had many opportunities to do so, as they visited quite frequently. According to the child protection plan, they were supposed to see the children every 10 days, and the Core Group meetings were held every 3-4 weeks. Becky, Laura's supervisor, and Laura visited us again one afternoon.

It was May, the weather was warm, and the children were happily playing in the garden. In the past month, Lilly had started nursery, but they could only take her in the afternoon group, which she did not tolerate very well, as she still needed/would have needed a short afternoon nap – she was barely two years old. As a result, Jack intended to transfer her to another nursery. To the morning group, so that Lilly could sleep in the afternoon. The social workers had previously agreed to this, but for some reason, it had now become problematic. Mainly because the other nursery was a 10-minute walk away, which would have been difficult for Cara to get to. It was already difficult for her to take the children to their current nursery and kindergarten because she had to walk up a „hill". Over the past month, Jack had also been looking for a child psychologist for Elsie, with whom he had consulted once via video chat. However, this caused a major scandal because the social workers believed Jack had done so without Cara's consent. They immediately jumped on this perceived parental mistake like dogs on a bone: How could Jack do this? How could he exclude the mother from such an important decision? He consulted a psychologist regarding the child's behaviour without the mother's knowledge or consent. Cara seized the opportunity, caught him out, and flatly denied ever having discussed with Jack that Elsie needed or would need a psychologist. But they had discussed it, and Jack remembered the exact date when they had done so. It was on Lilly's first day at nursery when they went together with their little girl. Thanks to Jack's foresight, there was even an audio recording of this, but unfortunately, he couldn't find his old phone, on which he had made it. So at that time, when he has been accused by the social workers, it was pointless to assert that Cara had already agreed to the psychologist's examination, just as she had agreed to the nursery change, and that the nursery Jack wanted to transfer the children to was the same institution they had chosen together two years ago, where Elsie started her education.

Later, when Jack found his old phone and could play the voice recording as evidence, the social workers refused to listen. They stated that Jack unlawfully made the voice recordings because she did not obtain consent from Cara; therefore, his evidence is not relevant. Which was a false statement. Everyone has the right to make voice recordings in public places, including those who are part of the conversation. But this was the way the truth was distorted.

No one believed Jack; no one wanted to believe him, and the social workers were clearly not interested in the facts or the truth. Becky and Laura's visit started nicely; the children were playing, the adults were chatting peacefully, and I was washing up in the kitchen. However, from the kitchen window, I suddenly noticed Becky leaning threateningly towards Jack, raising her voice, almost shouting at him:

- "Why did you do that? Even if you had the right to, why did you do it? Be honest! Why did you have the children tested without their mother's knowledge, and why did you transfer them to another nursery? You did it on purpose, didn't you? To make Cara's life difficult! You did it on purpose, didn't you?"

Jack couldn't speak. He tried to defend himself, to explain what had happened, but no one was listening anymore. Becky announced that another PLO Assessment would be launched because they believed that Jack wanted to alienate the children from their mother...

PART VII - RECKONING

Summer began, and the new investigation started. The appointed solicitor urged Jack to agree to everything because it would be better for him to cooperate (i.e., obey); social services would take the children away from him. The social services twisted Jack's words, and the minutes contained both simple lies and sophisticated gaslighting. The lies were sometimes blatant: for example, at the next child protection conference, the social worker stated that Cara had been in a healthy relationship for more than two years. Meanwhile, we knew because Cara had informed Jack in messages that she and Andrew had broken up three times in the past two years and that their relationship was definitively over this summer. The social network was not bothered by the lies. The social workers themselves did practise dishonesty, both in subtle and crude forms. I don't know how all this could happen, don't ask me, in a civil democracy at the beginning of the twenty-first century. I don't understand the system, and I have become deeply disillusioned. I can no longer trust any official.

The social services have stated that the mother has the same rights to the children as the father and that Jack must agree to increase the mother's contact time; otherwise, they will seek further legal advice, go to Court, change the Order, and might remove custody from him. Social services were preventing the transfer of the children's data from their former nursery to the new institution and had instructed the employee responsible for this task at the former institution not to transfer the data at the father's request unless the mother also agreed. The social services asked Jack not to discuss the past, including the events that occurred.

They forbade him from taking photographs of his children if they were injured. They forbade him from recording the children's handover on video. They said they could visit him at his home anytime, but did not specify how they would do so. However, we have observed that during these visits, the social service staff may have behaved toward him in any manner, and he must have tolerated it. These demands, prohibitions, and orders seriously violated Jack's fundamental human rights.

We trust that all this will come to light. How can you intimidate a parent? A father? A man who has never had any other motive than to raise his children in love and peace, safely! Cara has vowed to ruin Jack's life. She has written this threat in countless messages. And Cara seems to be keeping her promise, with the social services doing the dirty work for her, carrying out Cara's plan.

Jack wrote letters of complaint. He wrote to the local council, his MP, and the ombudsman. Based on these letters of complaint, an investigation is currently underway against the social services, who, in addition to their discriminatory comments and treatment, acted in a biased and unlawful manner towards Jack, on several occasions, falsely accused him, blamed him, distorted the truth in their reports, and in doing so endangered the safety and well-being of the two minors. We could only hope the independent investigator would prove all this.

The children spent two nights a week with Cara until mid-September, after which Cara declared that she would exercise her parental rights and retain the children in her care for the third overnight. This was a breach of the existing Court Order, but the Children's Services called it „Cara is just exercising her parenting rights". They declared that they had not encouraged Cara to do this, namely, to retain the children in her care for the third overnight, but, obviously, they did not advise her otherwise, so they accepted the breach of the Order.

The goal is 50/50 shared custody, which is less than Cara would like, but I believe social services would be satisfied with that result for now. The mother would receive benefits, would not be required to work, and the council flat would be funded by the state. Cara wrote to Jack on the Parenting App: I want at least two nights because then I will also receive the benefits. I hope you understand. But she didn't put it that way on the platform where the court can monitor their communication. Instead, she slyly wrote the following sentences so that what she wrote would not reflect badly on her, but rather on Jack: *"If I get at least two nights, then I'll get the child support too, and they won't take it away from you, we'll both get it, - that's what they told me - you'll continue to get it just as before, if that's the problem, that's why you don't want to..."*

Cara was getting increasingly skilful. She's becoming increasingly insidiously manipulative. That's what came to mind when Jack showed me this message. And in a way, I felt sorry for Cara. She had no idea that Jack was forced to work in addition to receiving child benefits because the benefits were not enough to raise children on – benefits are just benefits in the United Kingdom, which is an expensive country. Jack worked, I worked, I supported the children as best I could, and even so, we couldn't give them everything we wanted to! I felt sorry for Cara because it seemed she had forgotten that when she was getting all the money, and Jack was paying her child support on top of that, it was never enough for her, never, for anything. However, at that time, the children were much younger, and the amount of support to which Cara was entitled was substantially higher. The support wanes as the children grow older. Cara will not receive as much money as she believes. And if she doesn't find a well-paid job, she will never be able to live the life she wants with her children...

The two-night stays began in early August. The three-night stays began in mid-September. The children have come to terms with the situation. Every morning, when it's time to go for the two and later three-night stay, Lilly declares that she doesn't want to go. She shakes her little head and says, "No, no." However, no one considers her opinion. Elsie goes, obediently, sometimes happily, sometimes sadly, but always with a heavy heart. One night before bed, she said, "Nana, Mummy doesn't hurt us anymore." I was happy to hear that. I remain satisfied, even though I know this may be only temporary. Cara, as long as the social workers are involved and until she doesn't get what she wants, she will play along to avoid mistakes and will not harm the children. But what will happen after? Only God knows. And Elsie's brief comment still hurts me: "Mommy doesn't hurt us anymore." This sentence also implies that Elsie remembers everything, remembers it well. Even when their mummy hurt them. Although she has come to terms with it and even enjoys going to Cara's on occasion, Elsie's face often conveys concern. Neither Jack nor I can wipe that look off her face.

When the children return to Jack after their two and three-night visit, they throw themselves into their games with unbridled joy. They hug the dog, run around the house, are loud, and carefree.

The children are well, and we hope they will remain well. But problems still arise daily.

Cara is only willing to take the children to the nursery if Jack pays her taxi fare. The nursery is 25 minutes by bus, but Cara refused to use public transport; she expects Jack to pay for a taxi. Although Jack paid, Cara did not take the children to the nursery for the past 3 months, stating they were not well, had a fever or an infection, or were too tired. Although Cara made this declaration, she did not consult a physician for the children and rarely sought medical advice. Each week, upon their return, Jack needed to take the children to the GP surgery to confirm that they were healthy and fit for nursery. But on one of the rare occasions, Cara could manage to make the pharmacist prescribe an antihistamine, she declared that Elsie is allergic to food and to pollens because her eyes are regularly teary, and Cara administered the antihistamine prolonged, completely unnecessarily for months, until Jack did not request an allergy test, which confirmed that Elsie is not allergic to anything at all!

Multiple other incidents happened. Elsie picked up an anti-stress ball one day and took it in her mouth in Cara's care. The ball broke in her mouth, and all the chemical jelly burst in Elsie's mouth. Cara did not seek medical advice; she merely rinsed her mouth. The children came back to Jack regularly with scratches, and most of the time their bodies were covered with ballpoint pen drawings.

In September, Cara's mother visited (for the second time in the past 5 years) and attended the handovers, during which she insulted Jack. She told Jack that Elsie calls him a devil while Elsie is in her mother's care, and she harassed him with the Social Service taking the children away from him, and will place the children into her care. Jack was devastated, even though he believed the harassment could be unfounded. In a good, relaxed moment, Jack asked Elsie why she called him a devil in mommy's house, and Elsie responded as follows: "I don't know, Daddy, Mommy always said that, you are a devil, and she said I will not see you anymore..."

The social workers did not care about all this. They were not interested in the missed nursery sessions or the missed medical advice; they did not consider FII; they did not ask questions such as: what does it mean if a parent uses the children's skin as a canvas, regularly drawing on them? They simply did not care. They just accused Jack of parental alienation, when Jack was raising safeguarding concerns and tried to ask them to postpone the overnights, or at least reduce them.

The social workers had a narrative and accepted only facts that fit that narrative. They disregarded all other facts and evidence.

Jack and the children had 7 social workers and support workers in the past 2-3 years. And I am only guessing why this fluctuation was necessary. It is likely that some social workers found the narrative inappropriate...

I don't know what the future holds. Now, Cara, with Social Services' support, plans to return to Court to obtain shared custody. She also seeks a Specific Issue Order to allow her to take the children abroad on holiday. Will she come back with them? Only God knows.

But if anything happens to the children, - for the children, - I know Jack will be responsible for it. And me, if I'm still alive. We'll have to explain to the children why we allowed it and why we didn't do anything to prevent it. Why did we permit them to be harmed? When Elsie grows up and asks Jack or me, "Why did you let us down?" we will have to answer them. Elsie already remembers too much, even now. Let this story be the one that contains all the facts.

I know; I believe nothing is over yet. Nothing is closed. For me, the most worrying thing about Cara's behaviour is not only the seriousness of the accusations she has made against Jack, and the possible sentences Jack could have received if he couldn't prove their falsity, but the very fact that the motive behind Cara's behaviour remained unclear. We know, of course, why she is doing what she is doing – to get full custody of the children, to get all the benefits, and to be able to leave the country with the children and live happily with them until everyone dies – but why is she doing this? She herself admits that Jack is a good and caring father. She has written this down several times. If that's what she thinks, then why does she want to take the children away from him? Why does she want to get Jack into prison, behind bars? What is this bipolarity in Cara's behaviour?

She is fighting her own battle against the fate she inherited, having to grow up without a father, but when she is in a bad state, I think, she is fighting to ensure that her children also grow up without a father. Why? What is this?

Everything she accused Jack of, she did herself:

She accused Jack of cheating on her, while she cheated on Jack and had had three relationships since they broke up with Jack, in the last three years, now she entered the fourth.

She accused Jack of being rude, hurled insults at him immediately after the wedding, and kept it up afterward.

She accused Jack of physically abusing her, while she was the one who pushed Jack against the wall, down the stairs, and hit him in the face, splitting his lip.

She accused Jack of lying, while she was the one who lied about everything when it suited her interests.

She accused Jack of using drugs, while she was the one using illicit drugs and smoking weed in front of the children.

She accused Jack of not caring for the children, while she did not bathe, feed, or care for them, and gave up Lilly.

She accused Jack of sexually abusing the children, while she had been sexually abusing Elsie since she was a small child by taking off her nappy in the evenings and caressing her naked little body "down there" and was constantly watching to see how wide each little girl's genitals were and what they looked like.

She accused Jack of parental alienation this year. While she said Jack wouldn't see his children, they wouldn't know his name, she removed the children from the UK, did not want to return with them, and now calls Jack a devil, promising the children they wouldn't see him again.

What are these projections?

What is this constant, almost pathological lying?

What is this manipulation?

What is behind all this?

And what else will happen?

The fear of the future will not abate until there are concrete answers to these questions. Jack is willing to accept damage to his own nervous system as collateral damage if there are real answers to the events of the past four years – he goes to therapy. But he wants to know that his children are safe, and until he has those answers, Jack lives in fear, constantly on alert, prepared to lose everything at any moment. His children, his financial security, his freedom. Jack has already lost some of his financial security: he had six speeding offences in one year (after not having any offences in the previous eight years), so he temporarily lost his driving licence and cannot work as much as he would like. His doctor diagnosed him with emotional exhaustion and persistent anxiety disorder. This makes his life so difficult that it is almost impossible to live.

We seek assistance, but we no longer know whether we can expect any from persons in this situation in the United Kingdom.

Cara could retain her parental rights notwithstanding what occurred and what she has done in the past 4 years.

If investigated and confirmed by the Police, the incidents that occurred could have been considered criminal offences, because:

More than two instances of harassment are a criminal offence.

Repeatedly making false accusations is a criminal offence.

Forging evidence for a false accusation is a criminal offence.

Making false statements under legal procedure is a criminal offence.

Child abduction is a criminal offence.

Neglect is child abuse

Inappropriate touching of the child's genital area is child sexual abuse.

Child abuse is a criminal offence

...

But for some reasons, the pattern of the events, incidents and behaviour was not seen or recognised by the professionals or by the Police. Each incident was treated as an isolated event, the dots were never connected.

The Judges were not made aware of the full family history.

The solicitors and barristers remained silent.

Facts and evidence have been ignored and Jack was forbidden by the social workers from speaking about past events and incidents.

I am left wondering, why. And how could be young children be kept safe in such circumstances?

And a final question: If Jack had committed the same criminal offences, where would he be today? Would he have kept his parental responsibility? Would he have been able to retain his parental rights?

Double standards should never be applied, - never, anywhere, at any time, - but especially not in social care or in the justice system when the safety and well-being of two innocent young children are at stake. There cannot be one law for men and another for women, one rule for fathers and another for mothers. The law must be gender neutral. Because:

Abuse, including domestic violence and child abuse, is a gender-neutral phenomenon.

According to the data, unfortunately, parents are the perpetrators in the large majority of child abuse cases. In 2023. approximately 189,635 children in the UK were abused by their mothers and 125,493 by their fathers...(ONS) - Statistics speak loudly.

Social workers repeatedly state that children need their mother. Then they often correct themselves and state, a child needs both parents. Which is basically true as a principle. But why do social workers automatically believe that - if it comes to a mother's reduced contact time, ordered by the family court, - their mission would be to re-establish the equal time and secure the long term or permanent equal parenting rights? Forgive me the painful question, but do children really need an abusive parent equal time in their lives, just to "keep the balance," and demonstrate fairness in the system? A parent, who endangers the children's physical safety, uses them as a means to obtain benefits, fails to meet their basic needs, and continuously seeks to take revenge and have their other parent sent to prison?

I have no more questions left.

I believe every child protection case should be managed very carefully, accurately and fairly, and professionals should act purely, simply in the best interest of the children, bearing in mind the Maslow pyramid,'s meaning and prioritising the children's safety.

EPILOGUE

What comes to mind when we talk about the victims of domestic abuse and violence? Suffering women, girls, and children? The bruises, blood, and black eyes left by punches and kicks? Probably, and that's where the train of thought ends most of the time.

But domestic abuse is far more subtle and complex than this, and it can also be more severe. The silent terror, the daily emotional and psychological abuse, doesn't leave any visible marks, and may continue unnoticed, behind closed doors, for long years or even decades. The victims and the abusers remain trapped behind those very same closed doors. Together. When such cases come to light, they can generate significant misunderstanding. Who is the abuser, and who is the abused? Finding this out is not easy. Because those who commit emotional abuse are either highly manipulative, sick people, psychopaths, or are simply traumatised, damaged souls, who don't even know themselves what they're doing.

Both the justice and social welfare systems can be misled. Relatively easily. Officials, lawyers, judges, and even social workers often think in terms of stereotypes and haven't received appropriate training. Is there enough time, money, will, and intent to find out the truth? Or is it simpler, based on past experience and precedent, to validate a hunch and close the case as quickly as possible by focusing on one or two points? Even if the resulting decision is devastating for the victim? It can easily happen. It does occur in more than a few cases. Emotionally abusive people are cunning enough to game the whole justice system. Time and priorities are also on their side. Many people believe that emotional and psychological abuse isn't serious, it doesn't directly endanger life, and there is no immediate crisis, no need to rescue anyone. The firmness of this belief among the vast majority is clearly shown by the fact that emotional abuse is not a criminal offence. If anyone, anywhere, reports incidents like these, no one will assist them. Not even the police. These incidents aren't assigned case numbers. Serial psychological abuse will not be investigated, and the abuser won't be reprimanded. They won't suffer any consequences for their actions. The abused, however, does suffer. The abused becomes physically ill and mentally broken, often seriously, and may even end their own life, seeing no other way out. The only help in such cases comes from psychologists and psychiatrists. Their advice is simple: terminate the relationship. Start a new life and avoid all contact with the abuser. Yes, this is a reasonable, understandable, and simple recommendation. However, complying with this recommendation is not easy. The reality is usually far more complicated. The abused may have already developed Stockholm syndrome, either from this relationship or a previous one, perhaps unknowingly. But the relationship may also have resulted in children. Children who need to be cared for, who the abused wants to raise, who they don't want to lose contact with, who they want to love. They might want their children to grow up in a complete family, or, if that isn't possible, to provide them with a harmonious, well-balanced childhood. This can also make ending the relationship difficult. The second reason why the psychologists' advice is hard to follow is that, in most cases, the abusers – to put it mildly – are not keen to split up and they are particularly against the idea of no contact. Because then, who would be left for them to abuse? So, the abused, out of fear for the children or for other reasons, remains behind the closed doors, stays with the abuser, who gradually, almost systematically, breaks them emotionally and physically, over the course of months and years. The outside world sees little of this. Or, if it does, the problem is trivialised, misunderstood, or left unacknowledged. It's difficult to escape from an emotionally abusive relationship, and few people can help with this.

Even fewer people participate in investigating the seriousness and scale of the abuses and related matters. Who are the abusers anyway? What kind of person abuses another person? And why do they abuse them? Here, too, most of the work is (or should be) done by psychologists and psychiatrists, but they only have access to the most extreme cases, the psychopaths and sociopaths who endanger a broader side of the society, those who have already committed crimes and progressed to physical abuse – in other words, they've already raped, beaten, or killed someone. Psychiatrists can't treat the ones who struggle quietly at home with mild paranoid schizophrenia, borderline bipolar, and narcissistic personality disorder, unless the patient themselves asks for help.

In the United Kingdom's national health system today, people with mental illnesses that are deemed mild, such as depression, bipolar personality disorder (BPD), and narcissistic personality disorder (NPD), cannot be treated or referred for any kind of treatment against their will. Nobody can examine them without their consent, so there's no way of securing a diagnosis. The only exception is if the court orders an examination. However, the complex psychiatric testing that this entails is very costly, running into the tens of thousands of pounds. It hasn't become standard practice, as judges need to account for this use of taxpayers' money. No one else may initiate such an examination. It's not considered appropriate. Anyone who openly suggests that somebody else might be suffering from mental illness is painted in a very bad light. This almost counts as harassment and abuse, and in the end, it's the one who dared to speak out who finds themselves in trouble.

This is the boomerang effect. You can't say that a partner is abusive and it's because they may have some kind of mental problem, because this is tantamount to abusing them, riding roughshod over their rights and their dignity. There is a vicious circle in play here, too. A person with narcissistic personality disorder will barely admit that they have any kind of mental problem. They barely ask for help or go to psychotherapy – any psychiatrist will tell you that. And thus, the circle is complete. Most of the people with cluster B disorders remain unnoticed, undiagnosed, and untreated inside the smallest unit of society, the family, and continue to abuse their victims unchecked.

No blood is drawn, and there are no bruises (at most, the children might have some, but these might be dismissed by biased and tender-hearted social workers as 'age-related bruises' – the result of normal rough and tumble for kids of their age), so nobody does anything. The victims, meanwhile, go on to develop PTSD, mental illness, weight loss, and malignant diseases, but there is no way of monitoring or gathering evidence that these were caused by emotional abuse. In this way, there is no crime, no consequences, and no charges.

"What doesn't kill me makes me stronger" – this saying doesn't hold up here. Emotional abuse doesn't make people stronger, but it is certainly more likely to kill them. In the United States, narcissistic abuse is now a recognised category. Emotional abuse is chargeable, and damages may be awarded. But this is not the case in Europe and in the United Kingdom. Here, even slander only gives rise to a lawsuit if it entails defamation of character and quantifiable financial losses. Emotional abuse, in any form, is generally of no interest to anyone.

It's easy to explain, but impossible to accept, that almost all emotional abuse is committed by women against men. Every year in the United Kingdom, about 4000 men lose their lives because of possible psychological abuse, by committing suicide. They were all young men, fathers in their prime, aged 25-45. Each of these lives is now just a memory, a statistic. However, their family members, siblings, and parents have created websites to commemorate them, and through these, their stories can be told.

I consider it admirable that Women's Aid, founded to protect women, has helped reduce the number of female victims of abuse in just a few years. This is the result of some seriously hard work. However, it pains me that there is no organisation effectively supporting men, despite numerous initiatives to establish one. The Mankind Initiative, for example. Their failure to work effectively is not their fault, though. Emotional abuse, as a form of domestic violence, remains hidden, especially when it affects men. Despite awareness campaigns, articles, and memorial websites, the voices of men who speak out fall on deaf ears. Because there is no blood, nobody knows about the victims, and they themselves feel ashamed and, most of the time, stay silent. But they are also scared, because when they do speak out, there will be revenge, and they can quickly find themselves in the position of the accused – just because they were born male! Abusive women are highly skilled at lying. Making a false accusation as a form of defence is no big deal for them. It creates a distraction, and it can be years before the accusation is proven false. Meanwhile, no one investigates the original complaint or report, and it fades into obscurity, whereas here there are virtually no consequences for falsely accusing someone else of wrongdoing. Today, making false accusations has almost become a gender-specific tactical move. And as a tactic, it is successful in almost every case. Most people would be terrified by the number of members in social media groups established to support falsely accused men today. See the Facebook group Accused.me.

So now it's time to take a fresh look at some of the myths that threaten to drown us. It's true that most physical violence is committed by men, but when it comes to the other forms of abuse, women come out on top. Both endanger life; therefore, both should have consequences, as neither is less serious or weightier than the other. All abuse should be treated as abuse!

This documentary novel is about a relationship. It describes true events without modification, supported where possible by direct quotations. In the book, I set out to find both the causes and solutions. I have also sought to show how the justice system can be derailed by stereotypes, and how the entire legal, safeguarding, and social welfare systems can be misled when those who work within them lack the necessary information, training, and skills. I also hope that this novel offers some help. For victims who still live in toxic relationships and see no way out, who find no help. For fathers who sleep on the sofa so they can at least hug their children every morning. And for sons, who caught up on their fathers crying in secret. For mothers too, on how – or how not – to raise their daughters.

This novel won't appeal to those who don't believe in gender-neutrality when it comes to domestic violence, and those who have a biased view of women's place in society.

This is because this documentary states something that perhaps no one has yet dared to say aloud: that the originator, cause, and committer of violent acts is not necessarily, and certainly not in every case, the man. Just because someone happens to be a woman doesn't mean she can only be a victim. So, when it comes to domestic violence, we shouldn't just accept and believe everything by default just because a woman says it. The other party, the man, also needs to be heard, and until the whole truth is revealed, nobody should be condemned, or if necessary, both parties should be sanctioned to an equal extent. Everybody has the right to be presumed innocent until proven guilty. This is a fundamental principle that also appears to have slipped from legal practice.

Finally, the woman must be a man's supportive partner, according to an unshakeable ancient law. A man and a woman tread their path together, side-by-side, and if this isn't the case, problems arise. And when problems arise, it's good to get to the truth of the matter and find out what the problems really are. Individually for every single case. We should remember that Lilith was also there in the Garden of Eden, not just Eve. And let's also keep in mind that not all of Nox's children were fragile, angelic, pure-hearted virgins. The Ancient Greeks knew all the tricks, and they seem to have known the secrets. The Bible doesn't omit them either, and we shouldn't forget what we learned from our ancestors in the past six thousand years. We mustn't throw away our fundamental values. These include our constant pursuit of justice, our willingness to make peace, our desire to love one another, and our desire to cure illness. If we want to live and raise our children in a healthy society and in healthy families, we need to remember.

We need to remember that a wounded soul can easily succumb to malevolent forces. And while nothing is ever black and white, pure black and snow white still exist within us and around us. Forever.

This documentary is the story of a young couple, Jack and Cara, who loved each other. Their story is not unique; their problems are more common than one could imagine.

Final Thoughts

"And forgive us our trespasses, as we forgive those who trespass against us" - this sentence has also been constantly on my mind over the past four years. Well, I am trying very hard, and I can only hope the person who wrote these lines for me sees my efforts. Because, unfortunately, that is all I can do. At least for now. It would be good to know what forgiveness really means. I suspect it also means not bringing up everything that has hurt you, everything you should forgive. Even if you can't forget, you don't bring it up. I try to do that. But actually, I feel the same way as the Hungarian poet once wrote: "I can't tell anyone, so I'll tell everyone!"- Because it's impossible to keep quiet about it. For the sake of my grandchildren and their safety, I must speak up. And I hope, I truly believe, that the Eternal One understands this and forgives me.

LEGAL AND DOCUMENTARY STATEMENT

This book is a documentary narrative based on real events. The events, dates, and circumstances described are presented to the best of the author's knowledge and personal experience.

To protect children's personal rights, the names, identifying information, and circumstances have been partially altered or anonymized. The purpose of the stories is not to accuse but to testify: to show how children can be left unprotected within a system believed to be functioning.

This book does not constitute legal, medical, or psychological advice. The content reflects the personal viewpoint of the author.

The safety, dignity, and future of children take precedence over all other considerations.

www.ingramcontent.com/pod-product-compliance
Lightning Source LLC
LaVergne TN
LVHW052031200926
848481LV00005B/1646